ArtScroll Series®

Rabbi Nosson Scherman / Rabbi Meir Zlotowitz

General Editors

by
Yair Weinstock

translated by
Libby Lazewnik

Published by
Mesorah Publications, ltd.

Upon a Story

A famous novelist retells classic stories with passion and spirit

FIRST EDITION
First Impression … November 2007

Published and Distributed by
MESORAH PUBLICATIONS, LTD.
4401 Second Avenue / Brooklyn, N.Y 11232

Distributed in Europe by
LEHMANNS
Unit E, Viking Business Park
Rolling Mill Road
Jarow, Tyne & Wear, NE32 3DP
England

Distributed in Israel by
SIFRIATI / A. GITLER — BOOKS
6 Hayarkon Street
Bnei Brak 51127

Distributed in Australia and New Zealand by
GOLDS WORLDS OF JUDAICA
3-13 William Street
Balaclava, Melbourne 3183
Victoria, Australia

Distributed in South Africa by
KOLLEL BOOKSHOP
Ivy Common
105 William Road
Norwood 2192, Johannesburg, South Africa

ARTSCROLL SERIES®
ONCE UPON A STORY
© *Copyright 2007, by* MESORAH PUBLICATIONS, Ltd.
4401 Second Avenue / Brooklyn, N.Y. 11232 / (718) 921-9000 / www.artscroll.com

Typography by CompuScribe at ArtScroll Studios, Ltd.

Printed in the United States of America by Noble Book Press Corp.
Bound by Sefercraft, Quality Bookbinders, Ltd., Brooklyn N.Y. 11232

Table of Contents

ONCE UPON a STORY

HONOR AMONG
Thieves

MENACHEM LEVINE'S FINANCIAL SITUATION HAD NEVER been worse. Until the year before, he had been considered a well-to-do individual, a property owner and man of means. His textile factory in Budapest had been considered a solid and profitable concern, until about a year ago.

That was when he had attempted to climb too high, too fast. His drive for expansion had led him to buy a failing textile factory, hoping to revive it and double his income. In fact, the opposite occurred: The failing concern nearly swallowed its more successful predecessor, and devoured all available capital. In dismay, Menachem saw the truth of the saying, "The camel went to ask for horns, and got its ears cut off." He had had a hundred, but had wanted two, and now he no longer had even the hundred. He was nearly bankrupt.

Menachem walked the streets of his native Budapest for a week without any idea of how to save himself. His bank manager was appalled at the sight of the textile manufacturer's sunken cheeks. "What's happened to you?" he asked.

Sadly, Menachem told him about the recent losses that threatened to bring him down completely. If he did not manage to pull his affairs together quickly, his wife and children were looking at a hungry winter. "I don't care about myself," he said in despair. "But my family ... !"

"Do you have any ideas about how to turn this around?" the bank manager asked cautiously.

"Yes!" Menachem said. "If I had 15,000 *pengo*, I'd buy a huge inventory of textile fabrics, straight from the factory floor. The stock's being sold just now at bargain prices. With the 15,000 *pengo* in hand, I could buy an enormous quantity and sell it at a good profit that will help me get back on my feet."

The bank manager had a kind heart. He invited his friend into the bank and issued him a big loan, in the sum of 15,000 *pengo*, on easy terms. In return, both of Mr. Levine's factories were transferred to the bank as collateral. At the last moment, the bank manager also had the Levines' home put up as collateral as well. After all, two failing factories could never cover so large a loan.

Menachem did not know how to thank the bank manager, who had tossed him a rope to help him out of the quagmire in which he was floundering. They parted with pleasant words on both sides. Menachem expressed the hope that he would soon be in a position to repay his debt.

Very carefully, he placed the large bills in his briefcase. He must be extra vigilant now. Word had it that the trains were teeming with pickpockets, and he had to take a train in order to purchase the textiles. He fervently hoped that nothing would happen to him on the way.

Maxi Marian and Yanysh Barko were the bane of the Debrecen police force.

The pickpocketing duo was the most daring in all the city. Their nimble fingers had already victimized many citizens, and the Debrecen police could not seem to be able to do a thing about it. The criminal pair was so careful and so slippery that the police detectives did not even know what they looked like! They had certainly never managed to catch them in the act.

There were garbled witness descriptions of a tall, thin man with black hair who had been seen at certain locations; there were unclear sightings of a short fellow with straw-colored hair, glimpsed for a moment in a train compartment, followed shortly afterward by the screams of some poor unfortunate who'd found his wallet stolen. None of these descriptions allowed the police to form a complete picture of either of the men they were hunting.

The Debrecen police force had to comfort themselves with catching small fish. The two big sharks consistently eluded their net.

Maxi and Yanysh used various ploys in their work. They were very careful never to be seen together. Only one of them went out on a "fishing" expedition at a time. The two had signed a blood pact swearing loyalty to each other to their dying day. It was this constancy that had earned them their success, and continued to confound the city police.

The pickpocketing pair lived in a small apartment in a medium-income part of town. To everyone's appearances they were just ordinary folk. Their neighbors would have taken an oath that there existed no more honest, upright citizens than the two tenants of the ground-floor apartment facing the main street.

Maxi and Yanysh made sure to keep their "work" and home lives completely separate; never once did they dip into their neighbors' pockets. This decision arose not from any sense of righteousness, but rather from an instinct for extreme caution. Though they had hundreds of opportunities to steal from their neighbors, they never used them. Hundreds of successes could not erase a single mistake. Getting caught once would be one time too many!

The Debrecen police lay in ambush for them on every street-corner, praying for just one slipup by the pickpocket kings. But the crooked pair were too wily for them. When they sensed the net closing in, they prudently stayed indoors for a while, waiting until the danger had passed before resuming their operation.

Such was the situation today. Due to some overzealous police detectives, the two were taking a long, enforced vacation from their line of work. They sat in their kitchen this afternoon, sipping coffee and making plans. Their coffers were empty, their cash was gone, and their spirits were low. All they had left was their mutual loyalty, but neither friendship nor honor among thieves will buy a loaf of bread. They needed food. And for that, they needed money.

"What do you say, Maxi?" Yanysh asked gloomily, running a hand through his straw-colored hair. "Do you have a plan, some way we can make a big 'killing' all at once?"

Maxi Marian studied his well-manicured fingernails. "You mean like in the good old days, when we swept up a profit of several thousand at one time?"

"Yes. Just like that!" Yanysh said eagerly.

"Where are the 'good old days' now?" Maxi sighed, inspecting his fingers — the tools of his trade — again. Ten fishermen had never caught as many fish as had his ten wonderful fingers. "We've always made our biggest catches on trains. Passengers usually travel with large sums of money."

"But the trains are swarming with detectives," Yanysh reminded him. "It's been two years since we've been on a train, because of the police."

"We'll just have to take that risk. Look at this place! We don't even have a fresh apple to eat. The house is empty. Soon the police won't have to bother searching for us — they'll find our skeletons!"

Yanysh was worried. "Do you really plan to board a train? Why don't you or I try our hand at the marketplace? Even a hundred or two is good money."

"First of all, you're not going anywhere," Maxi said. "They chased you a few times already, and you were nearly caught. You have to lay low for at least half a year, until they forget about you. Second, I want to try a train. I'll hunt me down a whale, then rest for a year. We'll get out of this city, Yanysh. We'll go see the big world out there, and by the time we get back they'll have forgotten all about us."

"Good!" Yanysh grinned broadly. "You've hit the nail on the head, as usual!"

They rose to their feet, in a buoyant mood. Maxi prepared to board a train the next day. He would travel to the next city, where he would then take the return train for Debrecen. On the way, he would pass carefully through each car, taking every precaution. Who knew? If he was lucky, he just might land a whale.

◦◦◦

Menachem Levine boarded the train for Debrecen and looked around for an empty seat. The compartment was filled to capacity. He went into the next car, which was also full. Finally, he found a single empty seat in a crowded car, next to the aisle. He sat down uneasily, his mind on the large bills in his briefcase. He was fearful and suspicious of the person seated beside him, but the alternative was to spend the next two hours on his feet, arriving exhausted at his destination. He was already very tired. He needed a nap.

He was afraid to let himself fall sleep, lest someone rob him while he slumbered. His eyes closed with weariness, then flew open with a start. Instinctively, his hand went to his briefcase. Again his eyes closed, and again his nerves forced them open. This went on for half an hour, until exhaustion overcame him at last and he fell into a deep sleep.

In the middle of the crowded railroad car stood Maxi Marian, humming contentedly to himself. This was it! The Jew in the dark suit was obviously carrying a large sum of money in his briefcase. All Maxi had to do was keep a sharp eye out for the detectives and get to work.

Cautiously, he glanced around. His senses, sharp and well trained, had taught him how to be alert to impending danger. With a newspaper in his hand, he walked slowly down the aisle in the direction of the sleeping Jew. As he reached the Jew, he deliberately let the paper drop.

Its pages scattered along the floor. Maxi groaned, and bent to pick them up. The Jew's eyes were firmly closed, and his seatmate was asleep as well. With an almost imperceptible motion, Maxi's fingers snaked out to the Jew's briefcase, opened it quickly, and pulled out a long envelope, which he concealed among the pages of his scattered newspaper. A moment later he was passing into the next compartment. When the train stopped at the next station, Maxi got off.

Strolling along the platform, he passed the compartment where his victim lay sleeping, and grinned to himself.

He wiped the sweat from his brow. In a private corner, he counted his loot. This far exceeded his expectations: 15,000 *pengo* in large bills! He'd never dreamed of such a windfall. For a fleeting instant, he contemplated not revealing to Yanysh the true extent of his haul. Instead, he could report only half. He'd give Yanysh 3,750 and keep the other three-quarters for himself.

Almost at once, he rejected the notion. Their utter loyalty to each other was the bedrock of their partnership, and the secret of their success. If they started lying to each other, they were finished.

When the train pulled into Debrecen with a blast of its whistle, Menachem awoke with a start. He broke into an enormous yawn. *I'm so tired,* he thought, and tried to fall back asleep. Suddenly, he remembered that he was traveling to Debrecen to conduct some business that just might rescue the remnants of his business and his standing in the business world. Then he remembered the money. He thrust his hand into the briefcase and felt for the envelope.

It was gone!

Impossible! Why, just minutes ago the envelope had been there, safe and sound. How had this happened?

He tried again. The briefcase was empty. A shriek issued from his lips.

The other passengers crowded around as he cried heartrendingly, "The money, the money! Someone's stolen my money. Someone's stolen my life!"

The passengers tried to calm him, but he continued to scream, inconsolable. Several people advised him to lodge a complaint at the police station.

"Who will listen to me?" Menachem groaned. "In a place where so much crime takes place, who will care about one more theft?"

He stepped down onto the platform and stumbled around like a drunkard. There was no longer any point in his coming here. No reason for him to be in this wicked city. No point to anything he might do from here on in.

With no other options open to him, he decided to take the advice he'd been given. He went to the nearest police station and lodged a complaint about the robbery. He pleaded for help in finding the pickpocket, but the police were just as much at a loss as he was. They suspected that this was the work of the infamous pair they'd been vainly seeking for so long.

But compassionate Jewish souls can be found in every place. Menachem was soon surrounded by Jews who refused to abandon him in this difficult hour. They gave him food and drink, and strongly urged him to travel at once to the holy Rebbe, R' Yitzchak Isaac of Spinka, author of the *Chakal Yitzchak*, who was renowned for the power of his prayer as well as his clever solutions.

"He can help where no one else can," they assured him. "Go to Selish." Selish was the Rebbe's place of residence at that time.

Menachem walked into the Rebbe's courtyard, bent with sorrow. The *gabbai*, taking pity on him, sent him in to the Rebbe without delay.

As soon as he entered the holy Rebbe's sanctum, Menachem burst into tears. All his anguish went into the twin streams pouring down his cheeks.

"What is it?" the Rebbe asked kindly.

"My money's been stolen," Menachem wept bitterly. He told the Rebbe about the state of his business affairs, and how he had taken a huge loan from the bank. "And it was all stolen by a pickpocket on the train," he sobbed.

"I have an idea for you," the Rebbe said. "I will tell it to you on one condition: that you accept it unquestioningly."

"Agreed!" Menachem said eagerly.

"In that case, this is what you must do," said R' Yitzchak Isaac. "Return to Debrecen at once. Place a large ad in all the newspapers, stating that your money was stolen on the train. Say that anyone who has information about the robbery should come to your room at the hotel and he will be rewarded. But instead of writing that you were robbed of 15,000 *pengo*, say that 30,000 *pengo* were taken."

Momentarily forgetting his promise, Menachem protested, "But only half that sum was actually stolen from me. When I lodged a complaint at the Debrecen police station, it was for 15,000 *pengo*. If I suddenly say that the amount was double that, they'll think me dishonest!"

The Rebbe scolded him gently. "Didn't you promise to accept what I say? In that case, here's what you do. Follow my instructions to the letter and you will not regret it. If the police come to you with a complaint, tell them that the Rebbe who lives in Selish instructed you to act in this fashion. With Hashem's help, you will see salvation."

Encouraged by the Rebbe's words, Menachem set out at once for Debrecen. On his arrival, he visited the newspaper offices and placed his ad.

Maxi went out on Monday morning to buy some groceries. He was whistling merrily. What a hit! He and his partner would be sitting pretty for a good long time to come!

Yanysh was at home, reading the newspaper. A bold ad, entitled, "They Stole My Money!" suddenly caught his attention. His jaw fell disbelievingly as he scanned the ad. His face flushed with anger. "That two-timing Maxi! That double-crossing sneak!" he cried out.

He sat staring at the ad, straining to think. What to do? After a time, he nodded his head decisively, and left the house with hurried steps.

Monday night, police officers visited Menachem's room at the hotel.
"Did you place this newspaper ad?"
"Yes, I did," Menachem replied nervously.
The policemen beamed at him. "The stolen goods were recovered! You are invited down to the station to identify your packet of money."

Menachem was on his feet almost before the words were out.

At the police station, he found that the recovered packet was indeed his own, and that the entire sum was present in the same large bills. Not a penny was missing.

"How did you do it?" he asked joyously. "How did you catch those crooks so quickly?"

"*We* did it?" chuckled the inspector. "*You* did it! You were very clever. How did you think of such a shrewd plan? You have some brains!"

"What are you talking about?" Menachem was bewildered.

"Do you know what you managed to do? Thanks to you, we caught the two biggest pickpockets in this city. We've been after them for years, without a clue. Then along comes a clever Jew and traps them both, just like that!" He snapped his fingers.

"I didn't do anything," Menachem said honestly. "It was all the idea of the Rebbe who lives in Selish."

"We've heard of the great rabbi from Selish," the inspector told him. "I always knew he was a very holy man. Now I know that he's also one of the smartest men in the country. Do you know what happened? You advertised that 30,000 *pengo* was stolen from you. One of the partners read the ad and was certain that his partner, who stole the money from you last week, had been lying when he said he took only half that sum. Their working relationship was based on absolute trust — and you broke that trust. Yanysh, the one who saw the ad, felt deceived. He raced out to confront his partner, Maxi, out in the street. He grabbed Maxi and began shouting, 'Trickster, liar, double-crosser! You told me you stole only 15,000, when it was really 30,000! You gave me 7,500, and took more than 22,000 for yourself. Thief!'

"Maxi tried to calm him down, denying that he had taken 30,000. But Yanysh didn't believe him. In his anger, he came to us, the police, and turned in his friend. That's how we got our hands on those two notorious pickpockets, along with all your money." The inspector's tone was reverent. "To tell the truth, I don't believe this was ordinary cleverness. I think that, along with the *rabbiner's* wisdom, it was his holiness that brought this amazing thing about."

"A wise man is preferable to a prophet, but a wise man who is also a prophet is even more! How did the Rebbe know that there were two partners involved in this crime, when we had been talking about a single thief?"

This was the question Menachem raised whenever he told the story. "Thanks to the Rebbe, I fully recovered from my financial losses. My factories began thriving again, and I returned to my former prosperity. The Rebbe's idea saved me, by restoring not only my stolen money, but also my life!"

Like a Dream

THE GROUP OF CHASSIDIM SURROUNDING THE HOLY R' Uri of Strelisk were unbelievably poverty stricken. R' Uri, renowned as "the Saraf" (angel), was as detached from the material world as a real angel. He was destitute, and it looked as though he had deliberately chosen to be that way. The Rebbe scorned money, and his chassidim, attempting to imitate his ways, clung to their poverty as well. For long periods, the Rebbe and his family suffered the pangs of hunger. As time passed, however, some more well-to-do chassidim joined the congregation, and these undertook to support the Rebbe and his family.

Living with the Rebbe were his son, R' Shlomo (who filled his father's shoes for a short time before passing away just months later, saying, 'How can one live without a father like that?'), his daughter, and his son-in-law, the *tzaddik* R' Yitzchak. During R' Uri's lifetime, his daughter and son-in-law were supported along with him and ate at his table. But after the Rebbe departed this world on 23 Elul, 5586 (1825), R' Yitzchak and his family began to suffer seriously from hunger. They would fast for whole days at a time, simply because there was not a crumb of food in the house.

R' Yitzchak accepted this suffering with love, and learned Torah through the pain. Like his father-in-law, the Saraf, he, too, viewed poverty as a valuable aid in his service of Hashem. This world and its pleasures, he believed, distance a person from his Creator. Not content with this, he undertook still another resolution: He would take no positive action in pursuit of a livelihood, and would ask for no man's support. This resolution derived from a powerful trust in Hashem, a trust he acquired through holy and devoted service. "If *HaKadosh Baruch Hu* wishes to support me, and I am deserving of it," R' Yitzchak reasoned, "He will send help even if I do nothing to interfere."

Seeing the way R' Yitzchak and his wife, daughter of the holy Saraf, suffered from hunger, the chassidim took up a collection from which the family could be supported. From time to time, when some pennies had been gathered together, one of them would bring the money to the house so that the holy Rebbe's descendants might not perish, Heaven forbid, of starvation.

The chassidim supported the family in this way for a number of years, while the children — and the expenses — were still small. Then, like a dream, the years passed and R' Yitzchak's two oldest daughters had reached marriageable age. The family could barely make ends meet.

R' Yitzchak's good wife saw her daughters growing older, and worried about them. She added up the costs of marrying them off, and her worry grew. If there was not enough money to cover their daily household expenses, how would they ever be able to pay for weddings, dowries, and the like? From that day on, the wife kept up a constant pressure on her husband: "You can't just sit with folded hands. You've got to do something!"

R' Yitzchak raised his eyes from his *sefer*, where they tended to be fixed at any hour of the day or night. "And exactly what," he asked mildly, "do you think I can do?"

The question was asked to remind her of the policy he had undertaken: to do nothing in pursuit of money, but rather to "toss his burden up to Hashem," the true Source of support.

The experienced wife was ready for the question, and had her answer prepared: "After my father passed away, you became a disciple of his foremost student, the Sar Shalom of Belz. Go to him now, and ask him for a *berachah* and some advice about our difficult situation!"

Her voice trembled as she spoke, and tears welled up in her eyes. For long years she had remained silent in the face of numbing poverty. She had suffered the lack and the deprivation without a word. But the situation had turned desperate now.

R' Yitzchak sensed his wife's hidden weeping that threatened to burst out from beneath the heavy covering of submission to the Creator and loving acceptance of suffering. He, too, felt like crying. He packed his things and set out on the journey.

He was welcomed in Belz with great honor. However, it was not honor he had come seeking, but salvation. He poured out his heart to the Rebbe. He told of his poverty, which had grown more severe now that his daughters had come of age, and of the pressure his good wife was rightfully exerting on him.

The Rebbe listened to him. When R' Yitzchak had finished unburdening himself, the Rebbe advised him to travel throughout the cities and towns of Galicia, introducing himself as the Saraf of Strelisk's son-in-law and asking chassidim for their help in meeting the expenses of *hachnasas kallah*. "I am certain that you will emerge from such a trip with a large sum of money that will allow you to marry off your daughters respectably. I will provide a warm letter of recommendation."

R' Yitzchak had the look of a man who had been pierced through the heart. "But how?" he cried out in anguish. "How can I do such a thing? I undertook not to ask for any man's help. *Baruch Hashem*, until today I've never had to cross that line. I do not wish to change the way I serve Hashem. I cannot ask anyone in the world for financial help or any other kind of help!"

"You won't have to ask for help," the Sar Shalom explained. "Just walk around the cities and towns telling people what you were to the Rebbe of Strelisk, whose name is known everywhere. People will understand on their own, and will shower donations on you like rain, without your having to say another word."

"I can't do that, either," R' Yitzchak said, hanging his head. "Traveling throughout the country waving my *yichus* in front of everyone's face is saying, loud and clear, 'Give me money.' This runs counter to my identity, my nature."

The Sar Shalom saw how deeply R' Yitzchak held this principle. He sat lost in thought for several moments, while the room was plunged into total silence.

R' Yitzchak sat silent, too. He dared not disturb his rebbe's reflections. At last, the Sar Shalom turned to him and broke the silence.

"I see that you are resolute about not asking for anyone's help. But how about if I were to send you to a rich Jew who would provide the money for all wedding and dowry expenses for both your daughters? Would you go to him?"

R' Yitzchak remained firm as steel. "I will agree only on the condition that I will not have to change my custom. That is, the rich man would have to donate the money of his own goodwill, without my having to say a word. Until now, good people — my father-in-law's chassidim — have supported me without my having to ask them."

"In that case, you must prepare yourself for a long journey — to Romania," the Sar Shalom said apologetically. "In the city of Yasi there lives a very rich Jew, whose name I do not know, who will host you with honor and provide all your expenses with a lavish hand, without any effort on your part."

"How will he know of my need? Will the Rebbe speak to him?"

"Yes, I will speak to him," the Belzer Rebbe said with a mysterious smile. Only after he had left the room did R' Yitzchak recall that the Rebbe had mentioned that he did not know the man's name. How, then, would he communicate with him?

But when the Rebbe speaks, one does not ask questions. R' Yitzchak returned home to Strelisk, told his wife about the amazing proposal, and with her warm blessing packed his things for the long trip to Romania.

He went on foot. Railroads had not yet been built to shorten the distance from Galicia to Romania, and R' Yitzchak had neither the money to hire a private carriage nor even the pennies needed to pay his fare in a public coach. So he walked the entire long way, only occasionally riding as the guest of some passing traveler who took pity on him and invited him to board his carriage.

Two and a half weeks after he set out, R' Yitzchak reached the city of Yasi, travel-stained, exhausted, and aching in every bone.

Before he had left home, his wife had counted out her meager savings — several coins that she had managed to hoard with great effort — and given them to her husband to pay for lodgings. "You can't sleep in the street," she had said reasonably. R' Yitzchak had thought he could simply lie down on a shul bench. Now, as he trudged painfully through the streets of Yasi, he admitted that his wife had been right. His aching body sorely needed some real rest on a decent mattress. He began to ask the way to cheap lodgings, and was directed to the home of R' Tuvia Ganz, where the poorest visitors stayed.

R' Tuvia provided his guest with a small, clean room furnished with a bed, table, and chair. Ignoring the demands of his terribly exhausted body, R' Yitzchak turned to his host and asked, "Do you have a *Gemara*, by any chance?"

"Certainly!" R' Tuvia beamed, though privately surprised that this obviously fatigued traveler would deny himself sleep. R' Yitzchak almost grabbed the *Gemara* from his host's hand, *le'havdil* the way a drunkard will snatch at a bottle of whiskey after a long period of abstinence. Oblivious to R' Tuvia's astonishment, R' Yitzchak pored over the *Gemara* as peacefully as if he were back home in Strelisk. His fatigue disappeared and his eyes shone with alertness as he studied the holy lines, just as though they had not been threatening to close of their own accord just moments earlier.

Only after he had slightly slaked his soul's thirst by learning several pages of *Gemara* did he grant his body the rest it craved. The following morning, after *Shacharis* and breakfast, he returned to his room and his *Gemara*. There he remained, learning until close to sunset, when it was time to *daven Minchah*. This was his routine on the next day as well, and the one after that.

R' Tuvia Ganz was astonished. He was accustomed to guests who came there to rest after an arduous trip. Usually, after *davening* and breakfast in the morning they would go about their business. Why stay in his lodgings and learn? He had never had a guest like this one. It was four days since his arrival in Yasi, and apart from Torah and *tefillah,* there was nothing happening in his life. Weren't there any *Gemaras* in his own hometown?

But R' Tuvia did not enjoy poking his nose into his guests' business. As far as he was concerned, let the man sit and learn until he would finish all of *Shas* — as long as he paid for his lodgings.

When Perele, R' Yechezkel Schmidt's daughter, was born, his joy knew no bounds. He and his wife had been childless for years, and had found no comfort in all his wealth. He owned many factories and had a great deal of money, but of what use was property and cash if there is no one to inherit it in the end?

At long last, after many years, the miracle happened: Perele was born. From day to day she grew and blossomed, to her parents' delight. As though to make up to them for their long agony of childlessness, the girl was blessed with every kind of good quality.

At 12 years old, Perele had reached her peak. Her fine character and excellent qualities were a byword. Perhaps too many people spoke highly of her; perhaps someone cast an evil eye her way. Perele, the favored and talented only child, was suddenly stricken with a mental illness that stole her wits away. She could no longer move about in society like an ordinary person.

Her parents' grief was inexpressible. After twenty barren years they had merited a daughter at last and then, just when they were beginning to enjoy *nachas*, she had turned into a broken vessel. Never one to skimp on expenses, R' Yechezkel hired the country's finest doctors to examine his daughter. They took their tests, formed their impressions, and threw up their hands in despair. Perele remained lost.

No medication seemed to help her. Though the doctors insisted that their prescriptions had the power to help even the profoundly insane, they did nothing for Perele. She was kept confined to her room to spare her the town's ridicule, but from time to time she managed to open the heavy metal bars over her window and stick her head out into the street. On those few occasions, the parents' overwhelming sorrow threatened to choke them.

Her father traveled to Vienna, and returned with one of the world's foremost experts on mental illness. He was a man whose reputation for curing even the very ill had spread far and wide. The Viennese professor examined the young girl and declared that he had never before seen such a difficult case. "She is hopelessly ill," he said gravely. "Her mind is irreversibly damaged."

Hearing this diagnosis by the world-famous doctor, the father's spirit died inside him. Only the hope that this expert would be able to help his daughter had supported him; now all hope was crushed. For days, he and his wife walked through the rooms of their stately home with shadowed faces. If there had been no limit to their joy before their daughter fell ill, there was no end to their agony now. They lost all taste for life and yearned only for death.

One day, R' Yechezkel Schmidt was sitting at home, sunk in his painful thoughts, when a wave of dizziness washed over him. Slowly his eyes closed and his head dropped to one side. He fell into a deep slumber. And as he slept, he had a dream.

In his dream, he was up in *Shamayim*, watching a large crowd accompany a man who resembled an angel. He was curious to know who the *tzaddik* was. Approaching one of the crowd, he asked about the great man's identity.

"That is the *tzaddik*, Rebbe Uri of Strelisk," he was told. "They're bringing him up from the hall where he was to a higher hall in *Shamayim*. We are all going along to accompany him."

This is a propitious time, R' Yechezkel thought. *I will seize this chance to ask for salvation for my sick daughter.*

He pushed through the crowd until he reached the radiant figure. With tears and pleading he begged the *tzaddik*, "Help me. Please ask for a complete recovery for my sick daughter, Perele bas Sarah Kreindel."

The *tzaddik* gazed at him in sorrow. "I cannot help you. I no longer belong to your world. My advice to you is this: Go to a *tzaddik* who is still alive, and make your request of him. Go see the Belzer Rebbe, the *tzaddik* the Sar Shalom. He can help you."

"But how will I get to Belz?" asked R' Yechezkel. "The distance from Yasi to Belz is very great."

The answer he received surprised him. "I am going to Belz, too. Hold onto my sash …"

In his dream, R' Yechezkel saw the two of them arriving in Belz, where the Strelisker Rebbe introduced him to the Sar Shalom, describing all the travails the father had undergone since his daughter became mentally ill, and asking him to help bring about a salvation for her.

The Sar Shalom listened to the request, and immediately promised to pray for her. Then he reminded R' Uri about his daughter and son-in-law, still living in this world and afflicted with terrible poverty. Two of the Rebbe's granddaughters had reached marriageable age, but their father had nothing for them.

R' Uri explained that he himself had risen so high in the upper world that he was unable to help his daughter. "From that place, I cannot influence a place so far below," he said. "I no longer have any connection with the affairs of the physical world. But I can make one suggestion: Ask R' Yechezkel of Yasi to cover the wedding expenses of my two granddaughters. In that merit he will find salvation for his sick daughter."

"I agree to the condition," the Sar Shalom said. He turned to R' Yechezkel, who stood trembling to one side. "Everything that you have seen and heard here now is not a dream, but is actually happening. It says that when Hashem returned the exiles of Zion, we were like dreamers. *Like* dreamers — not actual dreamers — for it was no dream, but reality. While we've been speaking, R' Yitzchak, son-in-law of the Rebbe of Strelisk, has come to Yasi. Seek him out, and shower him with gold. Give him everything he needs to marry off his two daughters, and much more than that, so that he and his family do not teeter on the brink of starvation every day, and he can learn Torah with peace of mind. In that merit, the good G-d will bless your daughter, Perele, with a speedy recovery so that she returns to her own mind, as she once was."

R' Yechezkel awoke with a start, shaking and perspiring. The dream echoed in his memory like something he had viewed in reality. What had the *tzaddik* said? "We were like dreamers ..." This had been not a dream, but a vision. With rising impatience he waited for morning, then sent his servants out at once to find R' Yitzchak. They searched in the better inns, moved from there to the middle-level ones, and finally entered the simplest lodgings and still, they found no sign of him. It was only after several days of searching, when R' Yechezkel had nearly despaired of finding the visitor from Strelisk, that it occurred to him to check at the home of R' Tuvia Ganz. And there, poring enthusiastically over a large *Gemara*, sat a man who answered to the name of "R' Yitzchak of Strelisk."

"Why have you come to our city?" asked R' Yechezkel.

R' Yitzchak replied briefly, "The Belzer Rebbe sent me here so that a wealthy man from this city can help me marry off my daughters."

"And why have you not sought out that wealthy man?" R' Yechezkel pressed.

"I have never asked for anyone's help — only Hashem's."

"Are you the son-in-law of the Saraf, R' Uri of Strelisk?"

"Yes," the visitor answered, taken aback. "How did you know?"

"The Belzer Rebbe told me," R' Yechezkel whispered, and related his dream.

Needless to say, R' Yechezkel indeed provided R' Yitzchak with everything he needed in order to marry off his daughters — and much more. Also needless to say, his Perele gradually recovered from her illness until she was back to her old self again, and when she reached the age of marriage she wed a successful young *talmid chacham*. Nor is there any need to state that when R' Yitzchak and the wealthy R' Yechezkel made the trip together to see the holy Belzer Rebbe, and R' Yechezkel laid eyes on the Sar Shalom for the first time, he shook with

fear and awe. "That's the man I saw in my dream!" he whispered to R'
Yitzchak. "The very same one!"

Counsel for the Defense

THE TAVERN IN THE TOWN OF TARKAN, HUNGARY, WAS
filled to capacity. Around each table sat several men, tankards
of ale in front of them. The large crowd talked and drank
energetically. It was the gentile winter holiday, when they celebrate
the birthday of the founder of their religion, and the townsfolk were
celebrating in their traditional way: with drink. From the local church,
where they had listened to the priest deliver his sermon, they flowed directly to the tavern to begin the serious business of slaking their thirst.

The tavern-keeper was not present. He was sitting in the *beis
medrash,* learning. He was *Hagaon Hatzaddik* R' Efraim Green, of
Tarkan, known throughout Hungary as a man with two crowns adorn-
ing his head. On the one hand, he was a holy man who had helped
bring about salvation for many of his fellow Jews. And, on the other,
he had merited the crown of greatness in Torah. The title *"gaon olam,"*
world-class genius, went as naturally with his name as the title "the
holy Rav." As testimony to the reverence with which he was held, after
his passing, nearly every Jewish home in Tarkan named a newborn
son Efraim, after him. Even the local gentiles esteemed him greatly.
Years later, when his grandson, R' Yisrael Aryeh Green — who related
the present story — came to the town, even the gentiles stood up to
accord him full honor.

As was common in those days, R' Efraim kept a tavern to earn his living. However, he did not personally stand about pouring glasses of whiskey. Every possible moment was dedicated to Torah study.

Behind the counter stood two women, serving the huge crowd. One was R' Efraim's good wife, and the second was his daughter, a capable young girl by the name of Frayda. The women were not afraid of the gentiles who swarmed over the place. On the contrary, it was the gentiles who stood in awe of them, and especially of Frayda, who had been blessed with extraordinary courage. Frayda would put every customer firmly in his place. Her sharp tongue was a byword, and she used it to maintain iron control over the tavern. Generally, matters proceeded harmoniously, to everyone's satisfaction. Tarkan's gentile drinking population provided the tavern-owners with a living, while the Green family did its part, making sure to keep a continuous flow and wide variety of alcoholic beverages available to them.

Sunday was the gentiles' day to drink. They returned from church and made straight for the tavern to wet their parched throats. As they drank their fill, it was of course not unusual for some of them to get drunk and while inebriated, to behave in an inappropriate manner. At such times, Frayda would take firm control of the situation. A good tongue-lashing made the crowd cringe even under the influence of the drink, and she was able to chase them outside before they turned the place upside down in their drunken wildness.

More than once, both Frayda and her mother had found themselves facing difficult situations in which intoxicated gentiles abandoned their humanity and began to behave more like monsters instead. Through use of their innate wisdom and life experience, coupled with vigorous action, the two women managed to dominate the situation without too much trouble, and to shoo the drunkards out of the tavern before any real damage occurred.

That day, though, something was different. This was the gentiles' big holiday, and in honor of the occasion the place was extra crowded with local residents who lingered in the tavern for long hours. Outside, a snowstorm raged, coating the town in a layer of white. The contrast between the bitter cold outside and the warmth indoors caused rivulets of condensed water to trickle down the windows, thickening from hour to hour until they turned into small streams that dripped down onto the ground and collected in little puddles.

The gentiles sat sipping, another tankard of ale, another bottle of whiskey. Their voices were raised in song and interminable chatter. Had it ended there, neither mother nor daughter would have minded. But on this special holiday of theirs, some of the gentiles went on to become quite drunk and unruly.

At first, nothing was out of the ordinary. A few of the drinkers collapsed on the floor in a stupor, lying there like dead men. Some engaged in a cursing contest, the winner being the one who could come up with the longest and most colorful string of curses without repeating himself. Three drunkards broke into dance and ribald song, while another group clustered around an old farmer who racked his memory for old jokes that had his cronies literally rolling with mirth. A man with a long beard began plucking the strings of his fiddle, leading a group of rollicking singers.

Up until then, nothing untoward or unexpected had occurred. Gradually, however, the situation began to get out of control. The drinkers began to argue, and verbal arguments quickly moved on to the exchange of blows. Fists flew as punches were delivered to midsections, chins, and noses.

"Mother, we must get them out of here," Frayda said, watching the outbreak of violence. "They'll soon be out of their minds."

"Do as you think best, Frayda," her mother said, with complete faith in her daughter's abilities.

Frayda left her regular post and approached the brawlers. Raising her voice, she berated them roundly. She ordered them to let go of each other and stop fighting. But they had drunk too much. All restraint was gone. Frayda's shrill cries were lost among the louder voices of much larger men.

"Enough! Get out of here! You've crossed the line," Frayda shouted, in an attempt to frighten them off.

This was her mistake. For the first time since she had begun to rule the tavern with an iron fist, she was unsuccessful in dominating the situation. She was at a loss before the drunken brawlers.

"We don't want to go. We like it here!" a red-eyed man yelled hoarsely. Lifting a wooden chair, he waved it menacingly in the air in front of Frayda's eyes. "Don't tell us what to do! We're not little children!"

Frayda was no coward. She stood proudly and courageously, and snapped, "Put down that chair and get out."

"And if I don't?" the gentile mocked her.

"I will call the police."

"By all means, call the police!" he chortled, slurring his words. "I'm not afraid of the police. Fill up our tankards again, until the foam spills onto the tables. Let's make merry, fellows!" And he broke into a raucous dance, still waving the chair about, sometimes dangerously close to Frayda's head. This was the cue for the others to begin behaving like real animals, breaking everything that came to hand. They threw chairs at one other. They hurled tankards to the ground or poured them out on the tables; they broke the windows.

The tavern roiled. Frayda knew that if she did not impose order now, not a thing would be left intact in the source of their livelihood. She screamed at the drunken men with all her might and managed — unbelievably — to shoo them toward the tavern door. But in her fury over the damage they'd caused, she began to revile their religion.

A sudden silence descended. The gentiles stared.

"She cursed our savior," one man shouted suddenly.

"Yes. I heard it with my own ears!" his companion agreed angrily.

"She said that our savior is accursed," roared a third.

"Death to the Jewess!" a fourth cried.

Once the words were spoken, it was impossible to take them back. The Jewish girl was surrounded by furious gentiles, all intent on venting their rage at her slight to their religion's founder. To Frayda's great good fortune, there were a few diligent souls present who raced to the police station to lodge a complaint against the Jewess. The police officers — faithful Christians, to a man — came running to see justice done. And so, though Frayda was arrested and thrown into a dank, dark jail cell, the police did effectively prevent her from losing her life to a lynch mob.

R' Efraim Green returned home that afternoon to the news that his daughter was languishing behind bars. His heart nearly burst when they told him that she was due to stand trial in the near future, on the charge of insulting the Christian "messiah." In the rabidly Catholic Hungary of the time, the punishment for this kind of offense was the severest that the courts could hand down: the death sentence!

R' Efraim and his wife sat on the ground and wept bitter tears. They felt as thought their Frayda had already been taken out and executed. Dozens of their "loyal customers" changed their spots in a single moment, and were now prepared to step forward and swear that they had seen and heard the Jewish girl cursing and reviling their revered one. All the judges were staunch Christians; no defense attorney, learned and experienced though he might be, would be able to save Frayda. In the natural course of things, she had no chance.

But there are other solutions, those that are beyond the bounds of nature.

Frayda had a brother by the name of R' Dovid Green. R' Dovid was an ardent chassid of the holy *tzaddik*, R' Yeshayahu Steiner of Kerestir, renowned throughout the land as "R' Yeshaya'le Kerestirer."

The holy R' Yeshaya'le was a towering spirited leader and personally proved the truth of the saying, "Hashem is close to those who call out to Him in truth." Though he did not stem from a prestigious family of rebbes, from his earliest days a desire burned in him to cling to his Creator. He found his way to the generation's *tzaddikim*, who nurtured him to completeness. His Divine service was based on the principles laid down by the Baal Shem Tov, and R' Yeshaya'le built on these a chassidic court that revolved around *chesed* toward his fellow Jews. Whereas other rebbes might serve their Creator from the privacy of their rooms, R' Yeshaya'le served Hashem while standing beside the stove, cooking food to nourish hungry Jews. His home was open to all, with a bowl of hot soup ready to welcome any visitor, from near or far.

Jews are not stupid. Beneath the chef's exterior, they "smelled" the great *tzaddik*. They streamed to him by the hundreds and the thousands, not to eat his food, but to learn his ways in Hashem's service and to benefit from his blessings, which made an impact on Heaven and brought about miracles here on Earth. Particularly famous were the *melaveh malkah* meals the Rebbe conducted in his *beis medrash*, which hundreds of Jews attended each week from Kerestir and its environs. In honor of the meal, a challah was baked that was as tall as an average-sized man. At the start of the meal the challah was laid on the table, wrapped in a huge white cloth and flanked on either side by burning candles in candlesticks. (A guest from Eretz Yisrael, present at the meal for the first time, nearly fainted at the sight of a "corpse" lying on the table surrounded by candles. Only after the Rebbe washed his hands, uncovered the challah, and cut it open, did the man breathe easier.) After he had eaten a *kezayis* of the challah, the Rebbe would dole out the rest to those present. There were enough of these *sherayim* to feed a hungry person after several days of fasting.

R' Yeshaya'le was also extremely intelligent and knowledgeable about the ways of the world, despite the fact that he had never personally dealt in the outside world. From near and far people came to ask his advice and to partake of his wisdom. (Incidentally, a well-known remedy for unwanted mice was to hang up a picture of R' Yeshaya'le of Kerestir. This custom had its source in two cases, in which Jews came to complain about a massive infestation of mice in their homes and shops. The pesky creatures were gobbling up everything in sight! R' Yeshaya'le suggested that his picture be hung in the problem areas, and the mice disappeared!)

When trouble hit the Green family, Frayda's brother, R' Dovid, did not delay for an instant. He boarded the next train for Kerestir.

"Don't worry. With Hashem's help, all will turn out well. Your sister will not be harmed," R' Yeshaya'le promised warmly.

R' Dovid was relieved. The Rebbe's promise lifted a heavy weight from his heart. Still, they were obligated to take any positive action they could on Frayda's behalf.

"The law will be very severe," he told the Rebbe. "The whole town is boiling. The gentiles are furious and want to see her punished. And the courts won't be reluctant to hand down a death sentence. To save my sister from the hangman's noose, we must hire the best attorney there is. Whom would the Rebbe recommend?"

A broad smile crossed the Rebbe's face, and his eyes sparkled with a special light. "Do not hire any attorney."

"What?" R' Dovid was stunned. "Without an attorney, the case is lost in advance!"

"Don't worry," said the Rebbe. "I'll send you an attorney. Come here a day before the trial to remind me."

After making sure that R' Dovid ate and drank something, the Rebbe parted from him without another word of explanation. R' Dovid traveled home and waited daily for a miracle to happen. But as the trial date drew nearer, the family grew more and more afraid. The winds of public sentiment howled incessantly through Tarkan. The gentile populace was thirsty for Jewish blood. The Rebbe's promise that "all will turn out well" seemed completely detached from reality. Hovering in the void was terror, along with the sense that a big pogrom was imminent, just waiting for the guilty verdict to strike.

The day of the trial arrived.

The entire area in front of the courthouse teemed with humanity. An enormous crowd continued to stream in from every direction. They came not only from the town itself, but also from the surrounding countryside: gentiles traveling in by train and coach to be present at the open trial.

A whole crew of prosecutors stood before the judges, their expressions grim and menacing. In their long black robes, the judges themselves resembled a flock of crows ready to rip apart their prey; in this case, a young Jewish girl looking vulnerable, defenseless, and scared to death.

All eyes turned repeatedly to the place where the defense counsel was supposed to be seated. To everyone's astonishment, the seat was empty. Everyone assumed that Frayda's family had simply abandoned her to her fate without ensuring that she was legally represented. Only her brother, R' Dovid, was calm. The Rebbe had promised to send him a lawyer, and he would do so! R' Dovid had returned to Kerestir the day before, where again the Rebbe had promised to arrange for an attorney to be present at the trial.

The judges took their places. The prosecution was prepared. All the witnesses were eager to tell how the Jewess had cursed their "savior." Apart from the missing defense attorney, all was in readiness for the trial. And yet, despite the intense air of expectancy, the trial did not begin. The judges sat idly by, doing nothing. They, too, seemed to be waiting for something.

This was a totally unexpected and unprecedented phenomenon. No one in the huge crowd of spectators understood what the delay was about. Whispers began to crisscross the courtroom: "If the family has not taken a lawyer, or if he's just late, there's no need to wait for him."

Suddenly, the courtroom doors opened. Every head turned.

Into the room strode a tall, handsome man. With his clean-shaven cheeks and fashionable haircut, he looked like a member of a noble gentile family. His appearance instantly snagged the spotlight. Mesmerized, everyone gazed at the figure, who exuded an overwhelming confidence and strength.

Without asking for the judges' permission or consent, the man walked up to the defense table and began to deliver an energetic speech in defense of the accused girl.

The courtroom seemed under a spell from his first word to his last. When he was done — after an hour and a half — there was total silence in the vast room. Every person there felt as though he had been paralyzed under the influence of the speech. Not even the judges succeeded in recovering their wits for some time. At last, the head judge pounded his gavel and ordered the first of the witnesses to step up and testify.

A shock was in store for them. The very witnesses who had earlier asserted that the Jewish girl had cursed their religion now changed their story, stating that Frayda had merely shouted at them but had not said a word against their "messiah." There had been no cursing or reviling. They had no idea why she had been accused at all.

"You are making a mockery of this court!" railed the judges as they dismissed all charges. "Frayda Green is innocent of any wrongdoing!"

Frayda was released. The gentile crowd left the courtroom with hangdog looks, while the Jews rejoiced. As for the mysterious and impressive defense lawyer, he vanished immediately after the trial as suddenly as he had arrived!

R' Dovid went directly from the courthouse to Kerestir, to thank the Rebbe for the miracle. As he walked into the room, the Rebbe asked with a twinkle in his eyes, "*Nu*, did I send you a good attorney?"

[Many thanks to my friend, R' Efraim Hacohen Weiss, whose father, R' Yisrael Weiss of Bnei Brak, is the son-in-law of R' Yisrael Aryeh Green, nephew of Frayda Green, who recalled the entire incident which happened when he was just a child.]

A Carton of Cigarettes

YOUNG MEIR DOVID LOOKED SAD AS HE CLIMBED DOWN the stairs. Not everyone would have been able to discern the sadness in his eyes, but R' Aharon was very perceptive. For some time now, he had noticed that the boy seemed preoccupied and troubled. R' Aharon had wanted to question Meir Dovid, but had held back. Sometimes, being precipitate can make you lose. R' Aharon did not hasten to pry into others' affairs.

Today, however, worry had completely vanquished the smile that Meir Dovid always tried to wear. R' Aharon noticed, of course. The courtyard of the holy R' Yisrael (the "Yanuka") of Stolin boasted many fine and modest young men, and Meir Dovid was one of the finest. He devoted every minute to Torah study, was pious in his behavior, scrupulous in his mitzvah observance, humble, and modest. Above all, he was outstanding in the fervent and emotional enthusiasm he brought to the chassidism. In short, he was an excellent boy all around.

In light of this, R' Aharon Halevi Kalminov (who later moved to Jerusalem, and became known throughout the city as "R' Aharon Turever" after his birthplace of Turev) was surprised by the anxiety that clouded the young man's face.

R' Aharon was a practical fellow, a chassid who was also a man of action. Without further hesitation, he approached Meir Dovid when they were unobserved, took him by the sleeve, and asked quietly, "Why do you look so downcast? Why are you so confused?"

Meir Dovid flushed crimson. Looking around to see if they were alone, he whispered brokenly, "I'm in big trouble. I've received a military draft notice. I don't have to describe to you what being drafted into the gentile army would mean. No Shabbos, no kosher food, no *tefillin,* and no Torah study. I'd have to separate myself from my *Yiddishkeit*, Heaven forbid. The worry leaves me no rest, day or night!"

"So what do you have a rebbe for?" R' Aharon scolded.

"You're sprinkling salt on the wound," sighed the youth. "I want to go in to see the Rebbe, to pour out my trouble and receive his blessing. I've already handed in my request to the *gabbaim* several times, but have received no reply. Day follows day, and people who came here long after me have been in to see the Rebbe and left satisfied. For some reason, I keep being put off."

Hearing this, R' Aharon stopped his scolding. In his rich experience, he knew that the Rebbe sometimes employed a policy of "the left hand pushes away." Only the Rebbe knew the reasons why.

Several weeks passed. Meir Dovid had nearly despaired of hope. In his mind's eye he saw himself drafted into the army and losing his Jewish spark, bit by bit. One evening, however, immediately after *Maariv*, R' Aharon was startled by the sight of the Rebbe speaking in an undertone with Meir Dovid. The boy's face turned pink with emotion. He went at once to the bookcase, took out a small *sefer Tehillim*, and began to fervently recite chapters of psalms from the depths of his heart.

R' Aharon squeezed into the space between the bookcase and the wall. There, in that hidden corner, he whispered to Meir Dovid, "What did the Rebbe tell you?"

Happily, Meir Dovid answered, "The Rebbe told me to come to his room tonight. As soon as he's finished seeing people, he will see me, too, to deal with my problem."

R' Aharon Turever didn't leave the *beis medrash* that night. He waited tensely to hear what the Rebbe would say concerning Meir Dovid's serious problem.

The line moved slowly. Meir Dovid waited hours for his turn to come. All this time, R' Aharon sat in the *beis medrash* and learned *Gemara*. Every now and then he stole a look at the youth, as though to say, "I'm with you."

Finally, the last petitioner left the Rebbe's room. The door was closed for a moment, and immediately opened again to let Meir Dovid in. R' Aharon sat on hot coals, eyes straying nervously from his open *Gemara* to the door of the Rebbe's room. He was eager to learn how the matter would be resolved.

Several moments later, the door opened. R' Aharon tried to read Meir Dovid's expression. To his surprise and disappointment, Meir Dovid left with his head down, walking very rapidly. He fled before anyone could exchange a word with him, scooting through the *beis medrash* door and into the night.

R' Aharon was astonished — and uneasy. Why had the boy ignored the warm bonds of friendship that had sprung up between them in these last few weeks? Had R' Aharon not provided a strong shoulder for Meir Dovid to lean on? Why was he behaving like a stranger now, not even glancing R' Aharon's way as he left the Rebbe's presence?

These questions troubled R' Aharon. He had no answers. None of the Rebbe's *gabbaim* had overheard their talk, so none were able to disperse the fog of mystery that lay over the matter.

But we can reveal just what passed between the Rebbe and his young chassid, and what occurred to Meir Dovid afterward. Here is what happened:

⌘

As he entered the Rebbe's room, Meir Dovid was seized with terror. People far greater than him trembled with awe as they stood face-to-face with R' Yisrael of Stolin. Shouldn't a young chassid — an unbearded fledgling — quake in his shoes?

He stood totally still, unable to say a word.

"What would you like to say?" the Rebbe asked gently.

New strength seemed to flow through the youth. He began to relate the problem that had brought him here. He described his pain and anxiety over the draft notice. What was he to do? Was it best to obey the summons and join the army? But, in that case, what would become of his *Yiddishkeit*? Or should he try to flee the country, despite knowing of the horrific punishments the cruel arm of the military meted out to those who were caught doing so, especially to Jews like himself?

The Rebbe heard him out in silence. Then, without a word, he entered his inner room for a short time. When he emerged, he was holding a carton of fine-quality cigarettes. "Take this," he told Meir Dovid, handing the carton to him.

Then the Rebbe checked his watch. "Look!" he told the boy. "The train will be leaving the station in a little while. You must hurry as fast as you can to catch it."

Meir Dovid was about to ask what he was to do next, but the Rebbe interjected. "Of course, you must take that train," he said briefly. He pressed the young chassid's hand in farewell.

Meir Dovid left the room with mixed feelings. He was totally confused. Was this his answer? He had presented a serious and focused question but had received virtually nothing in return. A carton of cigarettes and instructions to travel away on the first train. Where to? At which station was he to leave the train? And what in Heaven's name was he supposed to do when he got there?

The cigarettes were another puzzle. What was he supposed to do with them? The Rebbe knew that Meir Dovid was not a smoker. Why, then, provide him with a box of first-class cigarettes?

At the same time, Meir Dovid felt enveloped by a strange peace. It was as though he were being borne aloft by a mother's gentle arms. But the Rebbe had urged him to hurry. Lowering his eyes to avoid meeting the curious ones of his friend, R' Aharon Turever, he raced out of the *beis medrash* as though someone was in hot pursuit. He ran to his room and threw a few personal belongings into a bag, including his *tefillin* and a few holy books, then made a mad dash for Stolin's train depot.

As things turned out, the speed turned out to be very necessary. He reached the depot just as the blast of the whistle announced that the train was pulling out. Fortunately, it was moving slowly. Meir Dovid was able to purchase his ticket and leap onto one of the cars. He found a seat on one of the inner benches, breathing hard from his headlong sprint.

He had done his part. From this point on, he could do nothing but pray for Heavenly compassion, observe developments, and hope that they would turn out to be for his benefit.

Because he did not know what to do, he did nothing. He looked out the window at the passing scenery. It was utterly new to him. Village after village passed by in a blur as the train sped along. Their names meant nothing to him. He saw trees and fields and listened to the monotonous chugging of the train. From time to time, the whistle blew a long blast, and the train stopped at one of the villages or towns. Meir Dovid was completely at a loss.

Many passengers passed him by, each carrying his luggage. Each knew where he was going, and why. Only one passenger was at a total loss among the bustling crowd of travelers. From time to time he glanced despairingly around him, as if hoping against hope that someone would come to his aid. But no one looked familiar. Most were gentiles whose language Meir Dovid barely followed.

An announcement was passed along the compartments: "Last stop, everybody off! We will be reaching our final stop in just a few minutes and will remain there until morning."

Having no choice, Meir Dovid got off the train. He could not have stayed aboard even if he had wanted to. Clutching his small bundle, he stepped from the platform into the street.

It was a small village, like all the villages that had preceded it on the long trip from Stolin. Where to go? The hour was very late. His fellow passengers hurried away in the darkness, each with a clear destination. One made his way to a local inn and another had relatives in town. Only he, Meir Dovid, had no place to go.

No! he thought suddenly. *I am a Jew! Perhaps there are other Jews in this village. If there are Jews, there will be a shul. Where there are shuls, there are benches. I can catch some sleep on one of them in the few hours left till dawn.* He approached a villager and asked, "Are there any Jews here?" The man replied in the affirmative. Meir Dovid sighed with relief. If there were Jews, he was not completely lost.

He began to wander through the streets of the small village, glancing at the doors to see if he could spot a *mezuzah*. His eyes raked the windows where faint candlelight could be discerned. Suddenly, he saw bright light shining from a large house. His heart told him that he had found his Jew.

Tentatively, he walked up to the door. His intuition had not led him astray: A large *mezuzah* was affixed on its right. A heavy weight rolled off Meir Dovid's chest as he knocked. The door was thrown open.

In the doorway stood a man with a long black beard and curly *peyos*. There was a pair of woolen *tzitzis* hanging over his clothes and a warm smile on his face.

"*Shalom aleichem!*" the man greeted him, shaking his hand. "Come in, come in!"

"I'm not from here," Meir Dovid said cautiously. "May I stay for the night?"

"Willingly! That is my business. I rent out rooms!" The man's smile remained fixed in place. "So there's nothing to worry about. I won't try to skin you. We can work out a price."

Meir Dovid felt his spirits lifting. Heaven was helping him. To come like a lost sheep to this village at the end of the world and immediately find his way to the home of such a warm-hearted Jew!

His host led him to a pleasant room. Meir Dovid set down his bundle and began to *daven Maariv* in his chassidic chant. When he was done, he recited the *Kriyas Shema* and prepared himself for bed, nerves still jangling from the events of the long, tiring day.

He did not sleep for long.

Some time after he had drifted off, a loud knocking on his door had him leaping out of bed and lunging for the doorknob. His host stood there, wearing an apologetic look.

"Forgive me for disturbing you," the Jew said in obvious distress, "but I had no choice. There are three tough-looking gentiles sitting in my tavern at this moment, drinking, smoking, and playing cards. They've just run out of cigarettes and are demanding that I find them some more at once!

"I tried to put them off. 'Where am I supposed to find cigarettes in the middle of the night?' I asked. But they're very stubborn, and insisted that I go from room to room, checking to see whether any of my guests has any cigarettes. To tell you the truth, I was afraid to wake the others, but you look like a nice fellow. Tell me, do you by any chance have a box of cigarettes with you?"

Meir Dovid remembered the carton of fine-quality cigarettes in his bundle. "As a matter of fact, I do," he said happily, and ran to fetch them.

His host's face filled with joy. "How much do you want for them?" he asked, a hand going to his pocket.

Meir Dovid refused to take a penny. "I don't even smoke," he protested. "If I have the chance to do another Jew a favor without any trouble, why should I refuse?"

His host blessed him profusely, apologized again for disturbing his sleep, and parted from him with a hearty, "Good night!" Meir Dovid returned to bed, covered himself again, and fell into a deep sleep.

Two or three hours later, he was again shaken awake by the sound of a vigorous knocking at his door. *What now?* Meir Dovid wondered groggily. He went to see.

In the doorway stood his host again. "I really hate to wake you up a second time," he said, "but those gentiles — the ones for whom you gave me the cigarettes — insist that they must speak to you before they leave. I couldn't refuse them."

Meir Dovid was seized with fear. A trio of hard-drinking, chain-smoking, card-playing gentiles wanted an interview with him in the wee hours? Perhaps they had some evil intent in mind. But if he didn't come to them, they would come to him, and the matter could end up even worse. Were they planning to trump up some charge against him and have him thrown into jail? That would not have been such an unusual event. Jewish blood was free for all.

Gathering his courage, he slipped on his shoes, put on his jacket, and allowed his host to lead him to the tavern hall.

The room was filled with cigarette smoke, and the fragrance of rich tobacco mingled with the scent of alcohol. The three gentiles were in a merry mood. On the table before them was the deck of cards they had been playing with all night, along with empty bottles of whiskey and wine, plates of cake crumbs, and an overflowing ashtray bearing the remains of dozens of cigarettes. The host led Meir Dovid forward and said, "Here he is."

They gazed at him through eyes reddened with alcohol and smoke. The oldest of the three spoke first. "Were those excellent cigarettes yours?"

Meir Dovid trembled. Jerkily, he nodded his head. "Yes, I gave you those cigarettes."

"So how much do we owe you?"

"I d-don't know."

The man seemed surprised. "How can you not know? Didn't you pay for them?"

Meir Dovid shook his head. "I didn't pay. They didn't cost me a cent."

"What do you mean?"

"I received the carton as a gift."

The gentile persisted in questioning him to the amusement of his friends, who seemed quite alert despite the hour. "Nevertheless, if you're a smoker, you must know how much a carton of cigarettes costs, even if you did receive this one as a gift. They were of very fine quality, and we've decided to pay you in full. Unless," the gentile's face darkened with sudden suspicion, "you stole them. If you don't smoke, why did you get an expensive box of cigarettes as a gift?"

Meir Dovid saw that brief answers would only increase his trouble. He decided to tell the three gentiles the truth. "I received a draft notice from the army. For an observant Jew like myself, going into the army would be a tragedy. Therefore, I went to my rebbe to ask for his blessing so that I might not have to serve. Instead of a blessing, he handed me this box of cigarettes and told me to take a train. I obeyed his instructions and here I am!"

The three gentiles broke into raucous laughter at his story. "Go in peace!" they said when they were done laughing. "You're a free man."

In the morning, after *davening*, Meir Dovid went to settle his bill. He asked his host whether he knew the men he had spoken to the night before.

"No, this was the first time I've seen them," his host replied. "I don't know where they came from or where they might be going. They came, asked for food and drink, smoked, and played cards. When I presented them with their bill, they went over it item by item, and asked why I hadn't demanded payment for the cigarettes.

"'That's because I didn't pay for them,' I replied. But they insisted on paying for the cigarettes themselves, and even demanded that I wake you for that purpose. 'It's already almost morning,' they said, 'and he'll soon have to get up anyway. Let it be an hour earlier.'"

After he had eaten a quick breakfast, Meir Dovid gathered his belongings and set out on his return journey. The future looked murky and unclear. The following few weeks passed in a fever of anxiety. When the time came for him to present himself to the draft office, he underwent the entire procedure with a hammering heart. Then it was time to undergo a medical exam, to see whether he was fit to serve in the military.

To his utter astonishment, the three doctors in the examining room were the very same cardplayers who had accepted his fine cigarettes a month before!

At the sight of him the three burst into laughter, as though suddenly recalling a hilarious joke. Then they consulted together in whispers, and without benefit of an exam or any medical questions at all, the doctors wrote in Meir Dovid's file, "Unfit to serve."

"Go in peace," they told him again. "You're a free man."

[Thanks to R' Yisrael Asher Halevi Krauss, *Shlita*, who told us this story that he heard from his grandfather, R' Aharon Turever Kalminov, who heard it from Meir Dovid himself upon the latter's return to the Stoliner Rebbe's court in Stolin.]

A Joyous Purim

ABOUT 10 KILOMETERS FROM THE CITY OF NIREGHAZA, Hungary, there was a small, remote town by the name of Ratzfert. Though few had ever heard of it, the place was gradually turning into a bustling center of chassidic life. On Shabbos, its streets were filled with men wearing *shtreimels*, white socks, and gleaming *kapotes*. Simchas Torah and Purim brought the chassidim out in droves to dance in the streets, much to the open enjoyment of the town's gentile populace. Over the course of time the vibrant chassidic community continued to flourish, until the town began to be called "Little Jerusalem."

During the First World War, a refugee arrived in Ratzfert from Galicia. He was the *tzaddik* R' Shalom Eliezer Halberstam, son of the Sanzer Rebbe, author of the *Divrei Chaim*. He settled in town.

Not far from Ratzfert was an even more remote village called Lokohana. This was the home of about twenty Jewish families, who lived there on excellent terms with their gentile neighbors. Yosef Moshe Farkash ran Lokohana's big general store. Rumor had it that he had money to spare; from time to time he would loan considerable sums to his good friends.

Late one afternoon, as Yosef Moshe prepared to lock up his store and go to shul for *Minchah* and *Maariv,* and the *shiur* that was given in between, a gentile by the name of Anton burst through the door, breathing hard.

Anton was something of a ne'er-do-well, and had been so all his life. He was a businessman whose businesses never succeeded. Nevertheless, he never gave up hope of making a "killing" and growing wealthy overnight. His friends laughed at him, and there was no one in all the village who would agree to lend him even a small amount of money.

"Moses, my good friend," Anton exclaimed, when he'd caught his breath. "How are you today?"

Yosef Moshe returned an impassive look. "Anton, you've come too late. I'm about to lock up."

"Don't worry, you won't be late for your prayers. I just this minute passed the synagogue and saw that the gate was still locked."

Anton came closer, face dripping with a cloying sweetness. Yosef Moshe sensed that this visit was going to cost him. "What do you want, Anton?"

"You're one smart Jew, Moses," Anton chuckled. "I need a loan. The deal of a lifetime is waiting for me just around the corner! A friend of mine has fallen on hard times and is forced to sell his flock of sheep. He's offered it to me at a bargain price. I need your help."

Yosef Moshe's nostrils flared nervously. "With your kind of luck, Anton, all those sheep will die the minute you lay a hand on them. How much do you need?"

"Five hundred gold coins, for three months."

"*Five hundred?* That's an enormous amount of money!"

Anton said calmly, "I have a guarantor for the loan."

"Then borrow the money from him," Yosef Moshe suggested. He began to close the heavy shutters.

Anton pressed forward. "You don't understand me, Moses. My guarantor is a judge."

Yosef Moshe stopped short and fixed Anton with a measuring glance. His hand paused in the act of reaching for the heavy lock. "Are you talking about Judge Parnatz?"

"Exactly," Anton beamed.

The storekeeper's expression softened. "That's a different story. Show me a letter of guarantee from Judge Parnatz, and you shall have the loan."

Judge Parnatz was the little village's ultimate authority. He was judge and supervisor over every area of village life. His signature on a loan changed the entire picture, for he had more than enough money to cover the sum.

The next day, Anton brought the loan agreement, written up in all the usual terminology and signed by the judge as guarantor. Yosef Moshe lent him the money for a period of three months. He lost no sleep that night, knowing that the money was solidly backed.

The loan came due on a Friday. Yosef Moshe was busy at home that day, packing a small suitcase. He planned to spend Shabbos in nearby Ratzfert with his rebbe, the *tzaddik* R' Naftali Hertz of Ratzfert.

A loud knocking on the door interrupted him. Opening it, he was surprised to find two visitors. One was Judge Parnatz, tall and silver haired. The second man, plump and fair, was Anton.

"We've come to return the loan," said the judge. "Will you let us come in, or do we have to talk out here in the street?"

Yosef Moshe stepped back hurriedly. "What a question! Please, gentlemen. Come in."

They followed him into the living room. "Why has the judge troubled himself to come to my house?" Yosef Moshe asked respectfully, thrusting the box containing his *shtreimel* into his suitcase.

Parnatz sat down and leaned back comfortably. "I came to witness the return of the loan," he said with a chuckle. Rubbing his hands with pleasure, he said, "Well, Mr. Anton, let's see you succeed at something for the first time in history, and repay your debt!"

Anton placed a bundle of bills into Yosef Moshe's hands. A quick count showed Yosef Moshe that he held the equivalent of 500 gold coins. His mind was on his upcoming trip. The wagon-driver was to pick him up momentarily for the trip to Ratzfert. Had he packed his *tallis*?

"Yosef Moshe!" called his wife, Tova. "Did you remember to pack your white socks?"

"Oh, I forgot!" Yosef Moshe exclaimed. Running over to the clothes cupboard, he took a pair of long white socks out of a drawer and absentmindedly put the bundle of money in its place.

The judge's keen eyes noticed the move. A malicious smile crossed his face, and was gone in an instant.

"I see that we've caught you in the middle of packing for a trip. Are we disturbing you?" he asked.

Yosef Moshe stammered something evasive.

"Where are you going?" Judge Parnatz went on, with apparently guileless curiosity.

"To Ratzfert. That's where my rabbi lives."

"Ah, very nice. Have a good trip," the judge said expansively. He and Anton took a hasty leave, apologizing for the interruption.

R' Naftali Hertz of Ratzfert was the foremost student of one of Hungary's greatest figures, the holy *gaon* R' Asher Anshel Halevi Jungreis of Tchenger, author of the *Menuchas Asher*, who was known as a tremendous *gaon* as well as a holy man of wonders. R' Naftali Hertzke himself was also known for his greatness in both areas, Torah and *kedushah*. As a young man, he had served as rabbi of a small village named Yanyshi, where he studied Torah day and night. In his humility, he did not permit himself to be addressed as "Rav" and sat in the center of the shul rather than along the coveted eastern wall.

Nevertheless, his reputation for piety and wisdom preceded him everywhere, until the people of Ratzfert chose him as their Rav.

R' Naftali Hertzke declined the position and remained in Yanyshi. Then, one day, the Ratzfert community learned that he was traveling to a wedding in a distant locale. They came to his home in the dead of night, loaded his furniture and *sefarim* onto wagons, and bore them off to Ratzfert.

Though his rabbinate in Ratzfert began against his will, the position ended up to his liking. He became known throughout Hungary as the Rav of Ratzfert, and stories about his righteousness circulated widely. Apart from his Torah scholarship, he devoted a great deal of energy to taking up collections for the poor, and particularly for the Rabbi Meir Baal HaNess fund. To this end, he used charity money to buy horses and wagons, which he leased to people who used them to earn money — all of which was expressly dedicated to the Rabbi Meir Baal HaNess fund. It was said that, in his eagerness to save money for *tzedakah*, R' Hertzke would get up at night to personally feed and water the horses.

This was where Yosef Moshe went for Shabbos, without a clue as to what was taking place behind his back in the village he had left behind.

R' Hertz behaved like a Rebbe, sitting down to a *seudah* on Shabbos night together with his many chassidim and spouting words of Torah on the weekly portion. Yosef Moshe sat along with the others, enjoying the spiritual experience. Suddenly, a silence fell. R' Hertz opened his eyes, which had been closed, and began to scan his chassidim's faces. He gave Yosef Moshe a long, penetrating look, and asked gently, "Have you placed wine on the table yet?" He was referring to an old, established chassidic custom of *"shtellen vine"* — a custom that was not usually practiced at R' Hertz's table. Flustered, Yosef Moshe replied in the negative.

"In that case," the Rebbe said, "You must do so now."

Without waiting for the astonished chassid to answer, the Rebbe turned to his *gabbai* and instructed him to announce, "R' Yosef Moshe Farkash *'shtelt vine.'*"

The wine was poured into small glasses. The chassidim sipped their wine and the *beis medrash* was immediately filled with cries of "*L'chayim!*" The Rebbe personally blessed Yosef Moshe, then ordered one of the other chassidim to sing "*Menuchah V'Simchah.*"

The moment the song was over, the Rebbe looked anxiously at Yosef Moshe. "You must *shtel vine* on the table!"

Yosef Moshe wanted to say, "I did that already," but the Rebbe gave him no opportunity to speak. Again without waiting for his consent, he ordered the *gabbai*, "Announce at once that R' Yosef Moshe is placing the wine."

The shul rustled with speculation. Clearly, there was something behind the Rebbe's unusual actions. Twice in one night, he had ordered his chassid to "*shtel vine,*" when he had never even practiced the custom before! The Rebbe obviously saw beyond the rest of them, beyond the limitations of time and space imposed on others. That, no doubt, was why he had issued these strange instructions. All would surely become clear in time.

As for Yosef Moshe himself, his heart missed a few beats as he wondered at the Rebbe's intention. He glanced down at his watch as the announcements were made, as though to etch the time into his memory.

The whole thing was repeated again at the Shabbos morning *seudah*. R' Hertz had the *gabbai* announce that R' Yosef Moshe was "*shtelling vine,*" then motioned for Yosef Moshe to offer the wine again. Taking the cue, Yosef Moshe whispered to the *gabbai*, who straightened up and announced that R' Yosef Moshe was offering yet more bottles of wine. Additional bottles were brought in, after which everyone sipped a bit of wine and wished each other a hearty "*L'chayim!*"

There was a tangible sense in the *beis medrash* that something had happened. Yosef Moshe himself, though he knew nothing, sensed that something bad had occurred back home and the Rebbe was attempting to sweeten the decree. Privately, he resolved to return home immediately after *Havdalah* on *Motza'ei Shabbos*. Perhaps, as he took leave of the Rebbe, R' Hertz would share the secret with him or, if he was unworthy of that, at least to offer a hint.

These thoughts were uppermost in his mind as he went in later to take leave of the Rebbe. R' Hertz pressed his hand warmly and wished him a good week and a safe trip home. Then he added a few significant words: "And celebrate a joyous Purim."

Purim, in the middle of the year, on any old weekday? What was the meaning behind the strange announcement, and the custom that had never before been practiced in the courtyard at Ratzfert? Surprise was piled upon surprise. But wondering at one's Rebbe was akin to questioning the *Shechinah* itself. Yosef Moshe did not permit himself to dwell on questions for long. He climbed aboard his wagon and set out for home.

"Judge" Parnatz had never attended a single law class at the university. In fact, he had never so much as laid eyes on the big university in Budapest, not even from the outside. He had been born in little Lokohana and had hardly ever left its precincts. His knowledge of the law was limited to the fact that lawbooks were big and heavy, and if he was not mistaken they were a sort of burgundy color.

He had earned his position simply by merit of the fact that there had been no one else in Lokohana willing to take on the job and settle disputes among the villagers. Not infrequently, he would settle the disputes with his strong arms and iron fists. Parnatz was a judge in name only, but he was still the village authority. His opinions (or his fists) were the deciding factor in settling cases and punishing criminals.

On Friday, when Yosef Moshe slipped the bundle of bills into the clothes cupboard, the judge had watched with interest. Afterward, he carefully studied the layout of the room and the entire house, paying particular attention to the placement of the cupboard.

That night, after all the villagers had gone to sleep, Parnatz went to work. Donning a mask, he tiptoed stealthily toward Yosef Moshe's home. He was certain of his success. First of all, he would work in total silence. Second, the mask completely concealed his identity. And, third, to whom would it possibly occur that the honorable judge was a thief?

The hour was well advanced. Apart from the stars peeking down from the black sky, all was dark and quiet. A few dogs barked on the outskirts of the village, but none was near enough to disturb him. He managed to open the old lock on the front door with ease, but when he pushed the door open, its rusty hinges squealed loudly. Parnatz froze. But the silence continued as before. After standing like a statue for the space of two endless minutes, his eyes grew accustomed to the dark and he found his way over to the clothes cupboard.

A muffled curse escaped him as this, too, opened with a protesting squeak. Every hinge in the house was in apparent need of a good oiling. His hands rummaged among the clothes, his nose sniffing like an animal's. He disagreed with the popular saying that claimed, "Money has no smell." He knew that it did! That afternoon, before accompanying Anton to the Jew's house to repay the debt, he had rubbed garlic on several of the bills. Anton had stared at him in astonishment and waited for an explanation, but none had been forthcoming.

A broad smile split the judge's face as he caught the scent of garlic. Soon the bills rustled in his hands. He hid them in his shirt front, just as a shadow abruptly moved closer.

Parnatz had a strong heart, and it was only this fact that saved him from collapsing on the spot when a shrill voice screamed suddenly, "Thief! Robber!"

Mrs. Tova Farkash was not deaf, and the double squeak of the hinges had woken her. She had been observing the masked intruder's movements, and decided to shake him up.

"Do you think I don't recognize you?" Tova shrieked mockingly. "Next time, get a more convincing mask or bend over, tall man. Judge Parnatz, what an honor! A judge by day, a thief by night."

Her small children were roused by her screams. They came running into the room in tears, and began shrieking along with their mother, "Thief, get out of here!" Tova Farkash yelled, "What an honorable reception you'll get in the village. I'm going to tell everyone just who our great judge is!"

With these words, Tova only worsened her situation. She had pushed Parnatz to the wall, leaving him no option but to resort to brute strength. Moments later, mother and children were trussed like chickens, with gags over their mouths. The thief made liberal use of the plentiful rags he found in the cupboard. Then he lit a kerosene lamp and used it to search the house. He soon found what he had been looking for: a strong, thick rope. He fashioned a noose at one end. In order to eliminate witnesses, he had decided to ruthlessly hang the mother and her children.

With the heavy noose in hand, he returned to the front room and began to look for a good place to hang the rope. The job was easy. Most houses in those days came equipped with a wooden beam arched over the doorway. He tested the wood with murderous pleasure. The beam was strong enough to support the weight of several hanging bodies.

When the noose was hanging securely from the arched beam, he decided to hang the mother first. At that very moment, in the Ratzfert *beis medrash*, the Rebbe was calling, "Yosef Moshe, you must '*shtel vine!*'" It occurred to the judge that it would be a good idea to test the noose out on his own neck first, to see if the rope was really strong enough. He dragged a chair under the arch, climbed up, and stuck his head through the noose. Yes, the rope was strong enough. He began to pull his head away.

At that moment, the Rebbe called a second time, "Yosef Moshe, '*shtel vine!*'" As the chassidim merrily wished each other "*L'chayim!*" the chair suddenly slipped from beneath the judge's feet. He found himself dangling helplessly in the air: the very fate he had planned for his victims!

For long hours, the mother and her children lay bound on the floor in the next room, unable to move. Then came the second Shabbos meal, and the Rebbe announced that Yosef Moshe should offer wine. Tova managed to remove the rag from her mouth. When the Ratzfert chassidim were drinking wine a second time, the neighbors heard Tova's cries and came to free her and her children from the ropes that were binding them. At the same time, they discovered the judge's body hanging from the beam. Only then did Mrs. Farkash understand why the thief had suddenly left them alone the night before.

Yosef Moshe heard the whole story from his wife on *Motza'ei Shabbos*. The timing had been amazingly precise, during both the nighttime and daytime meals. Now, at last, he understood the Rebbe's final instruction, "And celebrate a joyous Purim," for his enemy was hanged instead of his family, just as Haman was hanged instead of Mordechai, and the Jews were not killed.

A Four-Part Parable

T HE SHUL WAS FULL. IT WAS SHABBOS AFTERNOON, AND THE crowd was waiting eagerly to hear the scheduled speech.

On the steps leading to the *aron kodesh* stood a man wrapped in a *tallis*. He was built along large lines, with a sparse beard that moved as he spoke. His hands moved continuously, emphasizing his words.

"Who's the speaker?" someone whispered to his neighbor.

Without removing his eyes from the speaker's mouth, the other man said, "You don't know? It's the Dubno Maggid!"

"Interesting," the first man smiled. "And here I thought the Dubno Maggid was a different man."

He continued listening, smiling his mysterious smile. He smiled because only he knew the truth: He himself was the Dubno Maggid!

The man delivering the talk was masquerading as the famous Maggid, hitching a ride on his coattails as so many others had tried to do in those days. And no wonder: The Dubno Maggid's wonderful talks and incisive parables, combined with his beautiful power of oratory, swayed people's hearts everywhere he went. The Dubno Maggid was unique in his generation — and perhaps in every generation — as a weaver of parables. His talks had a special style, illuminating the holy texts with wonderful clarity, and without unnecessary embellishments.

The Maggid continued to listen to the imposter. With incredible self-restraint and patience, he had become used to hearing various professional speakers use his own sermons, and especially his original parables, without attributing them to him. With even greater restraint, he would listen to someone use his material without benefit of his own verbal grace and ability, ruining the beauty of his ideas and obscuring their meaning.

In the case, however, of a speaker misusing his thoughts and imbuing them with values and ideas never intended for them, R' Yaakov Kranz, the Dubno Maggid, would sometimes stand up and stop the lecture in midstream, pointing out the speaker's error. Alternatively, he would leave the *beis medrash* in order to avoid publicly shaming the speaker.

The present counterfeit speaker had apparently listened to one of the Dubno Maggid's talks in one of the Lithuanian town shuls, memorized it, and was now going about from town to village — places where no one knew R' Yaakov Kranz personally — pretending to be the renowned Maggid and collecting the appropriate fee for his services. As he went on, the false maggid began to distort R' Yaakov's original thought. Still, the Maggid listened patiently. When the speaker began to spout real nonsense, however, his patience came to an end. R' Yaakov rose to his feet.

"*Rabbosai*! I must reveal to this holy congregation that the speaker to whom you are listening is not the Maggid from Dubno. He has heard me speak, and is imitating me!"

He did not say, "I am the Dubno Maggid." There was no need; all present understood his meaning.

The speaker was flustered for a moment, but quickly recovered his wits. No one in this town was personally acquainted with the real Dubno Maggid, or had ever seen him. Brazenly, the imposter announced, "That man is a liar! *I* am the Dubno Maggid, not him!"

The audience was electrified. Here were two men, each claiming to be the Dubno Maggid. Who was the imposter? Were either of them speaking the truth, or was the true Maggid someone else entirely?

R' Yaakov gazed at the crowd with a small smile on his lips. "Let me propose a simple way for you to determine which of us is the Maggid and which is not. It is known that the Dubno Maggid is like a flowing fountain, able to come up with an original talk in the blink of an eye, replete with fitting parables. Let us open two *sefarim* to whatever page you wish. The man who succeeds in constructing a *drashah* on the spot, without any prior preparation, asking a question through use of a *mashal* or parable about something that's written in the first *sefer*, then enlarging the issue by asking another question on something that's written in the second *sefer* — again, using the same *mashal* — and continuing the thread of the parable until he has used it to answer both questions, *he will be the man you will know as the true Dubno Maggid!*"

The audience liked the proposal. A few energetic *bachurim* jumped up and went to the bookcase, returning with the first two *sefarim* that came to hand. These were a *siddur* and a *Chumash Devarim*. The *siddur* was opened at random to the *Selichos* for the days of "Bahab" (the Monday - Thursday - Monday fast observed by some individuals a short time after Pesach and Sukkos, as an atonement for possible excesses over the holiday; the entire congregation recites the pertinent *Selichos* on these days). The *bachur* read aloud the first line on which his eye fell:

"He Who responded to Avraham Avinu on *Har HaMoriah*, respond to us!"

Then a second, solemn-faced young man opened the *Chumash* at random and chanted, "An Ammonite and a Moabite shall not enter the congregation of Hashem, because they did not greet you with bread and water on your way out of Egypt, and because they hired Bilam, son of Beor of Pethor, to curse you."

"We'll stop here," said the Dubno Maggid, lifting a hand. "That is enough."

"Well? What do you say? Can you deliver a *drashah* on what we've just read?" the *gabbai* of the shul asked the imposter. "Can you offer a question and answer on the words we've read from the *siddur* and the *Chumash*, explaining your approach through use of one or two parables?"

The speaker glanced around in confusion, making it clear to even the simplest folk that he longed for a hole in which to hide. The *gabbai* then turned to R' Yaakov, who began to deliver a talk at once, beginning with this parable:

❧❧

Uriel was an extremely wealthy man. He dearly loved his only daughter, and when she reached the age of marriage, he arranged a match for her to a brilliant young Torah scholar.

As the wedding day approached, he bought his daughter clothing made of silks and velvets, in the manner of rich folk, and saw to the outfitting of both bride and groom in Shabbos and Yom Tov finery, again as per the custom among the wealthy. Expert tailors were summoned to his mansion, which hummed with activity in preparation for the big day.

At the height of the preparations, the head tailor came to Uriel with the news that his daughter's wedding gown was short a yard of pure white silk. Brimming with happiness at the upcoming event, the father spared no expense. He immediately ordered one of his servants to go to the biggest fabric store in the city and buy a yard of the best white silk. The servant traveled to the big city and found the store, which counted Uriel as one of its valued patrons. There he purchased the required amount of material and paid its price of 10 gold coins.

The white silk was carefully wrapped in clean paper, and the servant prepared to leave the store.

"Just a moment, if you please," called the shopkeeper.

The servant returned to the counter. The shopkeeper took out his purse.

"Listen, I was hoping to attend the wedding in person, seeing as Uriel is one of my oldest customers. But my doctors have forbidden me to travel because of my uncertain health. Please tell my friend Uriel that I send my warmest wishes — along with this modest gift." He held out a note worth 100 gold coins.

A beggar, witnessing this scene from the doorway, was struck by inspiration. Walking up to the counter, he said, "Can you measure me one yard of pure white silk?"

"Certainly," the shopkeeper said courteously, and hurried to fetch the silk.

The beggar paid the cost of the silk — 10 gold coins — and waited by the counter.

"Yes? How else can I help you?" the shopkeeper asked.

The beggar grew angry. "What's this? I also paid 10 gold coins for white silk. Why don't *I* get a 100-gold-coin note, too?"

The shopkeeper laughed. "You fool! Did you think that every customer who pays 10 gets 100 back? What kind of business practice would that be? I'd soon go bankrupt!"

"So why did you give the last customer the hundred?" demanded the beggar.

"He is the servant of a rich man who's been my business customer for many years. I must have made a profit of thousands through his business by now. He is about to marry off his only daughter, so I felt the need to send a special gift. But who are you? A stranger who's never done any business with me. This is the first time I've ever laid eyes on you, and you instantly demand a large gift?"

"The interpretation of this parable is also the question I'd like to pose," said the Maggid. "We say, 'He Who responded to Avraham Avinu on Har HaMoriah, respond to us.' This request is surprising. Don't we appear like that beggar in the fabric store? Avraham Avinu *deserves* his reward! He withstood 10 ordeals, was the first man to invite guests into his home in a cruel world of Sodomite values, converted souls to belief in the Creator, and spent his entire life engaged in acts of charity and *chesed*, even to the point of praying on behalf of the people of Sodom. Hashem 'made a profit' of many thousands of mitzvos from him. And so, when Avraham cried out to him for help, Hashem always responded.

"But who are we? We are like beggars knocking at the door: people who spout baseless hatred, engage in controversy and dispute, are consumed by egotism, meager in mitzvos and rich in *aveiros*. On what basis are we asking *HaKadosh Baruch Hu* to respond to us the way He responded to Avraham Avinu? Is this not the height of chutzpah toward Heaven?

"Let us return now to the wealthy Uriel and his daughter," continued the Maggid.

〜∂∾

The great day was at hand. The entire family set out for the *chasan's* distant city for the wedding. This arrangement had been agreed on beforehand, as the *chasan's* parents were getting on in years and unfit for the rigors of the road. It was the end of winter, with the world still caught in winter's icy grip. The rivers were frozen; in order to reach the *chasan's* home it was necessary to cross one very wide, deep river.

The family traveled in two carriages, one spacious and the other smaller. In the smaller carriage sat Uriel, his brothers, his assistants, and his servants. In the second, larger one were the bride and her mother, the maidservants, cooks, bakers, and all the bridal clothes for both *kallah* and *chasan*. There were also numerous gold and silver vessels, gifts to the young couple from relatives who were unable to make the trip. In addition, packed in this second coach were fine wines, pastries, and many other delicacies for the wedding.

The first carriage, being lighter than the other, crossed the frozen river without incident. But when the heavily laden second carriage began the crossing, catastrophe struck. The ice, already partially thawed, cracked beneath the wheels. The coach, horses, and everything inside sank into the depths.

The drowning servants raised their voices in terror, alerting some farmers from the neighboring village. After a great deal of effort, the farmers succeeded in rescuing all the passengers. The nearly drowned men and women were brought shivering and faint up to the riverbank, where their rescuers worked to revive them.

One of the servants, not blessed with excessive intelligence, hurried to inform the bride's father of the incident. He reached the city, where he found Uriel beside himself with anxiety.

"Ah, Master!" the servant cried out. "All the fine wines and pastries have drowned in the river!"

"Oh, no!" Uriel beat his head in distress. "What else happened?"

"The bride's wedding clothes sank, too," sighed the servant. "And the *chasan's* expensive suit and fur coat — all are now at the bottom of the river."

Uriel advanced on the servant with pale face and trembling lips. "You are telling me about property. What about my wife and my daughter, the bride? Are they all right?"

The servant retreated a step. "The whole carriage sank, along with your wife and daughter ..."

Uriel let out a shriek of agony.

"But they were pulled out of the water," continued the servant. "They fainted on the riverbank, in the deep snow."

Uriel slapped the man soundly on both cheeks. In a fury, he screamed, "Fool! You've put the trivial part before the important one. First you tell me about the food and clothes, about all the wedding finery that sank. Only then do you speak of my wife and daughter, lying unconscious on the riverbank."

"That," said the Dubno Maggid, "is the second part of our *mashal.* And it brings us to our second question. In listing the crimes of Ammon and Moab, the Torah seems to go from the lesser to the more important. First it reminds us that Ammon and Moab did not greet us with bread and water, just like the servant who began by talking about wines and pastries. Only then does it mention the much bigger crime of hiring Bilam to curse us. This is curious. After all, our Torah is the fount of wisdom. It ought to mention only the major point, Bilam's curse, which was meant to utterly destroy every remnant of the Jewish people!"

"And what is the answer?" the audience asked with one voice.

"Wait a bit. I will go on to the third part of our parable," replied the Maggid.

The wedding was finally conducted with pomp and ceremony, after everyone had been revived and had returned to their full strength. The *chasan* and *kallah* moved into Uriel's palatial home, where they lived in luxury. All too soon, however, trouble reared its head in the new family.

The young wife wanted to spend her time taking walks and out-ings, while her young husband, an outstanding man, wished only to learn Torah. The wife insisted that he join her in her outings, but he refused. They soon quarreled, and the new husband fled the house. He moved in with a friend, where he continued to devote himself to Torah.

The in-laws, hoping to repair the breach, sent over a lavish meal to the friend's house each day, with fattened geese and stuffed fowl. Weeks passed, and then months, but the young husband did not return home. The rift turned into a genuine break. There was a real fear that the husband would make his escape entirely, leaving his wife an *agunah*!

Uriel and his wife considered their options for obtaining a cheap *get* from their absent son-in-law. They were afraid that he would demand an exorbitant price in exchange for giving their daughter her freedom. From day to day they decreased the lavishness of the meals they sent, until in the end they were sending over only a meager piece of bread. Seeing that the young man still refused to divorce his wife, Uriel began to plot against him in earnest.

Heaven forbid that a Jew raise a hand to harm a fellow Jew! But Uriel heard of a great magician who lived in a nearby village, and whose curses and enchantments were capable of killing. Uriel went to see him, to request that he use his black arts to curse the errant son-in-law. As the young man had no brothers, his death would mark the end of Uriel's daughter's problems, and would free her without cost. The magician demanded a steep price for his services. Uriel handed over the gold without blinking an eye.

The young husband, hearing that a magician was seeking to curse him, immediately fled to the yeshivah in which he had learned before his marriage. He told the Rosh Yeshivah everything that had happened to him.

A month later, Uriel arrived at the yeshivah. He confronted the Rosh Yeshivah and complained, "Look at what you have produced! I took a poor boy, dressed him in silks and fed him delicacies, and in return he's run away from my daughter, leaving her an *agunah*. By a miracle, I heard where he had gone."

Innocently, the Rosh Yeshivah asked, "You obligated yourself to feed him in a rich manner. Why, then, in these last months, have you fed him only bread and salt?"

"Believe me, Rebbe," Uriel said plaintively, "I've lost a lot of money lately. As long as I was rich, I fed him stuffed fowl and gave him fine old wine to drink."

"I see. Well, if you've lost your money, how did you manage to pay the magician for cutting off your son-in-law's young life?" the Rosh Yeshivah asked, a fleeting smile playing on his lips.

"The Torah," said the Maggid, continuing his amazing performance, "complains about Ammon and Moab's failure to greet us with bread and water. Ammon and Moab are trying to claim that they had nothing to give. They'd had a hard year, a year of drought, and were therefore lacking the funds to buy bread and water for the *Bnei Yisrael*.

"'Oh?' says the Torah. 'How, then, did you pay Bilam, who demanded his full measure of gold and silver from Balak?'

"I will now come to the fourth part of my parable, in which I will answer the first question," continued the Maggid, as his admiring audience sat spellbound.

❧

The young *chasan* was divorced from the rich man's daughter. He continued to toil diligently in Torah, growing in knowledge of the Talmud and *poskim* until his reputation as a Torah light began to spread. His Rosh Yeshivah suggested a *shidduch* with the daughter of a rich man who was more upright than our old friend, Uriel. The young man went to live in his new father-in-law's home, and everyone in town — especially those learned in the Torah — respected and esteemed him.

When, some time later, the Rav of the city passed away, the community voted unanimously to appoint our young man as Rav and *Av Beis Din* in his place. The young man agreed to accept the job, but only on one condition: that he receive no salary.

A few years later, there was a great rejoicing: A son had been born to the Rav! The city's Jews, wishing to demonstrate their love and appreciation for their young rabbi, presented him with a special gift at the baby's *bris*: a rabbinical contract for the child! Here is what it said:

"After the Rav's long life, if this son is worthy of taking his place in Torah, wisdom, and piety, the rabbinate is assured him from this date!"

The father read the contract, and laughed. "Is this the way you demonstrate your appreciation for a rabbi who does not take a penny for his services?" he asked the community leaders. "If my son is worthy of taking my place in Torah and wisdom, what would be so amazing about your appointing him to do so? If you truly wished to show me that your hearts are with me in my moment of joy, you should have promised that my son would inherit my seat even if he is *not* as great as his father!"

"Now we can answer our first question," concluded the Maggid, to the amazement of the crowd who had of course already seen who was the true Maggid and who was the imposter (who, incidentally, had fled in shame). "We asked why we request that Hashem respond to us the way he responded to Avraham Avinu. It's logical: Were we as great as Avraham Avinu, sacrificing ourselves for the sanctity of Hashem's Name as he did, standing up to 10 ordeals, and sowing charity and *chesed* in the world, then we would not need to plead for Heavenly mercy in his merit. We would *deserve* to be answered! But it's precisely because we do not have Avraham Avinu's accomplishments to our credit that we ask Hashem for compassion, that He remember us because we are children of Avraham, who served his Creator so devotedly without any desire for reward. In his merit, we ask that Hashem respond to us the way He always responded to Avraham!"

Confessions of a Jewish Priest

THIS STORY TOOK PLACE IN THE CITY OF KROLI, ROMANIA, about eighty years ago. The city featured a liquor factory, which adjoined a tavern that supplied the locals with whiskey at discount prices. The tavern-keeper was a pious Jew who valued the mitzvah of giving charity. In a corner of his counter sat a pile of small coins, ready to be handed out to any beggar who chanced by.

Winters in Romania are very cold. Many destitute Jews would come shivering into the tavern to warm themselves with a shot of the fiery liquid. The tavern-keeper kept a special store of small shot glasses for them, beside the pile of coins. And so, any freezing Jew who entered the tavern would benefit doubly: a drink to warm his bones, and a coin to warm his pocket.

One winter's day, the tavern-keeper and his brothers stood behind the counter, serving the customers. Outside, the wind shrieked, and snow fell in a swirling white sheet. Inside the large room, men sat warming themselves with a glass of whiskey and the pleasant glow of camaraderie.

A blast of cold air pierced the room as the door opened wide. All heads turned and stared at the entering figure. None of them had ever seen a creature like this in their lives.

The newcomer was a man in his mid-40's. His face was pinched and sallow, as though from the effects of malnutrition. No comb or brush had touched his hair in many months, and his beard had turned into clumps of tangled hair dangling limply from his withered cheeks. The skinny body was wrapped in a torn priest's robe, and tattered shoes hung from his bare feet. A large skullcap covered his head. Seeing the large crowd of gentiles enjoying their drinks, he looked flustered.

Hesitantly he approached the counter, where he gratefully accepted the coin and the drink. This he downed in a single long swallow. Then he thrust the coin into his pocket and began to retreat.

"*Reb Yid*!" called one of the tavern owner's brothers, a curious youth. "Where are you running off to so fast? Stay with us a while. It's cold outside, but it's nice and warm in here."

"No! I'm in a big hurry," the poor man said firmly. "I have no time."

The tavern-keeper smiled ironically at this beggar who "had no time." Where was he off to in such a hurry: his executive office at some big factory, or the bank, to deposit his vast profits? "Sit down a bit," he urged. "Have a bowl of hot soup with dumplings. It'll give you strength."

"No! I can't!"

The tavern-owner's eyes strayed to the man's bare feet and the too-large shoes clinging to them. To walk around without socks in such cold weather was certainly not one of life's pleasures. "At least let me give you a pair of new socks, so you won't go barefoot."

"Absolutely not," the poor man said, his face registering sudden deep and inexplicable sorrow. Clearly, he longed to be able to accept, but could not do so for some hidden reason.

The tavern-owner's brother rose to the challenge posed by the stranger's obstinacy. "Why won't you?" he demanded. "Do you like walking around in the cold without socks on?"

The man saw that he would not easily be able to leave these two warmhearted Jews who were trying so hard to help him. Casting an irritable glance at the packed tables of drinkers, he motioned for the tavern-keeper and his younger brother to join him in a quiet corner.

The owner of the tavern brought along a bottle of liquor and a bowl of hot soup, which he set on a table. The man began to tell the story of his life.

I am the son of Yanysh Kovetz, head priest of a large city in the Zibenbergen region. Zibenbergen was a large tract of land in Hungary on which seven cities were situated. The word "berg" means "palace":

These seven cities bore the names of seven royal palaces. My father belonged to a Protestant sect, which permits marriage for its ministers. My father did marry, and I was his only son.

Apart from being a high-level minister, my father was considered an upright and honest man. He spent a great deal of time studying the Holy Scriptures, and raised me with a burning belief in everything that is written there.

I had always been blessed with a sharp mind and a quick grasp, and in my youth I studied hard and began to climb the ladder of the priesthood. In time, I became my father's right hand and was considered his heir, to the envy of my fellow seminary students who had neither my talent nor such an important father.

The predictions proved well founded. One day, my father died, and after the Church eulogized him and mourned his passing, the priests held a conference in which they decided, unanimously, to appoint me my father's successor as head of the Zibenbergen church. This was a great honor for someone as young as I, who was of an age when most men have hardly begun to think of their status in life.

As head of the Church in the region, I became famous. Many great people came to see me, and it was not long before they proposed that I wed the daughter of one of the country's most illustrious figures. I married her, and we had three daughters. I was a happy man and a proud father.

And then, as I stood at the peak of my powers and my exalted position, something profoundly significant occurred in my life.

I had a custom of sitting up at night, reading the Bible, until sleep overcame me. That night, too, I sat at the table and studied from a book of the Holy Scriptures, until my eyes began to droop and I sank into sleep.

In my dream, a strange woman approached me. She was dressed in Jewish clothing. "My Avishai," she whispered sorrowfully, "don't you recognize me? I am your mother. I died just after your birth, and a year later your father died, too. The priest is not your father. You are a Jew. Return to your Judaism!"

I woke up thoroughly shaken — completely beside myself and trembling like a leaf. With difficulty I dragged myself to bed, where my disordered thoughts whirled around my head for a long time. At last, I fell asleep again. In the morning, when I remembered the dream, I decided to ignore it.

The following night, I sat once again studying the Holy Scriptures with great concentration, as was my habit, until I fell asleep with my head on the book. I had no sooner dropped off than the Jewish woman from the previous night's dream appeared again. Her face was sad.

"My Avishai, my beloved son. Do you think that this dream is nonsense? That is a mistake. I am your birth mother. For nine months I carried you beneath my heart, but I did not merit the privilege of raising you, for a short time after you were born my soul was borne up to Heaven. Orphaned of your mother, you lived with your father — my husband — only one year before he, too, passed away. You are not a gentile. You are a Jew, and you must leave this false religion and accept the yoke of Heaven. I cannot rest as long as you cling to your false beliefs."

I woke up. This time, the dream had been much clearer. My ears still rang with the woman's voice, which stayed with me for many hours. Reeling as I was with the reaction, sleep eluded me. Toward morning, when the sky began to turn light, I collected myself and thought, *I have been a gentile ever since I can remember. I grew up in the home of a priest and never knew anything connected to Judaism. I have been appointed head priest of this great city. Many other priests bow to my authority. Whole churches do not crook a finger without my permission. From where, then, did these nonsensical thoughts come, trying to topple my firm world? This must be the devil's work. He must envy my success!*

During the course of the day, I behaved as usual. I dealt with many church matters and made important decisions. I sat on my Olympian heights.

But that night, again, I was hurled from the heights back down to earth, where I was as tiny as an ant. The moment I closed my eyes in sleep over the Bible I was reading, the Jewish woman returned. This time she looked angry and was holding a wooden rolling pin in her hand. "Avishai!" she said sternly, "don't you know how to accept favors? Must I beat you with this?" And she struck me in the ribs with the rolling pin, a sharp, painful blow.

This dream left its mark. Not only did the vision itself stay with me, so did the pain in my ribs. I was forced to remain in bed all that day, suffering bitterly.

I tried to examine the matter from every angle. Where had this pain come from? There was no natural cause that I could see. I had not fallen out of bed or been beaten up. I was aching with the pain of a blow such as I had never sustained in my life. Yet, apart from the woman who struck me in the dream, no one had hit me. It must be that the dream was true!

In the fourth dream, which came that night, the woman in the Jewish clothes came again. I recoiled in fear, afraid that she would strike me with the rolling pin as she had the night before. But this time she smiled and said, "Now that you've learned the hard way, your ears are open to listen and your heart is beginning to believe. I will now give you explicit information about your identity, your birthplace, and your parents' names."

She named a town in Hungary. "Your father, Tzemach, son of R' Yosef, made casks and barrels for a living. He was a man of medium height with a brown beard and long, curling *peyos* that reached his shoulders. My name was Chaya Rickel, daughter of R' Avraham Asher Halevi, and I looked exactly the way I appear to you now. We lived in a house that stood on the corner of the street, near the green well.

"When you were a year old, your father passed away, leaving you an orphan with no one to take care of you. One of the Christians in town took you away that same day, with an evil plan in mind. 'The great priest, Yanysh Kovetz, has no children. I will give him this child. The priest will have a son, the boy will have a warm home, and his soul will rejoice in Paradise!'

"Yanysh Kovetz was beside himself with joy and surprise. As a sign of his gratitude, he gave the man who had brought you a heavy bundle of cash and precious gems. As I say, you were a tiny boy, just a year old. Yanysh began to teach you Christianity from the moment you were able to understand and since then, neither your father nor I have known a moment's peace in the upper world. I have now been granted permission to rectify matters. Therefore, know this: As long as you refuse to renounce your false faith and continue to live as a Christian together with your Christian wife, I will not leave you in peace. I will come to trouble your rest every night and will beat you soundly with my rolling pin."

As she spoke, she turned to face me fully, and I saw that she was carrying the rolling pin again. I cringed with fear, for the previous blow I had received from that source had hurt almost unbearably.

Two or three more nights passed in this manner, until at last I decided to travel to the town she had named and investigate my roots.

I told no one about my plans, not even my wife. She saw that I was agitated but did not dare disturb me. Even the family of the church leader had learned to tiptoe around me.

In the middle of the night, I packed a few things and departed while my family slept. I left my priestly robes buried in a closet and wore a layman's clothing instead. A carriage awaited me outside. I had chosen the driver carefully for his reticence; he would not reveal a secret even if you knocked out all his teeth. We traveled through the night and came to the town at dawn. It was a place I had never heard of before my dream.

I saw now that the place existed in reality. We rode through the streets by the pale light of the rising sun. Looking around, I noted many Jewish homes. They were easy to identify because of the *mezuzah* on the doorpost. Suddenly, I saw something that made my heart stop and my eyes bulge. There, on a corner, stood a house whose front yard was littered with old rusted barrels and casks, some of them clearly only half-finished. Making a sweep of the area, I found the well, now a rapidly fading green.

Tears sprang into my eyes. Every detail of the dream had been validated. Still, I clung to my uncertainty. Had I actually been born here? Was the barrel-maker really my father, who had died a young man, and were these the casks and barrels on which he had been working when death had overtaken him?

I waited until the sun was blazing in its full glory and the streets had begun to stir with people. Then I signaled the driver to take me to the judge's house.

In those days, the local judge served as the absolute authority in small towns and villages. He was the unofficial "crown prince" of the place, and his word was law. I sought him out for one reason alone: The judge kept the archives in which every birth and death under his jurisdiction was recorded. I longed to know whether the names of Tzemach, the barrel-maker, and his wife, Chaya Rickel, appeared in his book.

It was still very early in the morning when I stood on the judge's doorstep and knocked tentatively at the door. Someone inside called out to me to wait.

After several minutes, the door was opened by a man with white hair and a wrinkled face. He apologized for the delay, explaining that age had made the simple act of getting out of bed difficult for him. I introduced myself, using an alias, and told him that it was important that I learn something about the residents of the town, dating back about forty years. The old man shuffled into the next room, returning with some dusty record books. We began looking through old records. We must have flipped scores — if not hundreds — of pages, scanning each line with interest. The elderly judge soon grew tired and handed the archives over to me. For long hours I sat in his home until I suddenly came across this line:

"A boy, Avishai, son of the Jew Tzemach, barrel-maker, and Chaya Rickel." The entry was followed by a date.

I summoned the judge and showed him the line. "Do you know what happened to that child?"

A sly look gleamed in the judge's aged eyes. "Why are you interested specifically in him?"

I thrust a glistening coin in the judge's hand. "If you'll tell me what you know, there's another coin waiting for you."

The man was greedy enough. He chattered on, telling me everything. That is how I learned what had been kept from me all my life.

The dream had been true. When I was a year old, my father, R' Tzemach, died. One of the gentile neighbors managed to get hold of me, and hastened to hand me over to the head priest, Yanysh Kovetz, who was childless.

I was a Jew!

The knowledge was bitter. I would have to give up my luxurious life, my position and authority, and take a step that would be irreversible.

I didn't feel capable of taking that step. Instead, I resolved to stay home, passively, and wait to see how events sorted themselves out. But my mother had other plans. She appeared in my dreams night after night, destroying any peace of mind I might have had left.

"But what am I supposed to do, Mother?" I asked her in my dream. "I don't know the Jewish world at all. To whom do I turn? What shall I do?"

My mother suggested that I travel to the city of Deizh, to ask the Rebbe there for advice.

I made the trip without delay. The Rebbe was astonished at the sight of his illustrious visitor: the head priest of Zibenbergen! His astonishment tripled when I told him my story. He paced his room like a caged lion, considering the best course for me to take. Apparently, he was very apprehensive about the Church's reaction were it to learn that a Jewish rabbi had had a hand in turning a priest from his faith. Pogroms and other anti-Semitic reactions were a real possibility.

After careful thought, he came up with the following idea:

"Go to Galicia and see a certain Rebbe (the teller of this story did not specify the Rebbe's name, though he did know that it was a famous Rebbe of the time). Tell him about your problem."

I went to Galicia. Well aware of the ramifications of what I was doing, I did everything in my power to conceal my movements, wearing simple clothes like anyone else. I presented myself to the Rebbe and again told my story, from start to finish.

This Rebbe was not hampered the way the Rebbe from Deizh had been. He spoke firmly: "You must leave your home quietly. Don't tell anyone in your family; just disappear one day. Your pure soul has been raised in a sewer all its life, though not voluntarily, and it is up to you to cleanse it if you wish to merit life in the World to Come. Therefore, go into exile for a period of three years. Where you sleep at night, do not linger during the day, and where you linger by day, do not sleep at night. For three years, wander throughout the country. Get rid of your priestly garments and dress as a Jew. However, in order to increase your mortification and make the necessary atonement, continue to wear your priest's robe over your clothes, to incite others to mock you. The garment which once brought you honor will now be a source of shame and mockery, for others will think you mad. Do not wear socks, but only shoes over bare feet. Live off charity alone."

"And after that?" I asked with quaking knees.

The Rebbe answered simply. "After that, everything will fall into place."

The traveler turned to the tavern-keeper and his brother, and asked, "Do you understand now why I am in a hurry? I was here during the day, so I may not sleep here tonight. I have wandered this way for two years already, and there is still another full year ahead of me. Now you can understand, too, why I refused to put socks on my bare feet, and why I'm walking around wearing a filthy priest's robe. On top of all that, I am deathly afraid that someone from my former flock will recognize me. Imagine the furor that arose when the leading priest of Zibenbergen, Anton Kovetz, diappeared one day and was gone."

With a nod of his head, the man stepped out into the frigid, storm-tossed street.

The teller of this tale — the tavern-keeper's brother — adds, "I was curious to learn whether the story was true. I investigated and asked questions, until I found out that indeed, two years earlier, the priest of Zibenbergen had vanished without a trace. I continued to follow up the story, and the sequel stunned me. Half a year later, the newspapers reported a shocking tragedy, in which a bolt of lightning struck the home of the missing priest. The house went up in flames, and from the rubble they later extracted the priest's wife and three daughters.

"Another six months passed. One day, an acquaintance told me that, in a poorhouse in one of the nearby towns, a strange, destitute wanderer had died. He had been wearing a stained and tattered priest's robe and shoes without socks. Avishai, the penitent, had apparently completed his atonement in this world, and on the same day returned his suffering soul to its place in Heaven."

[Source: The brother of the storyteller moved to Eretz Yisrael afterward and, in 5716-5718, recounted the entire episode to R' Shmuel Mordechai Schwartz, of Jerusalem, from whom I heard it.]

Boys at Play

THE DARK SKY STRETCHED OVER THE *KOSEL HAMA'ARAVI* as a group of men, over 100 strong, met there to recite *Tehillim* for the recovery of Simcha Yonasan ben Basha Rachel. They cried out to the Master of the Universe, pleading with him to lengthen the ill man's days. He was the head of a large household: Three of those praying at the *Kosel* were his sons-in-law, young *talmidei chachamim* of whom two taught Torah in yeshivos. Six others were the sick man's sons, the oldest having just come of marriageable age and the youngest sitting in a stroller, pacifier in his mouth. Along with them had come the patient's brothers and brothers-in-law, as well as his father, uncles, cousins, and friends. In all, over 100 people had traveled in chartered buses from a distant city, coming to Jerusalem to pour out their hearts in prayer at the Western Wall.

R' Simcha Yonasan was very ill, and his grave condition was extremely worrying for his family. Their heartfelt prayers and tears reverberated through the *Kosel* plaza, touching the hearts of everyone praying there. People came over to the group to inquire curiously about the identity of the sick man. One or two relatives offered details: He was a young man, at the peak of his life, and the father of nine. A growth had been found in his stomach, going on to send offshoots in all directions. His condition was critical and called for a tremendous outpouring of Heavenly compassion.

The questioners nodded sadly and said with a sigh, "Ah, our people need a great salvation. So many tragedies and illnesses. It's hard to hear of a new one …"

Two weeks later, the group returned to the *Kosel*. The group was larger this time, and its cries and tears were truly heartrending. The patient's condition had worsened dramatically, and his beloved family members were doing everything in their power to help.

But Heaven's gates, it seemed, were firmly shut to their prayers. Just a few days later the ill man passed away, and the announcement about the *levayah* (funeral) of R' Simcha Yonasan Rochelovski was made (identifying details in this story have been changed to protect the privacy of the protagonists).

Among the many who attended the funeral was one man who walked alongside the body weeping bitter tears, despite the fact that he was not a relative. It was Rabbi Gershon Meir Plotkin, an old friend of the departed man, dating back to their childhood. R' Plotkin had lived near R' Simcha Yonasan, and the two had learned together daily. The love between them was comparable to that of Dovid and Yehonasan — an unconditional love. They had frequently visited each other's homes and participated joyously in each other's happy occasions.

Their wonderful friendship had lasted nearly five decades, until the Angel of Death cut it short in one fell swoop.

Less than two months after R' Simcha Yonasan's passing, a fresh tragedy swept the community. His dear friend, R' Gershon Meir Plotkin, died suddenly of a heart attack. Both in life and in death, the friends were not parted.

The community reeled. Apparently, the friend who had been left behind could not bear the pain, and his overpowering grief had led to yet another tragic loss of life.

Well-known rabbinical figures rose to eulogize R' Gershon Meir, and to speak of the passing, in their prime, of both of the scholars and friends. They eulogized and wept until, in the audience, tears flowed like a river. People repented of their sins and returned to their Creator with full hearts.

One man there — R' Nachman Halevi — was prey to a paralyzing terror.

R' Nachman Halevi had been the third side of the beautiful triangle of friendship. In his modest way, he had remained concealed in the shadows so that, while many knew of the powerful bonds of friendship that existed between R' Simcha Yonasan and R' Gershon Meir, only few were aware that there was a third childhood friend in the picture. A restrained personality, R' Nachman did not generally show his feelings in public, not even when his spirit felt as stormy as a ship tossing at sea. Wordlessly, eyes wide with shock, he followed R' Gershon Meir to his final resting place. As he listened to the speakers eulogize his friend, the fear threatened to overwhelm him. This was not only because of the *Chazal* that warns, "If one member of a *chaburah* dies, worry about the rest." Two of his friends had just died, one right after the other. But there was also another reason why R' Nachman was so afraid.

He returned home that evening with long-forgotten memories of his youth rising up before his inner eye. Nearly forty years separated him from that time, but the memories were as fresh as if the events had taken place that very day.

The three boys lived on the same block. A short distance divided the Plotkin home from that of the Rochelovski's, and from there to the Halevi house on the corner was just a few more steps. The three had been close friends from the day they first held hands and sang songs together in kindergarten. As they grew older, they attended the same neighborhood yeshivah. Gradually, they graduated from childish games, sprouted hair on their upper lips, and became more serious and measured in their behavior. It was time for them to justify their families' hopes for them.

One morning, the three walked happily to their yeshivah. On one corner they found a new beggar dominating the street. He had spread a stained red blanket on the pavement, through whose torn fabric glimpses of dirty wool could be seen. The beggar held two tin cans in his hands and was shaking both at once. "A donation for a poor man — a big mitzvah!" he called.

He appeared slightly elderly, his face crisscrossed with lines that testified to a life filled with suffering. The black eyes told of much pain and anguish. Readily, the three boys reached into their pockets and took out the few pennies they had there, handing them to the beggar.

"Where did he come from?" wondered Gershon Meir.

"From Turkey," Nachman said soberly.

"Why Turkey?" Simcha Yonasan was surprised.

"Well, we're from Turkey, and my father said that all the beggars come from there." Wearing the same serious expression, Nachman added, "They have beggar factories over there."

His two friends broke into merry laughter. Nachman himself did not so much as crack a smile. He was always able to make his friends laugh while he remained sober as a board. A few minutes later, the three passed through the yeshivah doors. They joined the others for *Shacharis* and completely forgot about the new beggar.

The next morning, they encountered him again. The tin cans rattled vigorously as he called out, "A donation for a poor man — a big mitzvah!"

Once again, the three boys offered their pennies. Nachman was curious to know if his previous day's guess had any basis in reality. "Tell me, where are you from?" he asked.

The beggar was startled. Clearly, he was not used to being questioned. Generally people took no interest in him beyond the tossing of a coin into his homemade *pushka*.

"I'm from here." He pointed innocently at the curb.

"From here?" Nachman repeated. "I see. And where were you before you came from here?" He pointed at the curb in imitation of the beggar.

The beggar did not answer. A hand searched deep in his pocket and pulled out a cucumber, which he was soon munching energetically. He consumed the entire thing, unpeeled, in front of the three amused boys.

"Twenty seconds," Gershon Meir said, glancing at his watch.

"Not true," claimed Simcha Yonasan. "My watch shows that it took him 18 seconds to finish off that cucumber."

The beggar, impervious both to their comments and their grins, pulled an onion out of another pocket and began gnawing it hungrily. The boys grimaced with revulsion. Muttering something about the onion's pungent odor, they walked quickly away.

From that day on, each morning found the three boys stopping at the beggar's corner on their way to yeshivah. They would throw a coin or two into his can and amuse themselves at his expense.

And that was just the beginning — the opening act of a much bigger drama, which began with the arrival in the yeshivah of "Kiva Zicher."

No one knew where the old man had come from. One morning he appeared in the yeshivah hall, seemingly out of nowhere. He came armed with a thick, ancient *siddur* and a threadbare cloth bag containing his *tallis* and *tefillin*. Big black glasses perched at the end of his nose as he incessantly murmured from the *siddur*. As the first *bachurim* entered the *beis medrash*, yawning and rubbing their eyes, the old man would already be wrapped in his *tallis* and *tefillin*, the aged *siddur* open before him on the *shtender*. He recited *Korbanos*, pointing in an irritated way at the place where the *ba'al tefillah* was supposed to stand, as though to ask, "And where is the *chazan*?"

The students gazed at him blankly. This was no *shteibel*. The yeshivah was regulated by its own internal rhythm. If someone was looking for a quick *minyan*, he could always *daven* at the local shul.

No one dared express this thought aloud to the irritable old man, who tried from the first day to change the usual pace and repeatedly attempted to hurry the *chazan* along. After *Shacharis*, several of the *bachurim* approached him, extended a hand in greeting, and asked, "*Reb Yid*, where are you from?"

They learned that his name was Akiva Schwartz and that he had come from Nahariya. Or maybe it was Rosh Pina. Then again, it might be Metulla. Or was it Kfar Saba? The old man was slightly addled, and though he piled detail on detail, no student succeeded in adding them all up to make a coherent whole.

Then Gershon Meir came along and turned things around.

In the newcomer, Gershon Meir discovered that he had unwittingly stumbled on a treasure trove. With lightning acuity, he supplied the important facts.

"He says his name is 'Kiva,'" he said with a wink. Turning to the old man, he asked guilelessly, "Isn't it true that your name is Kiva?"

"*Yuh, yuh, zicher* (Yes, yes, of course)," the old man replied eagerly, happy that someone understood him at last.

Gershon Meir asked several more questions and listened to the answers with eyes closed in concentration, isolating the important words. He then turned to his friends with a serious mien: "He's retired, all washed up, and his name is Kiva Zicher. Do you want some breakfast, Kiva Zicher?"

"*Yuh, yuh, zicher.*" The long white beard bobbed back and forth as the old man nodded.

"Well?" Gershon Meir prodded his friends. "Kiva Zicher wants to eat something, and you're all asleep! Get him some salad, an omelet, bread, jam, and some coffee."

His two lighthearted friends, Nachman and Simcha Yonasan, were happy to prepare "Kiva Zicher's" breakfast. From that day on, the old man continued to be the yeshivah's guest. His home was close by and he insisted on joining the students for *Shacharis* at the yeshivah each morning, where he received a hot breakfast and served to amuse the three friends. Each morning, after a few minutes of kidding around beside the streetcorner beggar, the boys would hurry along to the yeshivah and the equally amusing company of Kiva Zicher. Though they did not deliberately wish to hurt the half-senile old man, they did not refrain from imitating and mocking his every move. With a mind that was rather confused and a memory that was now all too short, Kiva tended to repeat himself over and over, much to the amusement of the merry boys.

They were clever boys, and certainly no pranksters or troublemakers. They never did anything overt to the addled old man. Their mockery was sometimes poisonous and always sharp and to the point, but never obvious. To the observer, they appeared to be all *chesed* toward their visitor, taking great pains to see to his breakfast each morning.

With time, the old man's memory became even more impaired. He could remember hardly anything at all now. This provided the three boys with fertile ground for their humor. They gave him breakfast each morning and sometimes, after he had *bentched* and no longer remembered that he had already *davened*, they would organize an extra "*tefillas nedavah*," non-obligatory *tefillah*, for Kiva.

Their hidden mockery, though hidden from most, was noted by the *mashgiach*, an experienced pedagogue who had a sharp eye for catching the winks and grins camouflaged behind innocent faces. One day, when the old man had mistakenly begun to recite the Yom Kippur *Ne'ilah* instead of *Bircas HaMazon*, the *mashgiach* stopped Simcha Yonasan in his mad dash to bring the old man a Yom Kippur *machzor*.

"I want to see the three of you after breakfast," the *mashgiach* said, his expression unreadable.

"What did we do?" Simcha Yonasan blurted worriedly. Without answering, the *mashgiach* simply repeated the order.

Simcha Yonasan returned to his friends without the *machzor*. He, Gershon Meir, and Nachman helped the old man say the *Bircas HaMazon*, which he recited in full form, complete with "*Al HaNissim*," "*Retzei V'hachalitzeinu*," "*Ya'aleh V'yavo*," and "*HaRachaman hu yakim lanu es sukkas Yankel hanofales.*"

The *mashgiach* was waiting for them in his office. His expression was stern as he began to criticize their cynical humor, all the uglier because they were using it against an old man whose memory had betrayed him.

The three boys were deeply insulted. How could anyone accuse them like this, when all they were doing was making sure the old man got a hot, nutritious breakfast each morning, including oatmeal sprinkled with cinnamon and sugar?

"Cynicism, wickedness — and falsehood also," the *mashgiach* berated them. "There are those who feed their father fatted chickens but still earn Gehinnom. Oatmeal with cinnamon and sugar … a nice joke. You've adopted that poor old man in order to amuse yourselves each day. Even the name you've got all the boys calling him is despicable: 'Kiva Zicher'! You are filled with mockery, and just pretending otherwise. Everyone thinks of you as the best boys in the yeshivah, but I know you from the inside out. I see past the hundreds of pages of *Gemara* you're hiding behind. I see you as wicked sadists, taking pleasure and amusement from others' weaknesses."

The boys' eyes grew round with shock. The harsh words pounded at them like sledgehammers.

The *mashgiach* gave them no time to recover. Opening a *Chumash Vayikra* to the 19th *perek*, he read them the verse, "*Mipnei seivah takum v'hadarta pnei zakein v'yareisa mei'Elokecha ani Hashem* — In the presence of an old person shall you rise and you shall honor the presence of a Sage and you shall revere your G-d — I am Hashem."

"The Abarbanel says, 'In reference to the honoring of the aged it says, "And you shall revere your G-d," because it is the nature of boys and youths to mock and make fun of the elderly, and therefore they are warned to fear Hashem. For if they do not do so, and do not honor the elderly, the boys may not, Heaven forbid, reach old age as they did!'

"Do you hear, boys?" asked the *mashgiach*. "It's not I who says this, but the Abarbanel. Stop making fun of the elderly. Did they choose to lose their memory? Is it pleasant for them to see their minds growing feebler every day? The process of aging does not exclude anyone. If you wish to reach old age, learn to honor the elderly, even if they sound silly now and then."

The boys left, still wounded to the core, and nursing an antipathy to the cruel *mashgiach* who had called them a bunch of wicked sadists. They continued to care for Kiva Zicher as before.

These words of the Abarbanel rose up from the depths of Nachman's memory after R' Simcha Yonasan's death. Still, there was a natural cause both for his friend's illness and for his dying. Sadly, there are many stricken by that dread disease, and many of these die young. But when his second friend, R' Gershon Meir Plotkin, passed away suddenly in his 54th year, R' Nachman remembered the *mashgiach's* stern message. All at once he understood that, unless he acted at once, he, too, was liable to meet the same end as his two friends.

"You'll never know what anguish I felt," says R' Nachman. "Leaving everything, I returned to the city of my birth to search for Kiva Zicher, who had almost certainly passed on decades before. No one knew what had become of Akiva Schwartz, and only after endless investigating in every possible and impossible place did I find an old man named R' Uri Schwartz, R' Akiva's younger brother, who agreed to show me where his brother is buried. I gathered together ten men and went to visit the grave of Kiva Zicher. In tears, I apologized for the mockery we dished out to him daily, and pleaded with him to forgive me so that I would not die with my sin."

R' Nachman was crying now, too. "And that wasn't all. Afterward, I devoted a full month to further investigation, until I managed to unearth a *gabbai* in a shul in Haifa — the son of that poor beggar with the tin *pushkas*. The man agreed to take me to his father's gravesite. Again, I abased myself in front of ten Jews, confessing to them how bad I had been in my youth. Believe me, I did not garner much respect from that.

"And therefore," continues R' Nachman, "to avoid your having to go through what I went through, honor every man, and do not mock the elderly or make fun of them! If you, the young, wish to grow old in honor and please G-d, honor the elderly in whatever state you find him — and Hashem will honor you."

Who Was the Doctor?

THE CENTRAL COURTYARD OF JERUSALEM'S BATEI UNGARIN neighborhood was filled with the tumult of children at play, as it was every Shabbos afternoon. Laughing girls jumped rope, braids swinging. A group of young boys in white yarmulkas climbed the shul steps on their way to their weekly *Tehillim* group. From a first-story window peeped an elderly man, begging the children to play more quietly so that he might take a nap.

R' Isaac Weiss (the name has been changed) cut through the neighborhood, oblivious to all the merry goings-on around him. For the past three days, he hadn't been noticing much of anything. His mind was too caught up in painful reflections of its own.

They were troublesome thoughts. For the past several months, R' Isaac — a leading citizen of the city and a man in the prime of life — had begun to sense that his eyes were not as they had once been. His vision was growing gradually weaker. At first, he thought he needed glasses, and went to see an eye doctor to confirm this. The doctor had placed a large chart facing him, containing letters and numbers of varying sizes, and asked him to read them out loud. Then he wrote out a prescription for R' Isaac, with the type of lenses he would be required to wear from then on. Without delay, R' Isaac — now no longer able to recognize people when he passed them in the street — went to the optometrist to order a pair of glasses. They were ready a week later. He placed them on his nose and was pleased to see the blurry world turn suddenly sharp again.

The pleasure lasted only a day.

By the next day, his vision returned to its former state. The glasses were no help at all. R' Isaac was beside himself with anguish. He hurried back to the optometrist's to complain about his glasses, but was assured that the glasses were correct in every way. The optometrist re-checked his eyes, then said, "If you can't see well even with the glasses, you have another problem. Go back to the eye doctor."

R' Isaac did just that. He returned to the eye doctor, who tested him again. It turned out that the glasses were, indeed, correct, but R' Isaac apparently had an additional problem apart from nearsightedness. "I'd recommend that you go see an expert," the doctor said at last. "I haven't managed to get to the bottom of the problem."

R' Isaac wasted no time. As soon as possible, he paid a visit to Jerusalem's top ophthalmologist. This was the famous Professor Ticho, whose clinic served Jerusalem's residents faithfully and well, and whose memory is remembered and respected to this day. His clinic still exists on Rechov Harav Kook, in Jerusalem, where the Ticho Museum now stands. Professor Ticho was not only an extraordinary eye doctor, but also a renowned eye surgeon who had saved the sight of many a patient.

The name of Dr. Ticho was spoken with reverence in the city, as much for his humanity as for his expertise. The poor and downtrodden came to his clinic alongside the wealthy and respected, and the good doctor accorded them all the same treatment. Some even claimed that the poor received better care. Dr. Ticho was very compassionate toward the simpler folk, and often treated them for free and outside of his usual office hours. Many ailments afflicted the eyes of Jerusalem's poorer residents, especially contagious infections such as trachoma, a result of the city's dismal hygienic conditions. Middle-Eastern Arabs were known as frequent sufferers from trachoma. Jerusalem's Arabs were no exception, and they often infected their Jewish neighbors as well. The illustrious doctor had only to glance at a pair of inflamed, infected eyes to write out a prescription for an ointment or eyedrops. Sometimes, if the patient was very poor, the doctor would take a tube or bottle out of his own desk drawer and hand it to the patient for free. Some days, the doctor would personally place drops into the tortured eyes of dozens of Arab sufferers.

When R' Isaac entered his examining room, Dr. Ticho asked routinely — his hands busy with patients' cards in a metal filing box — "Is your eye infected? Do you need drops?"

"No," R' Isaac sighed. "If only that were my problem."

Dr. Ticho put down the patient files and transferred his gaze to R' Isaac. He saw a silver-bearded Jew with a refined countenance. He submitted R' Isaac's eyes to a thorough examination and asked questions about the progress of his condition. Then the doctor sighed too.

"You have a very complex eye disease," he explained to his distraught patient. "Only an operation can save your sight. Unless you undergo surgery soon, you will lose your vision entirely."

"What are you saying?" R' Isaac asked in agitation.

"I don't want to frighten you," the doctor said, "but you religious people are accustomed to learning things together with a commentary. So, I'll offer one now: If we do not operate quickly, you will become blind!"

❧

These painful words hammered in R' Isaac's head as he crossed the large courtyard on Shabbos. He weaved like a drunkard as he walked, and it was only with difficulty that he was able to manage the stairs to the Beit Ungarin shul.

"R' Isaac, don't you feel well?" several of his friends asked, alarmed by his white face and unsteady gait.

"It's nothing," he said evasively. He succeeded in pushing off all of the group, except for one sworn friend, R' Chanina Fisher, a zealous and respected Jerusalemite. R' Chanina knew his friend well, and would not leave him alone until R' Isaac had confessed his secret.

"Listen, my friend," R' Chanina said, his face solemn, "this is a very serious matter. You must go see a great *tzaddik*, a genuine *tzaddik*!"

"I am prepared to go to someone," said R' Isaac. "Just tell me who."

"Let me tell you a story that happened to me. Then you'll understand everything."

R' Chanina launched into the following tale.

"About a year and a half ago, my family had a difficult and complicated problem. I went to see the *tzaddik*, R' Shloimke of Zh'vil, who instructed me to travel to Tel Aviv to see the Husyatiner Rebbe, R' Yisrael Friedman, grandson of the Rebbe of Rizhin. I went at once. Now, I am a sworn zealot, and have never been used to seeing a Rebbe wearing a tie, as well as other manners I did not understand. I was positive that R' Shloimke had made a mistake and sent me to the wrong address. I returned to Yerushalayim and told the Zh'viler Rebbe that I did not understand why he had sent me to that kind of Rebbe. Do you know what R' Shloimke answered?"

"What?" asked R' Isaac, riveted.

R' Chanina took a deep breath, offering testimony to the fact that he had not yet recovered from the impact of what he was describing. "He told me, firmly and clearly: 'Don't be too smart for your own good, and do exactly as I tell you. Your problem is so serious that, in our generation, I do not know a single person who could save you — except for the Husyatiner Rebbe. Go back to Tel Aviv, enter his presence humbly, and ask him for advice and a blessing.'

"That's what I did, and I was saved, by Heaven's grace. I realized how shallow I'd been, judging a person's greatness by the style of his clothes or the length of his *peyos* and beard. Now I know that the Husyatiner Rebbe is the holiest of the holy!"

"So you're suggesting that I go to Tel Aviv to see the Rebbe?"

"Exactly," said R' Chanina. "He is a holy man of G-d. The Zh'viler Rebbe, R' Shloimke, calls him a 'great fire covered with ash'. We have no grasp of his greatness, but he is capable of helping save your vision."

R' Isaac breathed a sigh of relief and thanked his friend profusely. At that moment, the *chazan* stood up and began to chant the beginning of the Shabbos *Minchah* service, putting an end to the friends' conversation.

R' Isaac prepared for his trip to Tel Aviv. He packed some food for the way, then went to the "Aviv" taxi service on King George Street to buy a ticket for Tel Aviv. The taxi would be leaving in about two hours. He would say *Tehillim* until then.

As he stood there, weighing the option of finding a nearby shul until his departure time, two religious Jews entered the office and bought tickets. In voices quite audible to R' Isaac, they chatted with one another about the Husyatiner Rebbe. From what they said, R' Isaac grasped that the Rebbe was not in Tel Aviv at present, but was staying in Haifa.

If a trip to Tel Aviv in the year 5700 took a full day, going to Haifa was like visiting the far side of the moon. It required complex logistics, including a transfer from train to bus, overnight arrangements for several days, and more. R' Isaac felt bereft of the strength the trip would demand. He approached the two men, asking whether they were certain the Rebbe was away from Tel Aviv. When they assured him faithfully that they knew this with certainty, he walked crestfallen back to the counter, canceled his place in the taxi, and was refunded the price of his ticket.

What to do now? It was inconceivable for him to undergo such a serious operation without first receiving a great *tzaddik's* blessing. He returned home, where he seriously considered the merits of traveling to Haifa himself, or sending his oldest son in his place.

Deep down, though, he knew that his weighty deliberations were useless. The trip to Haifa was a very difficult one, and he was not up to making it.

Suddenly, he remembered R' Menashe Kaplan, a close childhood friend. R' Menashe lived in Haifa. He could serve as a liason between R' Isaac and the holy Rebbe!

On second thought, the plan seemed extremely difficult to carry out. In those days, no one had a telephone in their home. In order to place a person-to-person call from Jerusalem to Haifa, one had to go to a post office run by the governing British Mandate and ask the clerk there to phone the parallel office in Haifa. The Haifa clerk then had to summon the second individual from his home to the post office, for a phone conversation to be arranged at a precise time.

Innumerable obstacles, therefore, stood in R' Isaac's way before he managed at length to reach his friend Menashe Kaplan in Haifa. The process took three days! There was much running to and from the post office, futile calls, and missed connections. In the end, however, R' Isaac managed to speak to his friend. He told him about his failing vision and Dr. Ticho's grim prognosis, along wih the doctor's insistence on urgent surgery. Menashe Kaplan had never heard of the

Husyatiner Rebbe, but for his good friend he was prepared to make every effort to find him. He promised to track down the Rebbe and ask for his blessing before R' Isaac's impending operation.

R' Menashe went directly from the post office to the city's religious sections, where he began asking around about the presence of an honored guest, the Husyatiner Rebbe. To his relief, he was told nearly at once that the holy Rebbe was indeed in their town at the moment, staying not far from the Rizhiner chassidim's neighborhood.

Menashe hurried to the address at once. The Rebbe's *meshamesh* told him that the Rebbe was currently engaged, but would be free to see him in just a few minutes.

When Menashe entered the inner room a little while later, he was astounded. Though he had never had much to do with chassidim, even he was forced to admit to himself that the elderly Jew before him was graced with a radiance he had never witnessed before. The Rebbe's hands were soft as silk, his eyes were warm and caring. A holy aura seemed to float around the noble countenance. Everything about the Rebbe spoke of dignity and grandeur. With a reverence he hadn't known he possessed, Menashe presented the sad case of his friend, R' Isaac, of Jerusalem.

"There is no need to operate," the Rebbe said. "Tell your friend to go to Dr. Weinberger, an eye doctor in Yerushalayim, and to follow his instructions implicitly."

Menashe Kaplan reacted automatically. "Rebbe, I didn't come here to ask for advice, but for a *berachah* before the operation."

Calmly, the Rebbe repeated himself. "Tell R' Isaac to go to Dr. Weinberger and not to undergo surgery."

Menashe restrained himself, remembering who he was and who the man was seated opposite. All he asked, quietly, was "And a *berachah*?"

"Certainly. I bless him with a *refuah sheleimah,* a full recovery," said R' Yisrael.

Menashe was already at the door when the Rebbe called, "You won't forget to tell him not to agree to an operation?"

Menashe nodded his head and left the room.

On his way back, he went over and over the Rebbe's words in his mind. He made a decision not to pass on the Rebbe's instructions, but only the Rebbe's blessing. Who had asked him to give advice? All they wanted was a *berachah*!

And that's what he did.

The phone call from Haifa to Jerusalem was more easily effected than the previous call, as the two friends had already, in their first conversation, scheduled the second. This saved both of them much time traveling to and from the post office. At the appointed hour, Menashe made the connection. R' Isaac was waiting.

"The Rebbe blessed you with a *refuah sheleimah*," said Menashe. "You can go ahead and have the operation."

"I'm glad to hear that," R' Isaac said. "You called just in time. My condition is worsening. These past two days, my eyes have grown seriously weaker, so that I can barely differentiate between darkness and light. I wouldn't even have made it here to the post office if my son hadn't led me the way you lead a blind man. By the way, was that all the Rebbe said?"

"He b-blessed you," Menashe stammered, knowing full well what he was concealing from his friend.

"And nothing else?"

"Actually he did say something else. But it's illogical."

"What was it?" R' Isaac pressed. "Tell me exactly what the Rebbe said!"

His friend in Haifa tried to think how best to transmit the Rebbe's message, while at the same time minimizing its importance. He offered his opinion that the Rebbe had ventured into foreign territory by offering advice when only a blessing was asked for.

"*But what did he say?*" R' Isaac nearly exploded. "I'm not a small child. Tell me what he said, exactly, word for word, and I will decide what's to be done. This is my business, not yours!"

Menashe repeated the Rebbe's instructions. He added, "My friend, listen to what *Chazal* say: 'You've found a pomegranate; eat the flesh and toss away the rind.' Accept the *berachah* and take it with you to surgery. Don't listen to his advice about the doctor."

"I will decide that," said R' Isaac, ending the discussion.

Emunas chachamim — faith in the words of our wise men — was not Menashe Kaplan's strong point, but it was R' Isaac's. How much more so, in light of what he had heard about the Husyatiner Rebbe from his friend R' Chanina. That same day, he went to see Dr. Morris Weinberger, ophthalmologist.

This eye doctor was hardly deserving of the title. He was an ephemeral presence in Jerusalem, recently arrived and soon to be gone. If we were to measure his expertise against that of Dr. Ticho on a scale of one to ten, Dr. Weinberger would fall into the negative numbers. But at that particular time, he was working confidently out of his clinic on a narrow street winding between Rechov Ben Yehudah — today's well-known *"midrachov"* — and Rechov Jaffa. R' Isaac came to him and related his problem.

The doctor took a special flashlight and shone it into the depths of R' Isaac's eyes like a world-class professional. "Well, it's nothing serious," he pronounced dismissively at the end of his exam. "You have to take eyedrops morning and night for two weeks."

"That's all?" R' Isaac asked disbelievingly, as Dr. Ticho's words echoed in his head: *"You have a very complex eye disease ... Only an operation can save your sight ..."*

"That's all," said the doctor, smiling. "Would you like some ointment, too?"

"No, no, there's no need," R' Isaac hastened to reply. He had little faith in the doctor, but complete faith in the Rebbe.

For two weeks, R' Isaac faithfully inserted the drops into his eyes, morning and night. By the end of that time, his vision had cleared completely, as though he had never had a problem at all. R' Isaac witnessed Hashem's salvation firsthand. In his heart of hearts, however, he was still afraid that the disease would return. Without delay, he returned to Dr. Ticho's clinic. He wished to hear that world-class doctor's opinion.

Dr. Ticho examined him thoroughly. He gave his patient a long measured look, and said, "All right, you didn't want me to operate on you; that's your right. But tell me, who did the surgery? Who did such a good job?"

"That's the whole point!" R' Isaac burst out. "I had no operation!"

"Nonsense," the doctor said sternly. "There is no way to escape the disease you had except through long and difficult surgery. I must say that the surgeon who worked on you did a completely professional job, even in terms of the stitches. There is no scarrring around your eyes at all."

R' Isaac all but shouted, "Of course not! Because I never had surgery!"

Dr. Ticho leaped to his feet.

R' Isaac told Dr. Ticho exactly what had happened, and what the Husyatiner Rebbe had advised.

"Now I understand!" Dr. Ticho exclaimed. In a jocular tone, he added, "Listen, between you and me, Dr. Weinberger is an eye doctor the way you're an army officer, and those silly drops he gave you are good for nothing but minor eye infections. They had nothing to do with the serious disease that was affecting your vision." Smiling, he added, "From now on, don't say that Dr. Weinberger or his drops cured your eyes. Say that it was the Husyatiner Rebbe who cured you."

A Gift From Rachel Imeinu

THE LARGE ZICHRON MOSHE SHUL IN JERUSALEM bustled with life on that winter night in the year 5752, a year that had been blessed with plentiful rain. *Minyanim* of men *davened Maariv* in a constant stream. The hour was late, but still they streamed into the shul, wrapped in their warmest coats.

R' Dovid finished *davening* and left the shul. Stepping out into the cold street, he glanced up at the heavily clouded sky to check if it was raining.

Suddenly, he remembered that he had a very good reason for gazing upward. Tonight was the last possible date for performing the mitzvah of *Kiddush Levanah* and he had not yet done so this month!

His glance became concerned. A thick bank of clouds covered the sky from end to end. Not so much as a crack allowed a glimpse of the sky to peek through.

R' Dovid continued gazing upward. Crossing the street, he looked up again, hoping against hope that things would look brighter from that vantage point. But the sky remained as dark and impenetrable as before. It was one of the most cloudy nights of the year.

As he stood there, neck craned back and eyes fixed on the clouds, a merry voice spoke near him. "R' Dovid, have you lost something up in the sky? Maybe you're looking for an angel or two?"

Lowering his gaze, he saw R' Yosef, whom everyone knew as Yosel, a cheerful young man who was rarely without a smile. He was smiling now.

"I haven't lost anything, and I'm not looking for angels," R' Dovid smiled back. "But I'm about to miss out on the last chance to say *Kiddush Levanah.*"

Yosel clapped a hand to his head. "*Oy, vey!* I also haven't said *Kiddush Levanah* yet. *Nu,* is there a moon?"

"That's what I've been searching for these past few minutes," said R' Dovid. "But the sky is completely black."

"Let's look together," Yosel suggested. "You know what they say: 'Two are better than one.'"

Both men stood staring up at the heavy cloud cover above. They gazed a long time but they could discern no change. "What do we do?" Yosel said in despair. "Won't the moon come out at all tonight?"

"Don't give up," R' Dovid calmed him. "What we need here is patience."

Anyone who knew R' Dovid well knew that these last words encapsulated his entire personality. He was a patient man, always even tempered and cheerful. Not everyone knew that he was concealing a nearly unbearable pain: Almost twenty years had passed from his wedding day, and he and his wife had not yet been blessed with offspring. No one who met him for the first time would ever have guessed. He always appeared so contented. Only those who were close to him knew that the habitual expression he wore, and his loving acceptance of suffering, were the result of continuous work in internalizing the principle of "Whatever the Merciful One does is beneficial." When he said, "Patience is needed," he was speaking as a man whose patience had endured for close to two decades without reaching the breaking point!

The minutes passed, and the cloud formation began to change. That is, the sharp easterly wind blew some clouds away but the same wind brought a new convoy of clouds, equally dense, to take their place. Jerusalemites have always rejoiced at the sight of this kind of damp cloud bank, but tonight those clouds concealed the moon from those who wished to serve their Creator. They stood with faces tilted upward, as though hoping to be bathed in moonlight, but only raindrops fell on them.

They were still standing there, in the rain, when a well-dressed Jew approached. "Why are you two standing in the rain with your faces up?" he asked with a heavy American accent. "Is there a custom of drinking rain tonight?"

"We want to say *Kiddush Levanah*," the two men sighed. "But we've been standing here for two hours already, and the sky isn't clearing up."

"*Oy*, I forgot!" the man exclaimed. "I have to say *Kiddush Levanah*, too!"

After the three of them had stood there for another span of time without a glimpse of the moon, they decided not to remain passive. For a mitzvah's sake, one must give his all. If there was no moon in Jerusalem, that didn't mean it wasn't visible in Bnei Brak, or Ashdod, or Netanya. Using a passerby's phone (in the year 5752, cell phones were new, and not yet commonplace), each of them called acquaintances and relatives in the various religious communities throughout the country, waking more than a few in the process. Those at the other end of the line found it hard to believe that they were "turning over the world" just for the sake of *Kiddush Levanah*.

As we have mentioned, this was one of the rainiest and most overcast nights yet that winter. Heavy clouds covered the entire country, nearly (emphasis on the "nearly") from horizon to horizon, with the moon hiding itself behind the clouds. From every side came negative responses. Bnei Brak: No moon! Ashdod: Nothing! Beitar: No! Netanya: No! Chazon Yechezkel: No. Komemiyut: No. Haifa: No … And so on.

The three men went out into the street once more, hoping that they would not have to take their quest afar. Perhaps the moon would reveal itself in its full glory right here, in Zichron Moshe.

Some minutes later, as they stood craning their necks to see the sky, a taxi stopped beside them to let out three young yeshivah men who wanted to *daven Maariv*. A short conversation elicited the information that they had just returned from Chevron, where they had gone to pray at the graves of our forefathers in *Me'aras HaMachpelah*.

"You've come from Chevron?" Yosel said. "Could you see the moon there?" It never entered his mind that what they were seeking might actually come about in this casual manner.

To his shock, the young men reported that the skies over Chevron were not cloudy at all, and the moon was riding high and bright. They had canvassed the whole country, but forgotten Chevron.

"There's a moon in Chevron?" all three cried.

"Yes, a beautiful moon," they affirmed.

"Maybe the sky's clouded up since then," they fretted, having become schooled in disappointment that night.

"There were no clouds on the horizon," the travelers said confidently.

With a sense of self-sacrifice on behalf of a mitzvah, the three decided to make the trip to Chevron. The question was: How?

"In a taxi," the American suggested practically.

"But what taxi driver will want to drive to Chevron in the dead of night?" someone asked. Chevron has always been known as a danger spot, quite apart from the present-day intifada.

The American refused to despair. Instead, he hatched a plot whereby they might get a driver to take them to their destination. "We'll tell him we need to travel toward the neighborhood of Gilo and beyond, without specifying exactly where. We'll give him garbled directions. Once he's well on his way, he'll have no choice but to continue on to Chevron."

The idea found favor with his companions. They hailed a passing taxi and climbed aboard.

At first, the taxi driver was unsuspicious. The directions they gave him were garbled and unclear, but this was not the first time he'd had passengers who didn't know exactly where they were going. He drove down the road as they asked, beginning to pass Arab villages. After passing Beit Jalla, however, he sat up suddenly, suspicions aroused.

"Go on," Yosel urged. "We're almost there."

The driver continued on in silence for another few hundred meters, then asked, "Can I know where we're going?"

"Go on," Yosel said again.

"I'm not going anywhere." Angrily, the driver stepped hard on the brakes. The vehicle slowed, then came to a full stop. "I'm not going another meter without knowing exactly where you want to take me."

R' Dovid was candid. "The truth is, we'd like to get to Chevron."

"*What*? Are you crazy? Dragging me out to such a dangerous place in the middle of the night? If I'd have known you wanted to go to Chevron, I never would have started out!"

His fury grew by the moment. "All of you, get out of my car. I'm not taking you anywhere. You have no conscience! Do you want to have me murdered?"

"You're not alone," they said, trying to calm him. But the driver refused to be soothed. Ranting angrily, he ended by evicting them from his taxi. They were left at the side of the road, surrounded by black hills, gazing after the departing taxi as it headed back toward Jerusalem.

They had no idea what to do next. The darkness was almost total. Proceeding on foot was something they dared not do, lest they run into a band of armed Arabs or terrorists with murder on their minds. Arab villages surrounded them on every side. They decided to stay at the side of the road. Though traffic was sparse, perhaps someone would take pity on them and take them back to Jerusalem in his car or, even better, take them to Chevron…

Meanwhile, how better to pass the time than to continue searching for the moon?

Once again, they tilted their faces upward, scanning the sky. Their hearts belonged completely to their Creator as they prayed silently for the moon to shine down on them before the time for the mitzvah's performance was past.

They never heard the police car approaching quietly through the night. Suddenly, the glare of headlights blinded them. Several police officers came at them, running. One — obviously the superior officer — shouted, "What are you doing here in the middle of the night? Identity cards, please!"

In their surprise, the trio said nothing. The policeman continued, "Why are you staring at the sky in the middle of the night? Have you dropped out of the moon?"

Admittedly, the scene appeared highly suspicious: Three men standing in the dark, near Arab villages, gazing skyward. They must be plotting some sort of reprisal against the Arabs, or something else that was strictly unkosher! And how had they gotten here, anyway?

"Actually, we are looking for the moon," explained Yosel. "We want to say *Kiddush Levanah.*"

"Do you think I was born yesterday?" The officer laughed scornfully. "Do you think I don't know that you make *Kiddush* on Shabbos? If you think you're going to sell me some old wive's tale, you've got another thing coming. I am an educated man. Think carefully about what you're doing, or it's going to end badly for you."

He sounded very authoritative and very threatening. All three of the accused turned pale. Unless they succeeded in convincing him, they might very well end up in jail that night!

"Listen, please," R' Dovid said in a soft, reasonable tone. He placed a hand warmly on the policeman's shoulder. "When Hashem created the world, he created the sun and the moon of equal size. But the moon complained, saying that two kings cannot wear a single crown."

His voice grew louder as the police officers listened, mesmerized, to the young chassidic rabbi spouting words of Torah to capture the imagination and the heart. His black *peyos* glistened in the flashlight beam as he continued, "... and that's how we arrive at the monthly mitzvah of sanctifying the moon — *Kiddush Levanah.* We recite the blessing, 'Who, with His word, created the heavens. Blessed are you, Hashem, renewer of the months.'"

The notion of sanctifying the moon, with its implicit acceptance of the Divine Creation, captivated the policemen. They were convinced. Just one problem remained: getting these religious folk back to Jerusalem.

But R' Dovid, Yosel, and their American companion were not about to give up their quest. There were still two hours left to the deadline for doing the mitzvah. Perhaps they would still merit performing it.

Seizing the moment, they begged the police officers to use their radio equipment to help them. Would they ask their colleagues, over the airwaves, whether any of them, anywhere, had caught a glimpse of the moon peeking through the clouds?

The senior officer agreed. Radio in hand, he began moving from one police band to the next. "I have a group of *chareidim* (ultra-Orthodox) here who want to perform the ritual of blessing the moon. Do you see the moon out there?"

Strange instructions flew over the airwaves, as every police officer in the area was recruited for the noble purpose of finding the chief suspect: the moon itself.

After a long round of questioning and listening, the answer they'd been waiting for for so long came at last. Over the radio came a report from the police station at Beit Lechem: "The sky here has just started to clear. The clouds have opened up, and we see a full moon."

"Yes!" crowed the head officer, sharing the religious men's joy. Who can plumb the mysteries of the Jewish soul? "We're taking them over to *Kever Rachel* right now, in armored police vehicles."

No one has ever experienced a *Kiddush Levanah* the way it was experienced on that wintry night in Beit Lechem. Never before had the companions felt such an exaltation of the spirit as they sensed the Divine hand guiding them from place to place, the way a father might lead his young child. It was as though not only the clouds, but the seven heavens themselves, had opened up for them.

They stood with the group of police officers on the Beit Lechem street, just outside *Kever Rachel* (which, in those days, had not yet taken on its fortresslike aspect and still wore its age-old, familiar look), and joyously sanctified the moon so loudly and exultantly that their voices woke the neighborhood Arabs and sent them leaping out of bed to their windows. It was a beautiful *Kiddush Hashem* to see how people went out on such a frigid night in order to peform a mitzvah. They might have been asleep in their beds at that hour, in a warm, well-heated home, wrapped in down quilts. Instead, they had ventured out into the cold and the rain, battling the winds as they rejoiced in performing the will of their Creator.

"*Tanna D'Vei* R' Yishmael: If Israel only managed to exalt their Father in Heaven once a month, it would be enough."

On this night, they had merited exalting their Father in Heaven. All their toil had been rewarded. Just an hour before the deadline, they had merited seeing the moon and sanctifying it as it rode high in the night sky. They prayed that the "light of the moon might be as the light of the sun and the light of the seven days of Creation, as it was before its diminishment," and ended with a storm of fervent dancing.

But all that was nothing, compared to what awaited them at the end of the mitzvah ...

Once they had arrived, in so unconventional a manner, at the site of *Kever Rachel*, should they not take advantage of the special opportunity to go inside and say a prayer?

They stood near the embroidered velvet hanging that covered the monument and recited chapters of *Tehillim*. At this moment they felt a special closeness, as though Rachel Imeinu was standing right there, listening to every whispered word.

Yosel had already finished his *tefillah*. He glanced over at R' Dovid, who stood with eyes closed beside the monument, lips moving soundlessly. Suddenly, he knew what R' Dovid was *davening* for. It wasn't hard to guess! Nearly twenty years, as we've said, had passed from R' Dovid and his wife's wedding day, and they had all gone by without the blessing of children. Surely that was what he was praying for.

All at once, Yosel's heart began to churn with his friend's anguish. His eyes began to water. With hot tears pouring down his cheeks, he cried piercingly, "Ima! Ima Rachel! Who, better than you, knows the pain of those who are childless? Who is more aware of the pain of the Jewish woman who has not been blessed with offspring? You, yourself, lived with that pain. You knew the anguish of those whose homes are empty. What was it that you said to Yaakov Avinu: 'Bring me sons, for if not I will surely die!' You experienced the pain of childlessness — oh, the agony and the tragedy that dominates their lives. Please, pray for my friend, R' Dovid, to be blessed with living offspring!"

Seizing a corner of the velvet cover, he wept uncontrollably. "Mama Rachel, please, I beg of you, I am asking not for myself, but for R' Dovid, my good friend. Let him have children soon. He has suffered enough! I am not leaving this place until you promise me, right here and now, that R' Dovid will merit the joy of fathering children!"

His friends stared at him as though paralyzed. Even R' Dovid was astonished. He had not believed that his private pain had so touched his friend's heart. Yosel, oblivious to what was happening around him, continued to plead and cry at length. It had been a long time since such heartrending cries had been heard in the darkness before dawn near the tomb of Rachel.

And, approximately 10 months after that memorable *Kiddush Levanah* — on the 11th day of Cheshvan, Rachel Imeinu's *yahrtzeit* — a pair of twin girls was born to R' Dovid and his wife.

Yosel's prayers had pierced the heavens. "Mama" Rachel had prayed that Hashem bestow a precious gift on her beloved sons, who had traveled through the blackness of night to exalt their Father in Heaven.

Shabbos Protects
Its Protectors

THE FIRST WORLD WAR STRUCK ERETZ YISRAEL A SERIES of deadly blows, the hardest of which was a devastating famine. Worst hit of all was Jerusalem. People wandered the streets, swollen and frail, begging for bread that was not to be had.

Together with the hunger came the disease. The unhygienic conditions gave rise to sweeping epidemics that further diminished the struggling Jewish population. There were some 50,000 Jews in Jerusalem and its environs at the start of the war; at its end, on Chanukah 5678, exactly half remained: 25,000 Jews in all.

Food shortages were rampant as early as the first year of the war. Each day was worse than the one before. As roads were closed, the supply of fresh merchandise was cut off. There was nothing to sell and nothing to buy.

One of the city's best-known industrialists at that time was R' Yosef Levi Chagiz. He owned a large paper business in Jerusalem, which was closed because of the war. There was no point in keeping it open when no one was interested in buying paper. Everyone was seeking bread to assuage his own hunger and that of his family. Who needed paper at such a time?

Seeing that there were no prospects for him in Jerusalem, home of his main paper outlet, R' Yosef Levi moved to Jaffa where a branch of his company was located. Jaffa was the country's primary port city at the time. As such, conditions there were many times better than in Jerusalem. People could still live there in relative tranquility, without the devastating effects of shortages and starvation.

Even in Jaffa, however, R' Yosef Levi's paper store enjoyed only a brief respite. Within a short time, the port became devoid of life as the cruel world war put an end to sea traffic. Merchant vessels no longer sailed into Jaffa. Supplies of flour and other food staples dwindled, and Jaffa began to feel its first hunger pangs.

R' Yosef saw that Jaffa, too, held out no hope of success for a business concern. He sought another solution.

And he found one!

There was a very valuable commodity in Eretz Yisrael at that time, and that was kerosene. The concept of electric light had not yet made its way to neglected Palestine; only from tourists from abroad did members of the tiny Jewish "*Yishuv*" hear about the recently discovered marvel called "electricity" that could power lights. In America, that land of wonders, one could read at night without a kerosene lamp that smoked tearfully into the reader's eyes.

The kerosene was imported in wooden crates. Each crate held two cans of oil, with each can containing 20 liters of the precious fluid.

Because merchant ships were no longer reaching the port of Jaffa, supplies of kerosene stopped completely. After food, oil for light and cooking became the most sought-after commodity in the land. Without it, one could not read so much as a single letter at night, or cook even the meager food that was left to them. With kerosene so much in demand, people began stockpiling it secretly in all sorts of hiding places.

The Turkish government in Eretz Yisrael declared war on the hoarding of kerosene. An urgent decree, created to meet the emergency, stipulated the exact quantity of oil that each person required for daily use, a quantity that must not be exceeded under any circumstances. An additional law stated that anyone found concealing kerosene, above and beyond the stipulated amount, would face severe punishment. The wording left no room for doubt: Offenders would face the death sentence!

There was a very valuable commodity in Eretz Yisrael at that time, R' Yosef Levi was a seasoned businessman. At the war's very start, his well-honed instincts told him that kerosene would surely become a desired commodity, and its price would skyrocket. He owned a large orange orchard in Petach Tikva which, in those days, was no more than a large residential neighborhood, commonly referred to by the previous Arabic name of Malabas rather than the name Petach Tikva, given to it by its founders. Among the fruit trees was a wide, deep well. In normal times, the water from that well had supplied the trees, but these were not normal times. The well was now designated for a different job.

R' Yosef Levi traveled to Petach Tikva early on at the onset of the war, where he bought a large quantity of kerosene, hiding the crates in the well's dark depths. He was shrewd enough and experienced enough not to complete the operation in a single day; he had no desire to draw suspicious attention to himself. Every few days, he purchased a few more crates of oil, using different sellers. Then, in the dead of night when there were no eyes to witness his actions, he climbed down the ladder to the bottom of the well, carrying crates of kerosene in his strong arms.

The secret cache sat securely at the bottom of the well in Petach Tikva, while R' Yosef Levi spent his days in Jaffa. Now, he began to plan how best to turn the supply of oil into cash, so that he might continue earning a living in those stressful times.

But Heaven had other plans for him. Bigger plans.

The Arab watchman sat at the entrance to R' Yosef Levi's orchard, humming to himself. What better job than to guard an orchard, sitting comfortably on a broad chair and leaning indolently at his ease, listening with half an ear to the birds' twitter as a gentle breeze caressed his face and brought the heady fragrance of citrus trees. From time to time he waved his stick in the direction of a cluster of children who had dared to snatch oranges off the trees without permission. Sometimes, he had to contend with starving adults, who eyed the oranges longingly but were deterred by the sight of the hulking guard ominously clearing his throat.

Suddenly, his eyes flew open. A sound had reached his ears: the clump of boots on the path. He leaped to his feet and brandished the stick, his face a mask of terror. This was no band of barefoot children or hunger-enfeebled men. A troop of Turkish gendarmes was approaching.

The soldiers had known better days. Their straggling beards and stained uniforms told a wordless tale of their own. The Ottoman Empire was nearing its final hours.

At the head of the troop stood its leader, whose uniform boasted the symbol of his rank, the Turkish equivalent of major.

"Let us in," the officer rasped, knocking aside the watchman's chair. The guard's strength evaporated instantly before these armed military men, who passed him as though he were invisible and began a meticulous search of the orchard.

Such searches were commonplace, happening every day in every sort of place. The Turkish authorities were seeking out lawbreakers and hoarders of forbidden goods. In addition, many young Turkish soldiers had gone AWOL, finding concealment in all manner of hiding places, and the army was searching them out assiduously so that they might receive their just desserts and serve as an example to others.

The watchman sensed big trouble looming on the horizon. He felt limp as a rag as he watched the soldiers at their search. When they reached the empty well, one of them descended with ropes. It was only a question of time before the cache of kerosene was discovered.

That time was at hand. The soldier's voice floated excitedly out of the well's depths: "I've found kerosene! A lot of kerosene!"

The watchman paled. He was well aware of the fate that awaited his employer, owner of the orchard. While he had no great love for Jews, he knew that trouble for his boss meant the end of his own job.

The major crooked a finger at the guard. "What's this?" he shouted, pointing into the well where the scores of kerosene crates lay.

Frightened out of his wits, the watchman stammered unintelligibly.

"I-it b-belongs to *affendi* Yusuf, the orchard's o-owner," he managed to croak finally.

"And where is he, the *affendi*?"

"He lives in Jaffa and comes here several times a week."

The major twirled his thick mustache, which made him look even more threatening than before. "Get on your horse and ride to Jaffa, to your master, *affendi* Yusuf. Tell him that, by order of the Turkish Army, he must come here at once to explain these hidden crates of kerosene. Otherwise, there will be trouble."

"The *affendi* is a Jew," the watchman said. "He can't come here today, because Jews are not allowed to ride horses on Shabbos."

This enraged the major even further. "Tell your master that if he does not come today, I will make sure to fetch him, and to punish him as only a Turkish officer knows how. No one ignores a Turkish officer's orders!"

The guard had no choice. He mounted his horse and galloped away toward Jaffa.

❧ ❧

Several hours later, he reached Jaffa's Neve Tzedek neighborhood. R' Yosef Levi Chagiz was at home, peacefully enjoying his Shabbos *seudah* and singing *zemiros*.

"Oh, Mr. Yusuf, don't ask what happened!" the watchman blurted out as he ran into the house. Rapidly, he spilled his news. "You must come to Malabas at once and present yourself to the major, to explain the meaning of the crates of kerosene you hid in the well."

If the Arab had expected R' Yosef to fall off his chair in a panic, he was mistaken. R' Yosef calmly finished his meal, recited the *Bircas HaMazon*, and only then deigned to respond to his worker.

"First of all, go outside, unsaddle your horse, and tie him to the tree in the courtyard. Who gave you permission to ride one of my horses on Shabbos? I've already told you a number of times that, just as work is forbidden for me on this day, the same applies to my animal. It is a day of rest for him, as well.

"After that, I want you to go to the Jaffa *shuk* (marketplace), find yourself a horse or donkey, and return to the major. Tell him that today is my day of rest, my Shabbos, and Al-lah's command obligates me more than that of a Turkish army officer. After all, he, too, believes in G-d."

The Arab blanched. "Mr. Yusuf, do you know whom you are starting up with? That officer can hang you from a tree if he wishes, and no one will say a word!"

R' Yosef Levi nodded firmly. "I am not afraid of a Turkish gendarme. I am afraid only of Hashem in Heaven."

The Arab gazed at him admiringly. "Ah, *affendi*, I told that officer that you wouldn't come, and I was right!"

He tied up the horse as instructed and set off for the *shuk*. There, he found another horse on which he rode back to Malabas.

Dusk had fallen by the time he rode, weary and dust covered, into Petach Tikva. The Turkish major was waiting impatiently. When he saw the watchman returning alone, he roared furiously, "Where is your *affendi*? Why hasn't he come with you?"

"I told you he can't come. It is forbidden for him to ride a horse on Shabbos." The Arab spoke softly, in a placating tone, which succeeded in easing some of the officer's wrath. The major left two gendarmes to wait for the Jew and to stand guard over the cache of kerosene to make sure no one tried to spirit it away. The next morning, the Major returned with his troops, ready to devour the Jew who had dared disobey his orders.

R' Yosef Levi came riding in on his horse on Sunday afternoon. Dismounting, he walked erect and unafraid up to the glaring Turkish major.

"You are the *affendi* Yusuf?" demanded the officer.

"I am he."

"Why did you not come yesterday, when I summoned you?" the major screamed. "Do you know what lies in store for a person who disobeys the order of a Turkish officer?"

"There is Someone superior to you, and He ordered me not to come," R' Yosef replied calmly, gazing directly into the Turk's eyes.

"Who ordered you to disobey me?" The major was almost choking with fury.

R' Yosef pointed upward. "*Al-lah-il-kabir*, the great G-d," he said quietly. "He warned us in the Torah to keep the Sabbath."

"But Al-lah also says that you must obey the authorities. Otherwise, everyone would do whatever he wanted and leave everything up to Al-lah!"

Without his being aware of it, the officer's anger had become less intense. R' Yosef Levi took advantage of this and continued to explain his actions. "True, but only in a case where the authorities do not order something that contradicts His commandments. The great G-d in Heaven is above you and above your king, His Majesty the Turkish sultan himself. Think about this: What if you issued an order to a soldier, then along came an officer inferior to yourself in rank and told him to do the opposite? You would not tolerate that, would you? In this case, we are speaking of the King of kings, Whose commands obligate every living being in the world!"

"And the kerosene that you hid in the well, you crafty Jew? Is that there on Al-lah's command as well?" the Major asked sarcastically.

"Certainly," replied R' Yosef Levi. "That kerosene is designated for the poor, who do not have the money to buy any for themselves. Do you think I kept it for myself? Had I done that, I would have found a better hiding place, one that would never be found, and would not have risked hanging."

"It's for the poor?" the officer repeated, astounded. "Not for you?"

Once again, R' Yosef Levi met the Turk's gaze bravely and directly. "Go to Jerusalem, and ask the people there who Yusuf Chagiz is. Ask if he is a person who lives only for himself, or one who is concerned about the lot of the poor."

"Didn't you know you were breaking the law and could expect a severe punishment? You could very well hang for this!"

"I am not afraid. He who helps the poor and the unfortunate is under Al-lah's protection. If you, major, will help the needy, then Al-lah will protect you as well. I don't think you would object to the protection of the blessed G-d during this time of war, when human blood is being spilled like water."

The officer's stony heart melted. For the first time, a slight smile appeared on his face.

"Listen to me, Jew," he told R' Yosef Levi. "I, too, am a religious man who believes in Al-lah. I respect believers, but I have no liking for people who perform all sorts of atrocities in the name of Al-lah. Had you come from Jaffa yesterday, riding on your horse, and told me that you collected that kerosene for the poor, I would not have believed a word of it. I would have sent you straight to the gallows. Too many criminals and thieves hide behind Al-lah's name and do things in that name that they shouldn't be doing. But you are a different sort. You proved to me that you are a genuine and serious person, a man whose heart and words are identical. You were prepared to sacrifice your life for your faith. You endangered your life yesterday when you disobeyed my orders. By that, you proved to me that your words of faith are genuine. You are not a liar."

The officer thumped R' Yosef Levi's shoulder. "You are free to go and you may keep all the kerosene in your well for distribution to the poor who cannot afford to buy it. In the merit of our compassion for those whom Al-lah wishes us to help, Al-lah will protect you and me in this mighty war."

As R' Yosef Levi stood thunderstruck, the Turkish officer and his troops turned and left the orchard. Watching the scene with slack jaw and disbelieving eyes was the Arab watchman.

R' Yosef Levi did distribute the kerosene among the poor, down to the last drop. Because he had said that the oil was intended for the needy — though the words had been spoken in an effort to save his life — he remained faithful to his statement, and did not leave even one canister of kerosene over for himself.

Paradise Lost

"YOU SHOULD KNOW, *KINDERLACH*, THAT IN ORDER to feel something on Shabbos, you have to put in some effort. The way you prepare for Shabbos, it's no wonder you don't experience any of the flavor."

Twenty *bachurim* sat in a room, surrounding their *mashgiach,* R' Kasriel Ricklis. The boys drank in his words the way a thirsty desert traveler might gulp water. He spoke directly to the students' hearts, in clear and simple language. The *sichah* (talk), in today's *va'ad,* (group meeting), revolved around the topic of laziness, a topic R' Ricklis never tired of discussing.

His remarks were offered in response to a question ventured by a student named Yoel Levi: "I'd like to understand, what happens to us on Shabbos?"

"Explain your question," R' Kasriel said. "What exactly are you trying to ask?"

"We learned in *Gemara,* and we believe with complete faith, that a person has an additional soul, a *neshamah yeseirah,* on Shabbos. We understand that this *neshamah yeseirah* is a spiritual power. Why, then, do we feel nothing? Why does our Shabbos look so simple and earthbound? Where is the exalted feeling that's supposed to envelop us on Shabbos, the complete detachment from all our weekday concerns? True, we learn a little more on Shabbos. We sit in the dining room and eat and sing *zemiros.* But it's all on the surface. Where are the inner changes that are supposed to take place? I'm speaking for myself, of course. But maybe some of the other *bachurim* have felt the same way."

Several of his fellow students smiled. Shuki Honig, seated near Yoel, poked him in the ribs, while Chilik Ben-Zakai winked at him. "What do you mean?" someone whispered loudly. "Don't you see us transformed into angels on Shabbos?"

Even before the laughter over that sally had faded, someone else joked, "Four ounces of sunflower seeds and some cold watermelon, my friend. That's all you're missing to make you exactly like me."

R' Ricklis listened to the joking and decided to grab the bull by the horns.

"I think that's correct. Who just said that about the sunflower seeds and watermelon?"

Betzalel Wasserlauf's cheeks turned rosy as a ripe watermelon, identifying him without any need to say a word. The *mashgiach* encouraged him, "You are absolutely correct. In essence, you've answered Yoel's question. He asked why we don't sense a spiritual exaltation and pleasure on Shabbos, why Shabbos is so grounded in the material. This is the answer: For us, Shabbos is a day of sunflower seeds and watermelon, a day sanctified for lots of sleep and unrestrained eating. We are caught in the cellophane that surrounds the wrapping of Shabbos. We haven't even touched the wrapping itself."

The atmosphere turned sober. The boys sensed that the *mashgiach* would tolerate no joking now. They listened quietly, in all seriousness.

"From personal experience, I'm telling you, dear *kinderlach*, that those who invest in the Shabbos are rewarded by the Shabbos. The same rule applies to any spiritual endeavor. You ask about Shabbos. Why don't you ask about *HaKadosh Baruch Hu*? Hashem's glory fills the entire world, so why do we not sense Him with every step we take? The answer is this: The degree to which we seek Hashem is the degree to which He reveals Himself to us. The more you long for Him, the closer He will come. '*Karov Hashem l'chol kor'av*' — Hashem is close to all those who call Him. It's up to us. Calling out to Hashem brings Him closer to us, in the precise measure of seriousness and truth that we invest in the calling! The results are the direct consequence of the investment. Begin to invest in Shabbos, and you will feel something else."

"How do you invest in Shabbos?" one of the boys asked. It was Betzalel, the one who had made the crack about the sunflower seeds.

"Try to free up your Friday afternoons from distracting activities. Go to the *mikveh*, learn the *parashah* with *Rashi*, say *Shir HaShirim*, and learn the eighth section of the *Yesod V'Shoresh HaAvodah*. Pay attention to what is written there about preparing for Shabbos, and we'll meet afterward. I think you'll be singing new *zemiros*," the *mashgiach* ended with a twinkle.

Yoel was happy. He had received an answer to a question that had been troubling him for some time. Most of the other boys in his *shiur* were not as disturbed by this as he was. For them, Shabbos was, first and foremost, a day of rest and, only after that, a day of holiness. But

Yoel had already tasted a genuine Shabbos, and there was something in his soul that would not let him rest.

Yoel came from a very simple home. His parents lived on a *moshav* in the south of Eretz Yisrael, where they raised a large herd of 300 cows. In a home like his parents had, Shabbos was certainly a day of rest. His father was a hardworking laborer who, in order to support his family and marry off his eight sons and daughters, engaged in other pursuits apart from the raising of cattle and selling their milk. All week he worked long and hard, and by the time Shabbos came he was nearly at the point of collapse. His children were used to seeing his head drop in the middle of the fish course. It was only with difficulty that he managed to finish the meal. From the table he made straight for his bed, for a deep sleep that lasted 10 hours or more. Until the age of 13, Yoel had seen no other kind of Shabbos.

After his bar mitzvah, he spent several Shabbosos at the homes of relatives. He discovered that there are people who also learn Torah on Shabbos and do not only eat and sleep. At the age of 14 he spent an entire Shabbos at the home of a man who was a genuine *tzaddik*, and the experience had stirred something in him. He emphathized with every word the *mashgiach* had said today, for the man who had hosted him on that memorable Shabbos had behaved in just the way the *mashgiach* had described. On Friday morning, the man had sat with his *Chumash* and reviewed the *parashah*, "*shnayim mikra v'echad Targum*," and with *Rashi's* commentary. Afterward, in the afternoon, he had gone to the *mikveh*. On his return, it was clear that something had been ignited in him. He dressed early, made all his Shabbos preparations in good time, in a spirit of good cheer and perfect family harmony, and then went off to shul.

Yoel had accompanied him, curious to see what would happen next. In his own home on the *moshav*, this interval was generally spent making phone calls, reading the newspaper, dipping into the *cholent* pot and kugel pan, and engaging in pleasant conversation. About an hour before the Shabbos siren blared, people began rushing around to get ready, to the tune of much shouting and bickering. Every minute was punctuated by cries of, "Have you seen my shirt?" "Who was the last one to use the shoe polish?" "Has the Shabbos clock been set yet?" and so on.

Yoel's host had completed all his preparations two-and-a-half hours earlier, without any need for anger or raised voices. Two-and-and-half hours before the onset of Shabbos, he was on his way to shul. First he learned *Gemara* for a full hour, then he picked up a *Shir HaShirim* and began to recite the beautiful words with heartfelt fervor and real longing. It was a *Shir HaShirim* from another world. When he was done, there was still time to learn several commentaries on the *parashah* and to prepare a couple of cogent thoughts to be shared at the Shabbos table later.

This was the head of Shabbos, and the rest of the body followed naturally along after it. The whole day wore an entirely different look from the one Yoel had seen in his own home. True, they ate and slept in this house as well, but those activities were not the clear preference here. Yoel left his host's home on *Motza'ei Shabbos* in a definite state of exaltation, and the knowledge that Shabbos could be different. He was certain that he would be a part of other such Shabbosos in yeshivah. To his dismay, he was disappointed in this expectation. While he and his fellow students experienced Shabbos in a far more powerful way than he had at home, it wasn't the same thing. The experience did not reach the fringes of that Shabbos in the *tzaddik's* home.

That had been a wonderful Shabbos. And it led, in time, to two more wonderful Shabbosos.

It came without warning, one Friday. Yoel was busy preparing wicks and oil for Shabbos, chattering with his yeshivah friends about *halachos* they had learned.

Suddenly, he had felt a sort of inner constriction. Something was burning inside, something he could not describe. All he knew was that his legs took him to the *beis medrash*, which was empty at that hour. He grabbed a *siddur* with a fervor he had never felt before, and began to recite *Shir HaShirim* as though he hoped the words would extinguish the flames burning in his soul. But the flames only grew higher. Overwhelmed with an inexplicable spiritual thirst, he began racing to and fro between the benches. Occasionally he would stumble over some obstacle, but he didn't care. He did not know what was happening to him, until his inner emotion became suddenly clear.

For the first time in his life, he was truly tasting the Shabbos.

When two other *bachurim* entered the *beis medrash*, Yoel felt that their presence was disturbing him in welcoming the Shabbos the way he wished to. He ran instead into a deserted *shiur* room, carefully shut the door against intruders, and *davened Minchah* and *Kabbalas Shabbos* while it was still daylight outside. He was in the grip of an indescribable exaltation, as though he was stepping on unsolid ground. From the depths of his heart he prayed, tears streaming unawares down his face. If only he need never step down from this lofty plane! Never to have to detach himself from this joyous and elevated sensation, never to have to live another mundane moment in his life. Only he and his Creator were present, wrapped up in his *tefillah*.

He was mistaken.

A boy stood on the other side of the door. Avrumi Weiss was Yoel's closest friend. He, too, liked the privacy that the *shiur* room offered. It was a place where he could sit and concentrate on a *sefer* in perfect silence. Just as he was about to open the door, he was startled by the sound of Yoel's quiet weeping. What had happened to his friend? Was Yoel undergoing some sort of crisis? Had something occurred back home?

After listening for a few minutes, however, he was stunned by what he was hearing. Yoel, a young boy in the first *shiur* of the yeshivah, was reciting fervent verses about Hashem, over and over with mounting intensity. Avrumi listened a while longer, then returned to the *beis medrash*. Some inner instinct warned him that Yoel would be very upset at being caught at such a moment. It was a secret between him and his Creator. Far better that he never know someone else was privy to the secret.

The following Friday was a repeat of the previous one. On that day, too, exalted emotions rose up in Yoel, surprising him no less than they had the week before. He had been certain that a gift like this does not come twice. Once again, he experienced a burning desire to be close to Hashem. Like the verse in *Tehillim*, he "thirsted for his G-d the way a deer thirsts for water." He ran back into the empty *shiur* room. The sweetness of the feeling was so powerful that he almost felt he could not bear it. He was not worthy of it! He prayed that these holy feelings might never leave him. It would be impossible to describe these ineffable emotions in words; he grasped that clearly. It was a whole spiritual world that could never be contained by ink on paper.

On the third Friday, Yoel waited impatiently for afternoon to come. He immersed himself in the *mikveh*, dried himself off, then sat and waited for the exalted emotions to descend upon him from on high.

He waited in vain.

It was an ordinary Friday this time, like all the others he had had up until two weeks ago. There was no need to hide in the *shiur* room this time. It was just another Friday afternoon.

So he waited for the *mashgiach's va'ad*, delivered to a small, selected group of *bachurim*, to raise his pressing question. Only one other student present knew the secret behind Yoel's question. Avrumi Weiss smiled quietly to himself, but didn't say a word.

Yoel was pleased with the *mashgiach's* answer. He understood now that he would no longer be the recipient of the Heavenly emotions he had experienced as a sort of spiritual gift. He must put in a great deal of hard work in order to merit the Shabbos light.

Over the course of the following weeks, he did work hard, very hard. In trying to recapture those precious moments, he spared no effort. The results, however, were unimpressive. The "engine" simply would not switch on.

After a while, he read in *sefarim* that, at the start of a road, a person is given a taste of *Gan Eden*, without any prior effort on his part. Heaven opens a vista for him, so that he may know what awaits him if he works toward it. Then it is all taken away. The person becomes despondent, thinking that he has undergone a spiritual fall — but that is not the case. He can have it all again, if he works for it. From that point on, he must labor hard to earn his spiritual rewards. Nothing ever comes for free, and certainly not an achievement of this caliber!

∾∾

All this had taken place three years earlier, when Yoel first entered the yeshivah. Since then, he had flourished in his learning and discovered how to unravel a *sugya's* mysteries. He collected many pages of *Gemara* under his belt and attained a certain mastery over some tractates.

It was then, as he neared the end of his yeshivah days, that he began to slip.

It started during the break between yeshivah *zemanim*, when a few secular boys in the neighborhood asked him some questions. Feeling very adult and confident, he believed himself capable of answering them. Indeed, he felt that it was his obligation to do so. Naively, he let himself be drawn into debates. The other boys did their homework, arming themselves with a host of confusing questions, confusing to someone inexperienced at dealing with this kind of argument. Some rabbis, when faced with such poisonous questions and claims regarding the words of *Chazal*, have recoiled at the heresy inherent in them and warned family members that anyone not well versed in the subject should not venture near. This is wily and deadly ammunition, far more sophisticated than anything encountered in the past.

Yoel was drawn from argument to argument, and believed that he was winning every one until, one day, he felt as though he had been struck a toxic blow. Unconsciously, the terrible things he had been hearing from those boys, and the brazen language with which they had debated the truth of all that was holy and precious to him, had made serious inroads. Without his being aware of it, his own *yiras Shamayim* had cooled off. He began to be negligent in his *tefillah* and the performance of mitzvos.

But the evil one who had sent the boys to lead him astray was not done yet. He had prepared a fine ambush for Yoel: a pleasant Thursday outing in the South, which was due to continue on into a severe desecration of the Shabbos. One sin would drag another in its wake, until Yoel was totally torn free.

When Tomer and Guy, two of the neighborhood youths, proposed the outing, Yoel hesitated a bit at first. But the temptation proved too strong for him. Blinded by the treats in store, he followed the others like a calf to the slaughter.

The beginning was terrific. They hiked and climbed and rode jeeps through the hills. It was on the following day, Friday, that things started to get out of control. Every link in the chain had been carefully planned. Each seemed natural as can be. From stage to stage, the atmosphere became freer. He who had plotted the trip wanted to ensure that it would be one way.

On Friday afternoon, the group reached a dead end. It was the middle of nowhere. There was no place to go, and nothing in sight but a natural spring where a group of teenagers might frolic the hours away, carefree. They slid into the water and began cavorting and splashing amid raucous cries. Yoel was right in the thick of the fun. He knew that he was poised to burn his bridges behind him, but he had lost his ability to think in a balanced way. He was too far gone to know what he wanted.

He dove deep into the water, then rose spluttering and laughing to the surface. Dove again, and rose up.

Suddenly, a thought popped into his head. "It's Friday afternoon, and I am dunking in a natural spring in honor of the holy Shabbos."

A single thought, no more.

The engine that had failed to turn on three years earlier began, all at once, to spin all its turbos at full speed. He came out of the water like a man crazed. He suddenly remembered those two other Friday afternoons, just before Shabbos, when *Gan Eden* had descended upon him uninvited. And he knew just what he was about to lose, in exchange for a moment's pleasure.

"Know what you are trading in exchange for what: an eternal world for a fleeting one." The words came into his mind, etched sharp and clear.

He found his clothes and hastily put them on. Tears stung his eyes and his emotions were in a state of turmoil. With all his heart, he longed for a *siddur*. He wanted to pray.

"Yoel, what do you think you're doing?" Tomer asked, racing after him. "Why are you running away so suddenly? What happened?"

Yoel fixed the other youth with a blazing look. "I have nothing to do with you guys. I'm sorry I came. I'm going home."

"Are you crazy? You can't!" Tomer shouted.

"I can and I will." Rapidly, Yoel tied his shoes and seized his knapsack. He checked his watch: three hours left to Shabbos. Without another word, he crossed the road and began running in the direction of a distant copse of trees, near the horizon. There he *davened Minchah* with an overflowing heart, amid purifying tears and cries torn from the depths. Once again, he was plunged into the same amazing vortex of experience as on those other two, unforgettable Fridays. For three years he had been seeking his lost paradise. Today, he had found it.

The light of Shabbos descended upon him — again, without invitation. It had waited for the right moment!

Only one *bachur* in the yeshivah knew Yoel's secret, when Yoel returned just a minute before crossing that bridge. Avrumi Weiss knew Yoel's secrets, both of them. One had taken place three years before; and the other, just yesterday.

One Letter, Three Miracles

R'MORDECHAI OF LIPOLI WAS ONE OF THE FOREMOST disciples of the "Middle" Lubavitcher Rebbe, R' Dov Ber (who was born on 9 Kislev, 5534, and passed away on his birthday in the year 5588), son of the Baal HaTanya.

R' Mordechai had a beloved son by the name of Yitzchak. Everyone who saw the boy was astounded by his diligence in Torah and the emotional prayer that emanated from his warm heart.

The toothache that afflicted 17-year-old Yitzchak one day did not overly alarm either him or his family. For several days, he was unable to chew on the right side of his mouth, and when the pain became worse he placed a whiskey-soaked sponge on the sore place until he felt some relief. He did this one day, then a second, and a third. After a week, the toothache vanished as suddenly as it had come. Yitzchak went back to his usual vigorous learning regimen.

Suddenly, a fresh problem settled on Yitzchak from an unexpected source. Coming home from the *beis medrash* one day, he felt as if his whole body was aflame. His glazed eyes were evidence of high fever. He collapsed into bed, extremely weak, and was hardly able to move. His mother hurried over to his side and placed cold, damp cloths on his forehead and burning skin. She also poured him a cup of hot tea, then another and still a third. Apparently, the boy had caught a chill, she thought. Let him rest in bed for a few days until he recovers. In the meantime, she would take good care of him.

But when six days had passed and Yitzchak still lay in bed like a stone, burning with fever, his parents began to worry. The mother raced to the local doctor's house and summoned him urgently to her son's bedside. After checking here and prodding there, he confessed to Yitzchak's anxious parents that he did not have a clue as to what ailed the youth. "Continue placing cold cloths on his forehead, and give him two teaspoons a day of this," he said before he departed, leaving behind a bottle of syrup that, if it didn't help, would not harm the patient. Naturally, the ineffectual doses did nothing for Yitzchak. Neither did the cold cloths. The fever persisted. He lay in his bed almost without stirring, the illness growing stronger and more serious.

"There's no point in leaving him here in Lipoli. This is a small town," R' Mordechai told his wife. "The boy needs a specialist. I want to take him to a big hospital in the capital city, Petersburg. There are several good hospitals there, with experienced doctors and world-famous physicians. I very much hope that they will get to the bottom of this mysterious illness."

Without delay, the anxious parents placed their feeble son on a wagon, laying him on an upholstered pallet and covering him well with blankets fearing that, if the illness turned out to be nothing more than a severe flu, the rigors of the journey could make his condition worse.

Several days' traveling through steep hills and dense forest brought them to a point where the dirt lane widened and became a paved road. Now they no longer traveled alone, but in a long line of plain wagons and opulent carriages, all of them making their way to the capital city. For another half a day their horses continued pulling the wagon until they saw, in the distance, the rooftops and tall buildings towering over the metropolis. At sunset, they stood at the gates of Petersburg.

R' Mordechai was a man of action. Wasting no time, he rode at a gallop to the largest and most prestigious hospital in the city. The moment he walked inside, he hinted to one of the minor doctors there that he was a very wealthy man and would not stint at the expense if the finest doctors in the place were quickly brought to examine his son.

The patient was brought to a private room, where he was examined by the hospital's top doctors. No effort was spared. They ran every test available to them, then held a whispered consultation among themselves. Afterward, they came to the father with grave faces.

"We are very sorry. The news is not good. Your son has developed a serious infection which has spread to his bones. There is nothing we can do for him."

"But — but what will happen to my precious son?" R' Mordechai asked in trepidation.

He received no verbal answer, just a meaningful look and a helpless shrugging of their shoulders that said it all. R' Mordechai stood by his son's bed, fighting with all his might the urge to burst into tears. His dear Yitzchak'l hardly had a chance for survival. The son, for whom they had all predicted such great things, would not live to grow up. Like a candle, he would flicker and fade away before his parents' stricken eyes.

Then his mind began to take charge of his emotions.

R' Mordechai had trained himself from his youth to control himself absolutely. This was the testing time, when he would know whether he had achieved genuine results and changed his nature, or had merely been fooling himself. His wife stood in the corridor, out of her son's hearing, and wept bitterly, but R' Mordechai stood strong as a lion and studied the situation through the eyes of a believing Jew and a loyal chassid.

As a believing Jew, he would not succumb to despair. He must pray fervently, as our Sages have said that even if a sharp sword is resting on one's neck, he must not cease to plead for Heaven's mercy. Second, he was a chassid. That very day, he sent an urgent letter to his Rebbe — the holy R' Dov Ber of Lubavitch.

He made a rapid calculation. It was a five-day ride from Petersburg to Lubavitch by fast mail coach. In ten days, then, he would have his answer.

Ten days later, he waited impatiently for the mail coach. Being so anxious to know his Rebbe's mind, he did not wait for the coach to reach his lodgings, but went outside and peered down the road. A powerful sense of anticipation took hold of him the moment he saw the mailman in his blue uniform with the gold ribbon at the cuffs. But the anticipation soon turned to bitter disappointment. The mailman had nothing for him.

The next day he stood in the road again, waiting with mounting impatience for the mailman, and was once again left forlorn. There was no letter for him.

On the third day, he went back out into the street when the mail was being delivered. But the mailman ran swiftly down the road, completely ignoring R' Mordechai.

"Do you have a letter for me?" R' Mordechai asked.

"Yes — but I'm very busy. I have no time to look for it now."

R' Mordechai did not waste a moment. He approached the mailman, grabbed his mailbag, and began to rummage feverishly through its contents. As he did so, his curiosity was piqued. "What's your big hurry today, Sergei?"

"That's a whole story in itself," the mailman replied, and raced down the street, R' Mordechai keeping up with him and not for a moment stopping his search through the pile of letters.

And so, as they ran and rummaged, the mailman told him that Fyodor, the czar's son, had fallen ill. Contemptuously dismissing all of Petersburg's doctors, the czar had sent for the personal physician of the Austrian emperor. The doctor had done his job well. Prince Fyodor had recovered. Now the mailman, who also served as a sort of travel agent at times, had been ordered to find an appropriate carriage in which to send the honored physician back to his own city.

The mailman finished his tale at the very moment that R' Mordechai's questing fingers found what they had been seeking. A letter from the Rebbe! He sped back to his lodgings, wound his *gartel* around himself like a good chassid, and only then found the courage to open the holy rebbe's missive.

"I have received your letter," the Rebbe wrote, "and I paced my room, to and fro, and saw that salvation is drawing near, from far and from near." And in the margins, he had added, "Do not be sparing with your money."

Thirteen days had passed from the time R' Mordechai had sent his letter until the answer arrived. Had he not been a believing chassid, he would long ago have despaired. During the intervening two weeks, his son's condition had drastically worsened. Yitzchak lay unconscious, and the doctors were saying that only a miracle could save his life. But R' Mordechai held in his hand a letter containing several words that were worth more than a bank check crowned with the royal seal. It was the Rebbe's blessing: "Salvation is drawing near!"

Suddenly, it occurred to him that Divine Providence had brought matters about so that the mailman had not delivered the Rebbe's answer until today, so that R' Mordechai would know about the presence in the city of the personal physician of the emperor of Austria. He threw on his fur coat and opulent hat, drew on a pair of white gloves, picked up his gold-topped walking stick, and set out for the palace of Prince Fyodor.

Outside the palace, he found a commotion. Word of the great doctor's visit had reached the ears of local patients, many of whom had gathered, confident that they would find a cure at his hands.

The palace guards permitted no one to enter. "The doctor will not be seeing anyone! He has finished his job here and does not wish to be delayed for even a moment," they announced to the crowd. "He is now taking his leave of the prince and his family, and the moment he is done he will get into his carriage and drive away."

Most of the people, disappointed of their hopes, left with a muttered curse. A few, more obstinate, lingered. Perhaps a miracle would occur. R' Mordechai, too, refused to give up. Approaching the guard booth, he asked to speak to the palace steward. R' Mordechai was an impressive and highly respectable-looking figure — and the coin in his hand had a significant value of its own. The guard went inside.

He returned shortly, bringing the steward, a rotund fellow who managed to move quickly despite his bulk. R' Mordechai came closer.

"Listen, my friend. I know that the doctor does not wish to be delayed here, but I have something important to say to him. If you let me in, I know he will agree to hear me out."

With a shrug, the steward led him inside.

The Austrian emperor's royal physician was in the midst of packing his belongings when the Jew walked into his room.

"Why did you let him in?" he thundered at the steward, who had accompanied R' Mordechai. "I told you I was in a hurry!"

The steward whispered in the doctor's ear, "Please don't be angry. This is a wealthy and honored Jew."

"Oh, all right." The doctor turned to R' Mordechai. "What do you want?"

R' Mordechai told him about his son's illness, and asked the doctor to come to the hospital to have a look at him.

"I told everyone that I have no intention of lingering here even one extra minute," snapped the doctor.

"Would you agree to linger for 1,000 *rubles*?" R' Mordechai asked with a smile.

The physician hesitated a moment. "I do not lack money, but when offered a fortune — 1,000 *rubles*! — I cannot say no. All right, I'll come to the hospital with you."

The Austrian emperor's personal physician left the palace with R' Mordechai. He entered Yitzchak's room, where he found the youth nearly on his deathbed. After a superficial examination, he summoned the trembling father.

"At first glance, the Petersburg doctors are correct," he said. "The infection has spread throughout your son's body, penetrating even the bones. On the surface of things, there seems to be no hope. There is no medicine for him in all of Russia.

"But," he added in the same breath, to the gray-faced father, "in one of the suitcases that I brought with me is a very effective ointment that can help us. I will send someone at once to bring my cases, along with the medical texts that I left at the prince's palace."

R' Mordechai urgently sent a messenger to get the physician's suitcases and books. A short time later, they were brought to Yitzchak's room.

The Austrian doctor looked through his textbooks and found what he was seeking. His lips murmured some incomprehensible Latin phrases. Then he lifted his head and met the frightened parents' eyes.

"Tell me. Before your son fell ill, did he have a severe toothache?"

R' Mordechai, who had been unaware of this episode in Yitzchak's life, did not know what to answer. But his wife cried, "Yes, indeed! He did!"

"And what did you do for it?"

"Nothing. The toothache went away on its own."

"Not exactly," corrected the Austrian medical man. "Your son had a serious infection in his teeth that spread to his gums. Because it was not treated at the time, the infection spread through his body and reached his bones."

The boy's mother slapped her cheek. "Oh, no. Who would have thought of such a thing? Is there nothing to be done?"

"I didn't say that," the doctor said with an enigmatic smile. "I will call a meeting of some of this hospital's best doctors, and I will teach them how one treats this disease."

Several prestigious doctors were summoned to the room. From one of his cases the Austrian physician took a box containing a yellowish ointment. This he spread generously over the patient's body. For several long minutes, Yitzchak continued to lie still as a stone. Then, abruptly, he began moving from side to side. He uttered a low groan of pain, and then another. Gradually, the groans turned to cries that increased in volume as the pain grew. At the same time, a sore spot suddenly sprouted on the patient's leg and began to exude liberal quantities of pus.

"*Oy, oy*," Yitzchak's mother wailed. "What is all this? Why is he screaming like that?"

"That's a good sign," the doctor said encouragingly. "If he had been lying quietly, then would have started to worry."

"Continue this treatment for several days," he instructed his Russian colleagues. "Spread this ointment on him four times a day, until all the pus has left his body. When his temperature has become completely normal, you will know that the infection is a thing of the past."

Whenever the chassidim retold this story, they would add: See how great a *tzaddik's* actions are. They counted three wonders in this tale:

The fact that the Rebbe delayed his answer by three days. If not for that, R' Mordechai would not have known about the presence in Petersburg of the Austrian emperor's physician.

The Rebbe's words, "Salvation is drawing near, from far and near." "From far" referred to the doctor who had come from a distant land; and "near" referred to the medicine that could be found close by.

The Rebbe's words urging R' Mordechai not to spare any expense. This advice persuaded R' Mordechai to offer a hefty sum, large enough to induce the doctor to accede to his wishes.

Rachel's Quest

THE HOME OF AHARON AND RACHEL, IN THE TOWN OF Pruzhan, looked like a colorful illustration from an old book of fairy tales. It was a small house with a thatched roof, adjoining a tiny yard in the center of which was a round well. The picket fence was painted purple, and fettered to it was a white goat placidly grazing the green grass. Muslin curtains adorned the windows and colorful flowers thrived on the windowsills. It was the small, warm nest of a family at the start of its journey. Their lives were peaceful and pleasant. The new housewife was happy and tried to imbue the house with as great a measure of cheerfulness as she was able.

Aharon, the young husband, left for work each morning peddling his wares in the neighboring villages, while Rachel kept house and prepared a tasty meal to warm his heart when he returned at night.

He always returned at the same time each evening, and sat down to eat supper with his wife, who looked forward to hearing how his day had been.

One day, Aharon did not return home. Rachel though that perhaps he had reached a far-off town and had decided to stay overnight. With a hopeful heart she waited for him all the next day, and near evening stood by the window, eyes trained on the lane leading to their house. An hour passed, and then two. Night fell, spreading its black cloak over everything and still, Aharon had not come.

Rachel's heart began to fill with foreboding. Something had happened to her husband. If not, he would surely have returned home by now.

That night, she could not sleep a wink. She spent the hours weeping with anxiety. When morning arrived, she wrapped a bit of food in a kerchief and set off to track Aharon down in the neighboring towns and villages. All her searching was in vain. Her food was soon gone, and were it not for the help of compassionate Jews, she would have starved. Rachel went from town to town, inquiring after her husband, but no one knew his fate.

Heavy of heart, she returned home to wait with rapidly fading hope. Had he been forced to travel a great distance and been unable to send her word? Two months slowly passed, and still no word or sign of Aharon. He had vanished like a stone in the depths.

The Rav of Pruzhan helped collect a large sum of money from the area's wealthier residents, and poor Rachel used this sum to undertake a long trek throughout Poland and neighboring countries, searching for her husband in every city. The trip made use of various modes of transportation. She started out with a horse and wagon and continued by boat to certain cities in Russia and Germany, but nowhere did she hear word of her husband. After a number of years spent in weary travel, Rachel returned home a broken woman. Despair had settled in her heart to stay.

She rested at home for a few weeks, recovering her strength after her protracted and exhausting journey. Then she went to see the Rav about alleviating her *agunah* status. "My husband is apparently dead. A wild animal must have eaten him, or else robbers took his life," she said bitterly. But neither he nor any other *rabbanim* were able to find a way to permit her to remarry.

In those days, everyone had heard of the *tzaddik*, R' Asher of Stolin (the first of that name, son of the "Great" R' Aharon of Karlin). He had earned a reputation as a holy man who could bring about salvations. One day, several loyal friends came to see Rachel. They advised her to go see the Rebbe. Perhaps he could find a solution to her troubles.

Rachel traveled to Stolin. On entering the Rebbe's presence, she began to weep bitterly over the curse of being an *agunah*. She poured out her turmoil along with her tears. The Rebbe waited until she had calmed down somewhat, then asked where she lived.

"I am from Pruzhan," she replied.

"In that case, this is what you should do," he told her. "There is a city near Pruzhan that you surely know. Its name is Shershov. Near Shershov is a gigantic forest called the Great Forest of Lobitch. It is vastly long and equally wide. Travel to this forest, and there you will find your husband. But," the Rebbe warned, "the forest is very dangerous! The paths are confusing and you must be cautious and alert, for danger lies on every side."

Rachel returned home. When she told her friends and family what the Rebbe had said, they laughed. "Go look for the wind in that forest! How does your husband come to be lost in the Great Forest?" But Rachel, with the bonds of her lonely status pressing in upon her, felt she had no option other than to follow the Rebbe's advice.

On the following day, she arrived at the wagon market in Shershov, where she tried to hire a wagon to take her into the Great Forest of Lobitch. But no driver was willing to enter the forest, which was known to be riddled with robbers, murderers, and ferocious beasts. Any fool knew that terrible danger accompanied any venture into the Lobitch forest.

But money can buy just about anything. On hearing that Rachel was willing to pay a huge sum, one gentile driver agreed to risk his life and enter the forest.

An hour's travel took them far from human habitation. Suddenly, the gentile stopped the wagon. A long knife gleamed in his hand. "The money!" he demanded.

Rachel pleaded for pity. "I don't have a lot of money," she wept. "I am an unfortunate woman, searching for my husband who has disappeared. I borrowed the money from compassionate people and must return it."

But the gentile had a heart of stone. He threatened her until she was forced to hand over all her money.

Rachel's troubles were far from over. Having gotten hold of her money, the man then wanted to kill her. "The minute you get back to the city," he roared, "you'll go straight to the police and lodge a complaint against me."

Rachel fell at his feet. Shedding copious tears, she begged for mercy. Her pleading fell on deaf ears. Knife in hand, the gentile moved menacingly closer.

Tall thick-trunked trees surrounded them like a fortress wall. It was midday, but the forest was as dim as though it were evening. But when the knife came near, it seemed to glint a desperate message: "Run, Rachel, run!"

With almost superhuman courage, Rachel managed to evade the sharp knife. She leaped from the wagon and raced with every ounce of strength she possessed into the heart of the forest. For a long time she cowered behind a broad tree trunk while the murderous wagon driver searched for her. At last, he gave up and drove away. Perhaps he, too, was afraid that some wild beast would leap out and surprise him.

Rachel sat on the cold ground, shaking like a leaf. She didn't dare to move. The forest around her was quiet. The only sounds she could hear came from the chirping of invisible birds and scampering of squirrels' feet. She began to feel hungry; she had eaten nothing since morning. But she had abandoned all her belongings in her frantic race for life, including the food that she had prepared for the trip.

The sun sank slowly westward. Soon, darkness would fall. With night, the forest would awaken. The wild animals would roar for their dinners. What was she to do? The most alarming pictures painted themselves in her imagination. She was certain that, when morning came, all that would be left of her would be a pathetic pile of bones. In despair, she began to wander among the dense trees, seeking some sort of shelter from the ravenous beasts.

The sun had already set by the time she discovered, to her joy, a small hut deep in the heart of the forest. *No doubt it belongs to some honest woodcutter,* she thought, knocking on the door. There was no answer, and no sound from within. Pushing open the door, she saw that there was no one inside.

Exhaustion overtook her. She fell onto one of the beds in the hut and fell asleep instantly. A deep, dark slumber carried her away.

She awoke suddenly to the sound of voices. Opening her eyes, she saw unkempt, long-haired men in the hut.

"Hey, guys!" one of them shouted. "You said there was no food. Well, here's some. The cow's walked right into the pot!"

What were they talking about? What cow? But the exchange of a few more remarks made the truth appallingly clear. She had fallen out of the frying pan and into the fire! This was a gang of flesh-eaters. Cannibals!

She began to shake with uncontrollable fear. The hulking figures debated the best course of action. Was it worth their while to wait and put some fat on those skinny bones or should they get down to the feast at once? Unable to reach a consensus, they decided to wait for the head of their group to arrive.

A short time later, he came. His men presented both sides of the question, and he voiced his opinion. "She's nothing but skin and bones. We'll lock her up in the back room and fatten her up."

A black cloud swam before Rachel's eyes when she heard of the fate that awaited her. Apart from her fear, she was mortally offended. Those cannibals were talking about her as though she were an animal or goose waiting to be fattened, not a human being!

A moment later, she was locked in a small room. The men began to feed her meat and fish and every delicacy, with the goal of putting some fat on her emaciated flesh. But Rachel chose only those foods that she knew to be kosher — fruits and vegetables — and put all the fatty meats aside, knowing the doom — spiritual and physical — that awaited her if she ate them. She dug a deep hole in a corner of the little room, and there she buried the meat and covered it up again, to camouflage what she had done.

The wild men divided their day in two. At night, they would rampage through the forest, preying on travelers. During the daylight hours they ate and slept.

One morning, Rachel became aware of a stir in the hut. Then, to her shock, there came a very Jewish cry of, "*Oy, gevald!*" The gang had snatched a Jewish businessman on his way home. They had stolen his money and now wished to do the same to his life. The businessman, seeing which way the wind was blowing, tried to save himself with a clever ruse.

"Why kill me?" he blustered. "The money I had with me now is just a fraction of what I earned in the Bialystok market. I sent all the rest of the money by post to my home in Grodna." As proof, the Jew presented a post-office receipt for the transfer of a large sum of money to an address in Grodna. Without pausing for breath, he continued. "It would be well worth your while to release me. One of you can accompany me home. When we get there, I'll give you whatever you want."

The proposal was greeted with shouts of bestial laughter. "Do you take us for infants or fools? You're setting a trap for us."

On consideration, the gang leader decided to take the Jew up on a part of his suggestion. "Listen, men," he announced roughly. "We'll keep him here with us and we'll see that he's well fed." He winked at his companions, who doubled over with guffaws at the witticism. "He will send a letter to his wife telling her to send 3,000 *rubles* back with the messenger, for use in his business affairs. If the messenger comes back with the money, we let him go."

The wild men liked the idea. "But don't even think of trying to hint anything in the letter about your situation or where you're being held."

The businessman sat down and wrote his wife a letter, signing it, "Yosef Galinka, d"l." The robbers read the letter carefully, but found nothing suspicious in the additional "d"l" after the man's name, assuming it to be part of his family name. They began to argue about which of them would take the letter to Grodna. None wanted to risk being seen in the city.

"Lazy fools! Cowards!" roared the leader. "You're a bunch of spoiled brats. I'll take the letter to Grodna myself."

He turned to his companions. "If I'm not back in a week," he warned, "you can take that as a sign that I've fallen into a trap. Kill the businessman at once — and the woman, too — and escape to a new hiding place."

The home of Yosef Galinka in Grodna was bathed in the light of dozens of candles in candlesticks of burnished copper or silver. Scores of people filled the place, their faces aglow with joy. One of the guests — a coarse-faced fellow — asked, "What's the party for?"

"The *bris* of R' Yosef Galinka's son is taking place today," he was told. "Surprisingly, though, the baby's father has not shown up for the *bris*."

"I want to talk to the lady of the house," the coarse guest demanded. "I have a letter from her husband."

"A letter from my husband?" the new mother hurried over to the guest. "It's been so long since I heard from him." Eagerly, she scanned the brief note. She was happy to have received some communication from her husband, and assured the messenger that she would give him the money the moment the festive meal was concluded.

Still, something seemed strange to her. After the *bris*, she returned to her room and showed the letter to family members. They, too, wondered at the "d"l" after Yosef's name. The wife's brother guessed that there was something behind it.

"I am very much afraid that something bad has happened, and that this letter was written under duress. He was forbidden to reveal his location, so he added the 'd"l' after his name — standing for '*dai lemeivin*' (a hint to the astute)? We must question the messenger until he reveals your husband's whereabouts."

These words, spoken in a calm, measured fashion, rang true in his listeners' ears. They approached the messenger, who was stuffing himself at the table and swilling down glass after glass of whiskey. At first, they spoke gently with him. Being half-drunk, the man stumbled over his words and hinted that Yosef was being held somewhere. The police were summoned immediately, and they took charge of the interrogation. When the man refused to speak, they bound him hand and foot and loaded him onto a horse-drawn cart. He was going to lead them to Yosef Galinka, they insisted, and if he tried to lead them astray he would pay dearly for the attempt. Ten police officers set out on the journey, well armed against the robber bands so prevalent on the roads.

At first, the robber led them in a roundabout way. Seeing through his ploy, the policemen were true to their word: They beat him until his bones were broken and he was bleeding copiously.

"Leave me be!" he screamed. "I'll show you the right road now."

This time, he led the policemen along back roads and lanes until they reached the little hut in the heart of the forest, where his gang sat and waited the return of their leader with the 3,000 *rubles*.

The policemen burst into the hut, taking the gang completely by surprise. The wild men put up no resistance. Yosef Galinka and Rachel were freed from their captivity.

Before the robbers were taken away, the wounded leader asked to speak to Rachel.

"Do you know who I am?"

"I don't know," Rachel said. "But from the day I came here, I've been convinced that you're a Jew."

"Very true," he replied. "I am your husband! I am Aharon!"

Rachel was speechless with shock. She wanted to ask how he had sunk into such depravity, but he offered that information on his own. "The robbers snatched me as I wandered between two villages, and threatened to kill me. I had no choice but to join them, until I became worse than any of them and the leader of the gang. I recognized you the moment you came here, which was why I didn't let my friends hurt you. If I don't die from the injuries these policeman have inflicted on me, I will surely be executed and you will be freed from your *agunah* status. I will send you a sign by two witnesses who have seen me die, and they will testify before the *beis din*."

He removed his clothes and showed Yosef Galinka and his Jewish assistant, who had arrived along with the policemen, a birthmark over his heart and on his right foot. Rachel identified these signs and testified in front of the two men that this was unquestionably her husband.

The police officers set out for the city with the robbers in tow. On the way, Aharon died in great suffering, and his burial was witnessed by both men. The rest of the gang was brought to justice and sentenced to hanging.

On the strength of the testimony of Yosef Galinka and his assistant, Rachel was freed from her *agunah* status. The blessing of R' Asher, the Stoliner Rebbe, had come to fulfillment: "Go to the forest and there you will find your husband."

[Source: the book *Meoros HaGedolim*, in the chapter on R' Asher, the Stoliner Rebbe.]

ONE FREEZING NIGHT

HE *BEIS MEDRASH* WAS PIERCINGLY COLD. FRIGID AIR tends to dissipate in the face of an oven's heat, but this particular cold was even stronger than what the most elderly Poles, well schooled in freezing temperatures and deep snow, could remember. Though the *shamash* of the *beis medrash*, R' Mottel, fed the flames with fresh logs every hour, they soon dwindled and submitted to the prevailing iciness.

Shacharis was long over. On the table rested a large bottle of whiskey and a few simple cookies. It was a *"L'Chayim"* in honor of the renowned *tzaddik*, famous through all of Poland: R' Dovid of Lelov. Despite the snow and the biting winds, most of the worshipers in that *beis medrash* had made the trip to distant Lelov to pray at the *tzaddik's* grave on his *yahrtzeit*. (Author's note: I have heard from several people who were in Poland before the Holocaust, that R' Dovid of Lelov's *yahrtzeit* fell in the depths of winter, for the *tzaddik* had prayed that he leave this world at that time in order to prevent a large crowd from attending his funeral (!) and honoring him, or traveling to his grave. Nevertheless, on his *yahrtzeit* there was "a gigantic crowd [who traveled there], like to Meron on Lag B'Omer.")

Only elderly chassidim who lacked the strength to battle the cold, and the young who were totally devoted to their *Gemaras*, refrained from making the trip. These young men sat beside the old ones, whose entire lives had been spent in an atmosphere of holiness and purity, and listened avidly to the stories they told.

Here is a tale that one of the old chassidim related. His name was R' Eliezer Lipa.

It was a Friday afternoon, just before the onset of Shabbos. Several men emerged from the bathhouse at a rapid clip, ready to welcome the Shabbos in the purity of ritual immersion. Others were already streaming toward the shul, dressed in their best, faces aglow with the radiance of Shabbos. In R' Mordechai Yudel's home, however, every face was pinched with sorrow.

R' Mordechai was on his deathbed, writhing in pain. His children stood by his bedside, weeping bitterly. His hour, it seemed, had come.

They hastened to summon the *Chevrah Kaddisha* to the house. These men examined the patient and agreed that the signs were there: He would soon be returning his soul to his Creator. Suddenly, to everyone's surprise, the sick man turned his face to the wall and stared at it as though he wished to see something. Then he turned back to face the *Chevrah Kaddisha* and said calmly, "You can go to shul. My time has not yet come to leave this world."

With this injunction ringing in their ears, the men had no choice but to agree. The light in the sick man's eyes began to shine again, and it appeared as though he had spoken the truth. The doctor, when he arrived and conducted his examination, announced that the patient's condition had improved.

R' Mordechai's children did not leave his side all Shabbos. After the third meal, when three stars twinkled in the sky and men were hastening to shul for *Maariv*, the ill man turned to his children and said, "It is time. Call the *Chevrah Kaddisha*, quickly."

The bed was quickly surrounded by people. The sound of weeping rose in the air again. R' Mordechai Yudel opened his eyes and shushed them all. "Why do you cry?" he scolded his children. "Do not place the cart before the horse. Hear what I have to say.

"Many years ago, I worked as a servant in a small village called Negiwa. My employer was a man who ran several different businesses. He had a tavern which the gentiles frequented, to drink whiskey to warm their bones on cold winter nights. My employer made the whiskey himself, and I would help him. He also traded in livestock: cattle and sheep. From time to time he would buy and sell oxen and cows, sheep and goats. One day, at the height of the winter, the cold was unbearable. Everything had frozen overnight and a heavy snow had fallen. There was nothing sweeter than curling up under warm blankets and sleeping. But I was a servant. My master woke me before dawn, shaking me hard: 'Get up, you lazy thing. You've got to go to the *shochet.*'

"I was shaking with cold. Outside, a freezing wind shrieked and hard pellets of snow rattled the windows. Before I had finished saying 'Modeh Ani' and rubbing the sleep from my eyes, a large, woolly ram stood beside me, regarding me with its innocent eyes and bleating pathetically. 'Take it to the *shochet,*' my employer ordered.

"I went outside into a bone-chilling cold. The wind shot icy darts at me, stabbing every exposed portion of my skin. Beside me the ram huddled, as though trying to keep warm and to escape its bitter fate. We walked toward the *shochet's* house on the other side of town. On the way, we passed the frozen river.

"Suddenly, I stumbled over something in the snow and nearly fell. Startled, I leaned over to see what had tripped me.

"Spread-eagled on the snow was a young man, facedown and motionless. I quickly turned him over onto his back. His breathing was labored. Despite the powerful cold, I ripped off my heavy woolen coat and wrapped the frozen man in it. I recognized him. It was my master's son-in-law. His name was R' Dovid, and later on he would be known throughout Poland as a holy angel, the *tzaddik*, R' Dovid of Lelov.

"The young R' Dovid served his Creator devotedly. Each day, before sunrise, he would go out to immerse himself in the river. He had done the same in that dark pre-dawn, going down to the river and breaking the ice with his axe in order to immerse himself in the icy water. But, as I said, during the night the cold had reached unbearable levels, and when he climbed out of the water he fainted onto the snow. It was obvious to me that, had I not arrived when I did, he would have died.

"But Heaven had sent me at just the right moment to save him. Abandoning my master's commission to take the ram to the *shochet*, I picked up the young man, placed him on my shoulders, and carried him to his home. There I tended him with great devotion. I heated water and massaged his body until, gradually, life began to return to his limbs. I had him drink a cup of hot broth and did not leave his side until I saw that he had recovered.

"'Mordechai Yudel,' R' Dovid said to me, when he had regained enough strength to speak. 'I want you to promise me that, up to the day of your death, you will not reveal to a soul what happened here today.'

"I nodded vigorously. But R' Dovid was not satisfied. Gazing at me, he continued, 'As a reward for saving me from death, you can have great wealth all of your life — or the World to Come.'

"I did not hesitate for even an instant. Lifelong wealth is a blinding temptation but we are believing Jews who know that this world is a fleeting thing of 70 or 80 years. It passes like a dream. But the World to Come? Eternity!

"'I want the World to Come.'

"'*V'amcha kulam tzaddikim*,' murmured R' Dovid. 'See how this servant, someone whose world is seemingly composed of nothing but the physical, is giving up fantastic wealth and choosing the World to Come. You have merited the World to Come and I will also promise you this: You will live a long life, and before you leave this world I will come to you and you will see me while awake. Then you will know that your time has come to leave this world. As long as you do not see me in your waking hours, you will know that your time has not yet come.'

"That is what R' Dovid promised me on that day," the dying man told his family and the *Chevrah Kaddisha*. "That is why, when you came on *erev Shabbos*, I sensed that my time had not yet come: I had not yet seen R' Dovid. I turned to face the wall, thinking that he would reveal himself to me. But this did not happen. Now, however, R' Dovid of Lelov has appeared to me in all his glory, exactly as he looked in life. He has revealed to me that the time of my death has arrived. 'When they came to summon me to you yesterday,' R' Dovid said, 'I did not wish to come. I told the messengers, "Today is Shabbos." But with the end of Shabbos, the time has come.'

"Therefore, my brothers and friends, please say the *viduy* with me," the sick man requested. And, indeed, as soon as they had recited the *viduy* with him and said the *Kriyas Shema*, he once again turned his face to the wall and his soul departed immediately, without any of the usual death pangs.

Another chassid, R' Yechiel Fishel, heard the end of this story and smiled.

"If we're talking about R' Dovid's father-in-law, the picture won't be complete until we fill in all the details. R' Dovid's father-in-law was a simple villager who did not understand his hidden *tzaddik* of a son-in-law in the least. He viewed all of R' Dovid's actions as madness and was furious with him for "wasting his time with immersions and suffering" instead of doing some honest work with his hands and earning his daily bread. That servant boy, R' Mordechai, did well on that frigid morning in not taking R' Dovid to his father-in-law's house, but to R' Dovid's own home instead. His father-in-law might well have thrown him out of the house.

"The father-in-law was particularly angry over the fact that R' Dovid did not break the river ice to immerse himself just once or twice: he did it every single morning. There were times when the ice was so thick that the frail young man lacked the strength to break it. What did he do then? He climbed up a nearby hill and rolled from the top, right down onto the frozen river. The impact of his fall would crack the ice beneath him, and he would immerse himself.

"Relations between father- and son-in-law, then, were not the best, until the day came when the villager's eyes were opened to realize that he had an awesome, angel-like being in his home. Here's what happened:

"The village in which they lived boasted scarcely any *sefarim* from which to learn. In the *beis medrash* were a few *siddurim* and *Chumashim*, some *sifrei Tehillim* — and that was all. There were no *Gemaras* or *midrashim*, *sifrei Zohar* or other works of kabbalah, *Rishonim* or *Acharonim*. To quench his thirst for Torah, R' Dovid was forced to travel to a nearby city — a journey of four hours by wagon in the summer, and double that on a snowy winter's day. He would sit in the *beis medrash* from Sunday through Thursday, learning with astounding diligence. Once, on a Thursday night, R' Dovid wished to travel back home. As usual, he didn't have a *kopek* in his pocket, but his *bitachon* was overflowing. Filled with trust in Hashem, he went out into the street to search for a wagon driver traveling to the distant village in which he lived. Though the chances of finding one were slight, R' Dovid believed with all his heart that he would find such a driver. He lifted his eyes and there stood a neighbor of his, hitching his horse to a closed carriage.

"'Are you going home?'

"'Immediately.'

"R' Dovid came closer. 'Unfortunately, I have no money to pay a driver for the trip. Would you take me with you?'

"'What a question!' the villager beamed. 'Climb aboard, and off we go!'

"R' Dovid climbed into the carriage. The horse began to move.

"A short time later, the horse seemed to be gripped by a trance. It stood stock still and refused to budge. The driver called out to it, using every term wagon drivers customarily used — to no avail. The horse's legs seemed riveted to the ground. Furious, the driver lashed the beast with his whip. The horse surrendered and began to pull the wagon again. The moment they left the city limits, however, and began to move along dirt roads, the horse began to lead the carriage on a twisted, circuitous route that considerably lengthened their journey — much to the driver's chagrin.

"'Whoa!'" he cried furiously.

"It seemed as if the horse had been waiting for just this order. Once it stopped, it refused to take another step. The driver lifted his whip again, when he felt a gentle hand on his shoulder.

"'Let him be,' R' Dovid pleaded quietly. 'You are transgressing the prohibition of causing an animal to suffer.'

"'What about *my* suffering? Look what this horse is doing to me! Either it refuses to walk at all, or it leads us around in circles. Our trip is already hours longer than it needed to be. I'll have to sit here and watch him all night. We won't be home before dawn, that's certain.'

"The young man gazed at him kindly. 'Who says it has to be that way? You are not obligated to watch the horse. Let it walk on its own.'

"'Sure,' the villager laughed. 'I'll have a nice nap, and that animal will roost here till next week! Listen, you go and learn Torah inside the carriage, and let me deal with foolish horses.'

"But R' Dovid would not back down. 'Come inside and sit with me. You don't have to do a thing. Just have a nice rest; the horse will know what to do on its own. Let it go where it will. Direct route or no, we will trust in Hashem to lead us in the best possible way.'

"The villager found himself unable to refuse R' Dovid. He entered the carriage and sat facing his passenger. Looking into R' Dovid's smiling face, he felt his anger melting away. The horse had barely taken a few steps when the driver suddenly let out a yell of surprise.

"'Impossible! We're at the door of your father-in-law's house. Am I dreaming, or do I really see what I think I see? There's Farmer Stephen sitting in the tavern, drinking down a glassful.'

"Stunned, the driver emerged from the carriage and raced into the tavern. No, it was no dream. They were in the village of Negiwa.

"The villager was no scholar, but he knew something about *tzaddikim*. Recalling the scornful tone the father-in-law customarily used when speaking to his son-in-law, his heart rose up. Running all the way, he came to the tavern-keeper's house.

"'Good evening, my dear neighbor. Do you happen to know where your son-in-law, R' Dovid, is right now?'

"The father-in-law made a scornful gesture. 'Dovid? Go to the frozen river and you'll find him dipping beneath the ice. And if he's not there, he'll be rolling down the hill.'

"'You fool!' the villager screamed. 'I wish such a son-in-law on myself, and on every Jew! He is a hidden *tzaddik*. Just a moment ago, we were an 8-hour drive away from here, but R' Dovid performed a *kefitzas haderech* (shortening of the way), and we came home in one minute. And you're heaping scorn on such a holy *tzaddik*?'

"From that day, the father-in-law's attitude toward his son-in-law underwent a complete change, and he began to treat R' Dovid with the respect and esteem that he so richly deserved."

[Source: "*Migdal Dovid*"]

The Outcast

THE SHIP'S DINING ROOM WAS FILLED TO CAPACITY. THE menu was not especially fine or luxurious, certainly not the kind of food that would be served at a king's table. But there was enough to satisfy the hunger. For the group of passengers — several hundred Jews traveling from Romania to Eretz Yisrael — it was more than enough.

This was an era when the gates of Romania were opened (the years 5715-5716/1955-1956), days of great upheaval. Before the Communist Iron Curtain clanged down upon the state for many years, thousands of Jews took advantage of the chance to flock to Eretz Yisrael.

The passengers sat and ate a hearty meal. They would have to spend several more days between sea and sky before they reached a safe shore, and then ... the future was shrouded in mist, but they hoped for the best. R' Yosef Reinitz, the ship's *mashgiach* responsible for the *kashrus* of its kitchens, had just stepped out of the kitchen for a moment when, right before his astonished eyes, a monumental human drama began to play itself out.

A passenger entered the ship's dining room — a frail-looking Jew with a beard that had turned white before its time. His eyes scanned the room for an empty table. At that moment, a silence fell over the huge hall. At once, all the other passengers began to cast looks at the newcomer that were sharp as daggers. Suddenly, the shouting began:

"*Sheigetz! Rasha,* despicable one — get out! Don't pollute this place with your filthy presence!"

The *mashgiach* was certain that the man would crumble under the stream of invective being hurled at him from every side. But he merely bowed his head, found a lone, empty table and began to eat serenely, despite the hisses of fury and hatred that threatened to drown him.

R' Reinitz was stunned. He had never seen such a focused laser-beam of enmity directed at one man. The passenger who sat eating, as isolated as a leper, had the appearance of an ordinary, good Jew. Why all the anger and the hatred?

He wished to approach a group of diners who were casting murderous looks at the man, but something in their manner stopped him. It seemed to him that he might deflect some of the anger at himself if he intervened. He decided to pretend he had not seen anything, and removed himself from the scene.

But the incident repeated itself the next day. All the passengers, as one, banded against that single man, who seemed frightened in the face of the open loathing and the appalling fury. The epithets that the other passengers hurled at him were enriched by colorful new additions, with such words as "kapo" and "traitor" becoming part of the lexicon of hate. Once again, the man sat alone in his corner and ate his meal.

R' Reinitz's heart ached with compassion for the individual being so mercilessly hounded. He wanted to speak with him, to learn what had given rise to all the anger, but something inside urged him to put off the question for another time. At any rate, it would not do to speak in front of the other furious passengers.

The next day, their rage rose to new heights in the face of the man's daring, as he brazenly entered the dining room to have his meal. Yesterday and the day before, they had only heaped curses and scorn on his head and allowed him to eat in peace. Today, they threw putrid eggs at him, and rotten tomatoes, and other wilted vegetables beginning to go bad. Everything they could lay their hands on they turned into a weapon to vent their loathing. The man fled from the attack in alarm, making with all possible speed for his own cabin below.

R' Reinitz could no longer restrain himself at the sight of that unfortunate man's plight. Turning to the group of passengers celebrating their victory, he asked, "Why are you torturing one individual like that?"

In response, the *mashgiach* was inundated with harsh questions: "Why do you have pity on that accursed *rasha*? Aren't you ashamed to empathize with such a low, despicable creature?"

R' Reinitz left quietly and made his way to the wretched man's cabin. Things had reached a breaking point. He must hear what lay behind this cruel persecution.

He knocked on the cabin door once, twice, and did not desist despite the fact that there was no answer. He knew that the man could be nowhere but here.

After five or six rounds of knocking, the man called fearfully, "Who's there?"

"Rabbi Reinitz, the *mashgiach*."

Even then, the man did not wish to unlock his door. He was afraid that the rabbi might be nothing more than a foil for the crowd that wished to harm him in his cabin. However, after a parlay that continued for several minutes, the man understood that he had nothing to fear. He opened the door and allowed R' Reinitz to enter.

The *mashgiach* sat down in the tiny cabin and gazed for a moment through the round porthole at the waves crashing against the ship's sides. He placed a hand on the tabletop, which was covered with a simple blue cloth embroidered with red roses. "I have been watching, with amazement, what's been going on here on the ship from the first time they attacked you," he began candidly. "I've never seen such a thing in my life. Why are they hounding you with such deep hatred?"

The man sighed, and spread his hands heavenward. "What can I say? They are in the right and I am mortified. They are correct."

"What?!"

"Yes, they are correct in every harsh word they've thrown at me — all the accusations. It's all true. They despise me with justification. This is not baseless hatred. I've earned it all — the hatred, the curses. If they do not beat me to death, they are complete *tzaddikim*."

"But why?" R' Reinitz cried. The man's words surprised and shocked him to his core. "What did you do to them? After all, you're one person, and they are hundreds!"

"I'll tell you the whole story from the beginning, and then you'll understand," the man sighed.

Yosef Halevi (fictional name) stood out in his hometown like a beacon of light on a dark night. His teachers and friends called him an *ilui*, and they were not exaggerating. When he became a bar mitzvah, his father sent him to yeshivah in the city of Vishova, headed by *hagaon hatzaddik* R' Menachem Mendel of Vishova, son of the Ahavas Yisrael of Vizhnitz.

In yeshivah, too, the boy's talents were outstanding. He pored over his *Gemara* night and day. After several years of inordinate diligence, he was well versed in all of *Shas* as well as every manner of study in which the average youth is not knowledgeable at all. His learning rose to a very high level, and when he reached marriageable age it was obvious that he would not make a match with the daughter of any simple householder.

Indeed, it was not long before he was taken into the home of an important Rav in one of the towns in the Marmarosh district. He married the Rav's only daughter and, as his son-in-law, became the natural successor to his seat one day. His father-in-law was no longer a young man.

Yosef lived in his in-laws' home and was supported at their table. Most of the day he spent learning in shul, or together with his father-in-law. But their learning was interrupted from time to time by townspeople, coming to ask their halachic questions of the Rav.

Yosef, listening curiously, was surprised at the people's ignorance. Gradually, it became clear to him from their queries that these men lacked even the most basic knowledge. They knew nothing. They barely recognized a few verses from the weekly Torah portion — and even those they read with numerous errors. Yosef, a brilliant young man accustomed to learning in yeshivah among others of his own caliber, was filled with scorn and contempt for these Jews who, though simple, honest folk, were ignorant *amei ha'aretz*. He mocked them and their questions. There was not one who escaped the lashing of his sharp tongue.

The more he was exposed to his fellow townspeople's ignorance, the more contemptuous he became. He never missed an opportunity to demonstrate his superiority in Torah in front of these uneducated innocents. Occasionally he would take a simple villager into a corner and explain the fundamentals of halachah and why his question was really no question at all, adding that if the fellow would just spend a few minutes a day learning the *Shulchan Aruch*, he would understand on his own how silly he had been.

The people of the town suffered his barbs in silence, knowing full well that in any debate that might ensue, he would be able to defeat them soundly. After all, he was a famous *ilui* while they were babies, beginners.

In the privacy of their own hearts, they began to cultivate a hatred toward the young genius. They waited for the day when they would be able to exact their revenge.

The day came.

Their elderly Rav became ill and died. The moment he was buried, the community heads met secretly and resolved — unanimously, with no exceptions — that one particular man would never become their new Rav.

That man was Yosef Halevi, son-in-law of their departed Rav, and his natural successor.

The community leaders traveled to the neighboring towns and cities seeking a new Rav. It was not long before they returned with a worthy candidate. A sterling young man and *talmid chacham* whose *yiras Shamayim* preceded his wisdom.

Yosef Halevi was stunned. Was it possible? How did these brazen folk dare steal from him the inheritance that had been designated for him ever since his engagement? He went out into the street and began to seek an explanation, but from the day of his father-in-law's passing, no one accorded him a shred of respect or courtesy any longer. Curtly, he was informed that the new Rav would be installed within a matter of days, and that the matter was not up for discussion.

Checking into his usurper's identity, he found him to be a *talmid chacham* but one who did not in any way measure up to his own level.

Impatiently he waited for the new Rav's installment ceremony. On the appointed day, he joined the throng in the largest shul and seated himself on the eastern wall, near the seat that had belonged to his father-in-law, the departed Rav.

The young Rav began to deliver his sermon, seeking to erect a pleasing structure of *pilpul* suited to his listeners' level of understanding. Like a ravenous lion Yosef attacked at once, demolishing everything the Rav said and destroyed the foundation he had built from the bottom up. Seeing their new Rav thus humiliated, the townspeople stood up in a fury and chased Yosef Halevi out of the shul.

Yosef ran home, his anger burning red-hot. For a few days, he wandered about in a haze of disbelief. How had this terrible thing happened to him? He had been guaranteed the rabbinical seat. His rage swelled until it surpassed the bounds of good sense and reason.

Yosef left town, abandoning his wife and children, and went directly to one of the largest churches in the land — where he converted.

It was not long before he climbed the ladder of the clergy and became a Catholic priest.

When an outstanding *ilui* such as Yosef Halevi converts, his burning hatred leads him from bad to worse. He placed all his awesome knowledge in the service of the Romanian church, publishing anti-Semitic essays in which he quoted *Chazal* profusely — out of context, and in a distorted and exaggerated fashion — in order to prove to the gentiles how the Torah nourished the Jews' hatred and scorn toward all non-Jews. As an outcome of his efforts, a fresh wave of anti-Semitism broke out in the land. One sin drags another in its wake, and during the dark years of the Holocaust, when the Nazis invaded Romania, this *meshumad* (one who has converted from Judaism) did not refrain from placing his complete mastery of the Talmud and Jewish lore in the service of the Nazi death machine.

After the war, Yosef continued his life as a gentile — until one night ...

Yosef had a dream. In the dream, he was once again a *bachur* in the yeshivah at Vishova. Together with his friends, he was seated at the table of the old Vizhnitzer Rebbe, the Ahavas Yisrael. The large crowd sang "*Kah Ribbon*" using a famous Vizhnitzer melody, and he sang along with the rest. The atmosphere was redolent with holiness, purity, and the peace of Shabbos. The Rebbe's visage was radiant as the sun as his eye fell on Yosef.

He awoke with a start, the song still echoing in his ears and on his lips. In an upsurge of emotion, he burst into bitter tears. For a long time he sat on his bed, shaken and emotional, and he assessed his soul.

That very day, he decided to repent. He abandoned the Christian faith and returned to the bosom of *Yiddishkeit*. Now, however, he was rejected on both sides. The Jews did not forgive his betrayal or the way he had thrust a knife into their backs. And the Christians were beside themselves with fury at the priest who had turned his back on his newfound faith. No one would speak to him. Everyone despised him. Yosef felt as though the very earth beneath his feet was on fire. Secretly, he sold all his property, and when Romanian Jews were granted permission to go up to Eretz Yisrael, he joined them on board the ship …

"Now do you understand," the man said, when he had completed his sorry tale, "why they're all so angry with me? I deserve every kind of scorn and rejection. May my mortification serve as an atonement!"

On their arrival in Eretz Yisrael, Yosef continued to suffer a great deal. Everyone kept him at a distance. No one wished to know him. Even his wife and children continued to behave toward him as strangers. He wandered from place to place. One day, he attempted to enter to see the holy Vizhnitzer Rebbe, R' Chaim Meir, but even the compassionate Rebbe refused to receive him. Finally, Yosef sent messengers with his plea. They told the Rebbe that Yosef had long since repented of his sins and that he now had nothing in the world and was dying of starvation, abandoned and rejected.

Then the Rebbe had pity on him and instructed his people to give him shelter and food. But even now Yosef found no peace. He traveled to Teveryah, where he lived for two or three years before he left this world, alone and lonely.

Rabbi Reinitz kept seeing one unforgettable picture in his mind's eye, one conversation that had been echoing in his head ever since he had spoken with Yosef in his tiny cabin that day.

"But how," R' Reinitz had asked, "could an *ilui*, an outstanding *talmid chacham*, abandon his wife and children and his faith, and stick a poisoned dagger into the backs of his brethren just because he wasn't picked as Rav of his town?"

Yosef's face was long and sad. Sighing deeply, he said, "It all came from pride. You think, no doubt, that it was anger that made me lose my mind, but I tell you, it was pride that did it. I took all the Torah that I had learned all those years and used it not to uphold the Giver of the Torah, but to bolster my own ego. I was filled with an overweening arrogance, and when the Jews of that town insulted me — with much justification — I was ready to let everything go up in smoke. The words of the *mishnah* were fulfilled: jealousy, desire, and honor remove a man from this world. Because of my pride, I lost my whole world!"

[Many thanks to the teller of this tale, my esteemed father-in-law, *Harav* Yaakov Moshe Spitzer, *shlita*, of Har Nof, Jerusalem, who heard the whole story about forty years ago from R' Yosef Reinitz, the *kashrus mashgiach* aboard the ship at that time.]

The Cure
Before the Ailment

RAFI ARBIV WAS A SWEET CHILD, FILLED WITH CHEERFUL enthusiasm. He was a source of great pride and satisfaction to his parents and grandparents. A tender blossom, only 4 years old, with all his life before him ... when suddenly, like a dark cloud blotting out the noonday sun, he began to suffer from worrisome headaches. The smiling little boy stopped smiling as he was taken to the hospital for a thorough examination.

After conducting their tests, the doctor told Rafi's stunned parents, Nissim and Odelya Arbiv, that their son's suffering was due to a tumor in his brain. While the parents were trying to absorb this shock, the doctor went on to add that the growth was malignant. Odelya was already half-swooning, when the doctor concluded with the worst news of all: the tumor was located near the brain stem, and if it were not removed at once it would quickly spread to damage the brain stem itself. Once that happened, it would be inoperable.

Nissim Arbiv, a diligent young *kollel* man, struggled to remain calm. He asked the doctor where such an operation should take place. The doctor explained that their son's condition called for complicated and difficult surgery. The tumor was touching many sensitive parts of the brain, and its removal called for a brain surgeon, one of the best in the world. His name was Dr. Abrahams, and he worked in Boston Hospital. He specialized in the removal of malignant growths such as this.

From that moment, the Arbivs' life changed drastically. Everything revolved around the trip to Boston. Needless to say, the Arbiv family was not well endowed financially and did not have a cent to spare. They were looking at surgery that cost the earth, plus an expensive hospital stay for their son, airfare to Boston, and lodgings in that city.

At this point, a number of *chesed* activists took up their cause. Within a short time, enough funds were collected to set in motion the complex undertaking of getting little Rafi Arbiv to Boston.

Time was of the essence. In order to save the boy's life, it was necessary to act with dispatch. Every day counted! The hospital in Boston sent its confirmation and set the date for the surgery.

Just two days later, Nissim Arbiv, his wife, and ailing son boarded a plane bound for the United States. Community activists were waiting for them at the Boston airport. A warmhearted Jewish family, for whom *chesed* was a lodestone, hosted them and made every effort to see that they had as pleasant a stay as possible. The father of the family, Shalom Dov Fuchs, a noted activist himself, quickly recruited a few friends to help make arrangements for Rafi's hospital stay as well as to track down additional sources of money for the expensive operation. Most of all, he served as an interpreter for the Arbivs, who did not speak English.

That same day, Rafi was admitted to the hospital. He underwent a battery of tests to determine his readiness to undergo serious surgery. By evening, preparations began for the operation, which would take place at 9 o'clock the next morning, if nothing went wrong.

～♪～

Something went wrong.

Nissim and Odelya Arbiv sat in their son's hospital room, *sifrei Tehillim* in hand. The child had already been prepped for his surgery and his hair was shaved.

"Why have they made me bald?" the boy asked his mother innocently, running a hand over his shorn head.

His mother smiled sadly. "They gave you a second *upsherin*," she joked feebly.

In just a short time, Rafi's bed would be wheeled into the operating room and the battle for his life would begin.

A male nurse, dressed in green, approached them. "Are you the Arbiv family? Parents of the boy?"

"Yes."

"Come with me, please."

The nurse brought them to the doctor's office. There, waiting for them, was the surgeon, Dr. Abrahams himself. The couple was surprised. The surgeon was apparently planning to fill them in on the upcoming medical procedure.

But what they heard was radically different. They suddenly became aware that the noted surgeon looked a bit stressed, twiddling his fingers restlessly.

"Listen carefully," he told Nissim and Odelya through the interpreter. "Your son was due to undergo surgery shortly. Unfortunately, a problem has arisen that makes the operation impossible."

Nissim stared at him uncomprehendingly. What sort of problem? What was the surgeon talking about?

"My special scalpal was damaged in the operation that I just completed," the surgeon explained. "Therefore, we will have to postpone your son's surgery."

The couple began a dialogue in Hebrew. Both were filled with apprehension. Their son's life hung in the balance, and now they were being told that the operation was to be delayed. For how long?

"How can that be? We're not in some rundown small town hospital," Odelya Arbiv asked her husband. "There must be dozens of scalpels here. Maybe the surgeon was trying to say that the operation will be postponed for two or three hours. You know these Americans, making a big drama out of every little thing."

Nissim's fears were not allayed. He wanted to hear this from the surgeon himself.

"Ask the doctor," he instructed the interpreter, "how long the surgery will be delayed."

The answer stunned the parents. The surgeon explained that his surgical knife was a rare and expensive instrument designed specifically for complex surgical procedures in the area of the brain stem. There was no place in the world from which to obtain another one except from its manufacturer, in Germany. Because it was impossible for him to attend to all the logistics, he could not guarantee just when the new knife would arrive. Therefore, the operation would be postponed for a week's time.

The Arbivs were beside themselves with anguish. It had been the unanimous opinion of every doctor they had consulted, both in Israel and here in the United States, that every passing day was critical. How could the surgery be postponed for a full week?

"Pray to G-d to help you." Dr. Abrahams concluded the difficult meeting and bade the fearful parents good-bye.

They walked into the corridor. Mrs. Arbiv sat down on a bench and burst into tears. The situation seemed to be teetering at the edge of hopelessness. Unless some kind of miracle occurred, their precious son's life would be in very grave danger! Nissim tried to comfort her, but he was equally distraught.

Suddenly, from the surgeon's office came alarming cries. It was the kind of shouting that belongs in a marketplace, not a hospital. Frantic nurses raced toward the surgeon's office.

A dismaying spectacle greeted them. Another family, this one from Chicago, whose father was also due to undergo brain-stem surgery, had just been summoned to the office to hear that the special knife had been damaged. But while the Arbivs' reaction had been quiet and restrained, this family responded with an emotional storm reminiscent of a typhoon. Before the surgeon and the medical staff's incredulous eyes, the patient's children began to rampage through the room. In their anger they shattered valuable crystal ornaments, broke armchairs, and smashed the doctor's expensive desk.

The hospital staff held an emergency meeting. Someone whispered to the hospital administrator that the family had a long arm that stretched into the criminal world.

The Boston hospital did not want trouble. With amazing alacrity, they suddenly discovered a way to obtain the special surgical knife from Germany without too much "logistical" difficulty. The first patient to benefit from the knife was that father from Chicago; the second was a little Jewish boy by the name of Rafi Arbiv.

But the Arbivs' suffering was not yet over. For seemingly interminable hours, they waited for the man's operation to be completed and their son to be brought into the operating room after careful prepping. As a green-garbed male nurse approached them, their hearts began to pound in their chests. What news this time? Had the new knife broken, too?

The knife had not broken, but the news was an equal blow. The renowned surgeon, Dr. Abrahams, was not feeling well after the lengthy surgery. Therefore, his backup, Dr. Waterman, would be the one to remove the growth from Rafi's brain.

"Then why did we fly all the way out here?" Odelya Arbiv fumed. "There are doctors of Dr. Waterman's caliber in Israel — and they come a whole lot cheaper, too! Nissim, maybe *we* should start breaking a few tables."

Nissim did not like this idea, both because he was a gentle-natured man, and also because shattering many pieces of furniture would not reenergize the noted surgeon.

"Let's hope that good will come out of the bad," he said hopefully. The words were hardly out of his mouth when a nurse came over to sweeten the bitter pill, informing them that, though Dr. Abrahams was not feeling well, he would make every effort to return to the operating room within a short time, where he would closely supervise the delicate operation. It was at least a partial comfort.

The parents sat in the waiting room for 12 hours. They murmured chapters of *Tehillim* and tensely chewed their fingernails. At long last, the doctors emerged from the operating theater to share the news that the surgery had gone very well. The tumor had been completely removed and Rafi's brain had sustained no damage at all. Rafi had his life back. Once he had recovered from surgery, he would be able to resume his normal life just like any other healthy child.

Ten years passed. Rafil Arbiv was now a youth of 14, learning in *yeshivah ketanah*. His sturdy build and pleasant-featured face radiated good health and strength.

Until the nightmare returned.

Once again, as though replaying old, dark scenes from the past, Rafi began to suffer the same symptoms he had suffered a decade earlier. He was rushed to the hospital for tests. To his family's anguish, the nightmare was back. The illness had reared its ugly head again, in the very same place as before. Once again, the boy — who just a year earlier had happily celebrated becoming a bar mitzvah — was in grave danger.

His parents threw themselves into battle mode again. This time around, they were seasoned veterans. But this time the battle was to be fought on more difficult terrain. Ten years earlier, Rafi had been a small child who had not understood what was happening around him. He had been unaware of the danger that threatened him. The entire burden had been carried by his parents. Today, Rafi was a young teenager who understood. He was in the picture now.

But Rafi rose to the challenge, revealing the essential soundness of his nature. Not only did he not succumb to fear or despair, but he was filled with an ardent faith in his Creator, Who he believed with all his heart would help him. This faith was contagious and touched everyone near him.

After consultations with noted activists and senior physicians, the decision was made to make the trip to Boston Hospital. It was the same illness. All of Rafi's files and medical charts were there.

And so was the surgeon.

In the intervening years, the Arbiv family had grown. Rafi, the firstborn, now had three younger brothers and two sisters. These children would have to be left behind while Rafi and his parents flew to the United States. Relatives were drafted to take the younger children temporarily into their homes.

The Arbivs arrived in Boston. This time, it was the Linker family that stood by to help them — a family no less wonderful than their previous hosts, the Fuchses. The Arbivs settled in briefly in the Linker home and then went directly to the hospital.

A great many question marks hovered in the air around them. Once again, there was the question of money. They had been told that the fee for the difficult operation had escalated. And what about the surgery itself? Would it be capable of saving Rafi's life a second time? And would they again be forced to suffer last-minute disappointments? Would a knife be damaged or Dr. Abrahams abandon them at the critical moment, leaving the job to his second-in-command, Dr. Waterman? Though Dr. Waterman, it must be said, had done a fine job, as fine as Dr. Abrahams himself might have done ...

The answers to the Arbivs' pressing questions began to be found by the local Jewish community. The Linkers, their hosts, pressed into service several important rabbinical figures who went door-to-door collecting money for the sick boy. They succeeded in amassing a significant sum. There was a feeling in the air that this time — as opposed to their earlier experience — things were starting off on the right foot.

The feeling sowed hope in their hearts. Nissim and Odelya could not help drawing a hopeful message, something on the order of a *"kal v'chomer"*: If last time, when things had looked so bleak, all had ended well, this time, with everything going smoothly, how much more so?

Parents and son arrived at the hospital, which had hardly changed at all in the ten intervening years. Rafi underwent the admittance procedure and the first battery of tests.

Mrs. Linker, their hostess, came to their room with a hot lunch for the family. Happily, she told them, "Here's the update. You've been expecting Dr. Abrahams to be the surgeon — but he's retired now. Today, the head of the neurosurgical department is Dr. Waterman. He's apparently the one who will operate on Rafi."

"Dr. Waterman?" Nissim and Odelya cried in a single voice. "He was Rafi's surgeon last time!"

"That's right," Mrs. Linker said. "He's earned a worldwide reputation. Over the years, Dr. Waterman has gained enormous knowledge and experience. He's known today as one of the world's foremost brain surgeons, largely thanks to his mentor, Dr. Abrahams."

Dr. Waterman greeted the Arbivs warmly. He looked through Rafi's file. As he turned pages and scanned notes, he suddenly smacked the desk with his hand. "Rafi Arbiv? The name is so familiar ... I remember now. He was my first operation!"

The surgeon was deeply moved. For a moment, he closed his eyes and communed with himself. Then he opened them and gazed benevolently at Rafi's parents. "I would like to make a special gesture in honor of my first surgical patient. I will operate on him for a specially reduced fee."

He mentioned a sum that shocked the Arbivs. It was a paltry amount, almost negligible. Even in Israel, surgeons received a higher fee for their work.

Thus was Hashem's compassionate hand revealed to the family. They saw with brilliant clarity how Hashem prepares the cure before the blow strikes — and then heals the blow itself.

The same thing happened as in the first time around, only, this time, with greater expertise. The second surgery was as successful as the first had been. Even the patient's full name, Rafael, hinted at a cure prepared before the illness. Today, Rafael is a healthy yeshivah *bachur* making great strides in his learning. Whatever headaches afflict him these days are only the outcome of an especially difficult *sugya*.

FORCED to LIVE

THE LIFE THAT R' SHALOM SCHEINKOPF SHARED WITH his wife, Gittel, was a peaceful and pleasant one from their wedding day to their old age. Their children were all grown-up by now, with grandchildren of their own — some of whom would soon be ready to stand under the *chupah*. R' Shalom was well known as a G-d-fearing Jew who set aside times for learning Torah. For many years he had served as a *gabbai* in his shul, and he worked on others' behalf with a warm Jewish heart. He was the same in his 80's as he had been in his 30's. As long as his legs had the strength to carry him, short, slender R' Shalom did not cease running through the streets of Jerusalem, calling out cheerfully to everyone he met, even if he didn't know them. He could be seen every Shabbos, coming down the stairs of the *Beis Baruch* shul in Meah Shearim, wrapped in his *tallis* and straightening the threadbare *shtreimel* on his head. He greeted everyone with a hearty, "*Gut Shabbos*!," even small children.

"And how are you today, R' Shalom?" his acquaintances would ask.

His rich, slightly hoarse laugh would fill the narrow street as he replied with a merry, "*Baruch Hashem*!"

A genuine Jew from old-time Jerusalem.

R' Shalom had passed peacefully through the circle of life. This world and its cares were nearly behind him now. Soon he would be gathered unto his fathers.

He and his wife were getting on in years. All their lives, it had been his wife, Gittel, who had been the weaker, sickly one, while R' Shalom was rarely ill and never even rested except for a few hours at night. Now, as they aged and began to near the end of their time in this world, R' Shalom began to entertain a profound fear that his wife would depart this life before him and leave him all alone.

One evening, as they sat down to their supper, he whispered to his wife, "Gittel, I have a good deal for you."

She was surprised, and curious. Since when was her Shalom a businessman, involved in "deals"? And why all the secrecy?

Shalom began to pour out the pain that was in his heart. "Our children, they should be well, are getting on in years themselves. It seems like our Shloimy had his *upsherin* just yesterday. Do you remember how I took him to Meron on Lag B'Omer, in the year 5672 (1912)? The trip took us three days. Well, just imagine: our little Shloimy will be retiring next month! He'll be 65 years old. Our aging children no longer have the energy to visit their elderly parents. Our many grandchildren have young heads; they don't understand the old. All week long we're alone, and only on Shabbos do our offspring come to visit. Can we go on like this?"

"So what do you want, Shalom?"

R' Shalom inched forward and whispered a question. "What will you do if I die before you? Would you want to live alone? Even the street cats will be happier than you. You'll sit marooned in the house and no one will pay the slightest attention to you."

The old woman began to cry. Shalom was right. Her strength was depleted. Her body had its day of glory and youth. Now it was just a bag of skin and bones which would soon be buried under a pile of dirt, with nothing but a cold slab of marble to tell the world that she had ever existed.

"So what do you want, Shalom?" she asked again in a quavering voice.

Shalom's eyes gleamed with a mysterious smile. "I want to make a pact. Whichever one of us goes first will hurry to tell the Heavenly Court that he or she wants to be reunited with his or her spouse. That way, neither of us will have to suffer from loneliness in this world."

"I'm afraid old age has made you senile," Gittel scolded. "Never in my life have I heard such a crazy idea!"

"Gittel, loneliness is more painful than death," Shalom declared. "You won't be able to bear life alone."

It was several days before the old woman gave him her answer. She thought the matter over and gave it her full consideration, until she found the idea to be a sensible one. Indeed, what would she do alone in the house without Shalom to sprinkle a bit of light into her world?

And so, the two made a pact. They promised each other that whichever of them passed away first would not rest until he or she had managed to bring over the other one, too. In them, the saying would be fulfilled: "Beloved and pleasant in their lifetimes, they were not parted in their deaths."

It was not very long afterward that the Angel of Death came for the frail Gittel. The Jews of Jerusalem attended her funeral and came to comfort her husband and children. Expecting to see R' Shalom in anguish, they came to believe that his grief must have unhinged his mind: He was as merry as a bridegroom on his wedding day. The sight of his cheerful smile astounded one and all. Had his friends and neighbors not known that he and his wife had lived for all these years like a pair of doves, they would have suspected him of having looked forward to her demise. Knowing that they had lived in peace and harmony all their lives, they could not fathom the reason for his present happiness. His reasoning, they concluded, must have become addled from the pain of her passing.

A small number of his closest friends were unable to restrain themselves or suppress their amazement. Approaching R' Shalom, they said, "R' Shalom. *Chazal* have taught us that the first three days of mourning are for weeping. Why are you not crying over your dear wife's death?"

R' Shalom smiled his mischievous smile and mumbled something they couldn't catch. How could he tell them that he was certain that his "airline ticket" would be coming through in just a matter of days? They would be certain that he belonged in a mental institution! So he just whispered something mysterious about a pact he had made with his wife before her death, a pact that would ensure the bond between them even though they were physically separated now.

No one understood his inexplicable words. The consensus was that R' Shalom had gone mad with grief, or else had become senile overnight. R' Shalom saw the winks and nods that his friends exchanged behind his back, but he cared not a whit. They would go on with their lives on this earth, fleeting lives in an ephemeral world. He would go on to eternal life.

He sat *shivah* with his children, but while they shed tears over the loss of a beloved mother, he was privately saying good-bye to this world. He trusted implicitly in the pact he had struck with his wife before her passing, and knew that he would very soon be leaving this earth.

The week of mourning passed. His family went to the fresh grave and watered it with their tears. Only R' Shalom did not cry. He just looked at his wife's grave with a concealed reproach, as if to say, "We made a deal. What's taking you so long?" He glanced surreptitiously over at the empty plot beside Gittel's, like someone getting acquainted with his future home.

R' Shalom sat home and waited for the pact to be fulfilled. A week passed, and then another, but nothing happened. Several times he visited her grave secretly. There, where no one would see, he shed bitter tears. "Gittel, why have you left me alone in this world? Without you, my life is no life. I want to die. Take me to you — today!"

These are not the kind of words one generally hears, but R' Shalom had lost his taste for life. Eighty-five years were enough for him. It seemed as though his wife, may her memory be a blessing, had forgotten their pact.

She must be preoccupied with her judgment, he thought. As it says, there is no *tzaddik* on earth who has not sinned. Even the best people have done some wrong in their lives. Apparently, when Gittel faced her judgment before the Creator of the world, some lack had been found in her behavior and she had not had the leisure to fulfill the pact she had struck with her husband in this world. He decided to wait a few weeks. She would remember then.

So old R' Shalom sat and waited, two months, and then three. Half a year went and he was still walking the earth, hale and healthy. He had never felt better. He walked around with an erect bearing, his senses functional and his mind clear as that of a 40-year-old.

Eleven months elapsed from his wife's death. R' Shalom had learned the meaning of the *mishnah's* dictum: "You are forced to live." The Master of the Universe did not wish to take R' Shalom's soul from this world yet. Not only was Gittel not working to fulfill their pact, but she would not even reveal herself to him in a dream, despite the fact that he thought about her a great deal during the day, and dreams, as everyone knows, tend to be linked to our thoughts.

As the year of mourning for Gittel drew to a close — a time when, in the natural course of things, pain and grief over a loss begin to diminish — R' Shalom experienced the opposite reaction. Whereas during the week of *shivah* he had been cheerful and lucid, he was now depressed and in pain. He looked like a candle that had gone out, a broken man.

His children and grandchildren saw their father's grief, but none of them had a clue as to the real reason. He was mourning his living. He longed to enter Heaven already, to be together with his Gittel and to say *Kaddish* over the whole world. He wanted to be finished with all of it. Let others continue running around down below, on this tiny ball that we call the Earth, full of their worries and empty concerns. He would look down on them from above and bask in the glow of the *Shechinah*.

On Gittel's *yahrtzeit*, the family went to visit her resting place. To their astonishment, R' Shalom wept copiously over her grave. He draped himself over the new monument and soaked it with his tears.

His weeping shook them all. He sobbed for a long time, until he fell to the ground in a faint. A sprinkling of cold water revived him. His children wondered anxiously whether they ought to take him to the hospital.

However, the old man quickly recovered, though he remained depressed and sad. His family was distressed by this strange, uncharacteristic behavior on the part of their beloved and energetic father. He had rejoiced during the week of mourning when everyone else was crying, and was dissolved in tears a year later. No one could understand it.

That night, R' Shalom had a dream.

In his dream, his wife Gittel appeared to him, dressed in pristine shrouds, her face radiant. The sight moved him deeply, and he sensed that even in his dream he was crying hard.

When the storm of tears had abated somewhat, he saw that Gittel was still standing before him. She smiled happily.

"What happened to you? What's been going on from the time you died till today?" The question burst from his lips with the force of water from a dam.

Gittel told him about her judgment, and told him that she already merited arriving at her rightful resting place.

"In that case," her husband asked in agitation, "why didn't you remember me even once? Why didn't you keep the promise you made me in our pact?"

"I wanted to keep the promise," she said, understanding his turmoil. "But then, your uncle, R' Moshe — your father's brother — appeared before the Heavenly Court and begged it not to accept my plea — to leave you alive in the world below. I said my part, and your uncle said his, and the Heavenly Court accepted his claim and not mine. What else could I do?"

Abruptly, Shalom awoke. He sensed that the dream had been genuine. It was not just a pack of nonsense. He believed that his wife's spirit had truly revealed itself to him that night.

Immediately after *Shacharis*, Shalom took a taxi to the cemetery on *Har HaMenuchos*. He needed no help in locating the grave of R' Moshe, his uncle, whose *yahrtzeit* he had been observing ever since his death some twenty years earlier. He went directly to the site, recited a few chapters of *Tehillim*, and then roared from the depths of his heart: "R' Moshe, my dear uncle. Why have you prevented me from being united with my Gittel? It is our holy wish to be together again."

He poured out his heart in a monologue, and then left the grave in a black frame of mind.

        ♏

That night, he couldn't sleep. Troubling thoughts disturbed his rest and prevented him from relaxing. After counting thousands of sheep, shearing their wool, and manufacturing coats for all of Jerusalem's poor, he finally fell into a brief sleep. In his dream, he saw his uncle, R' Moshe.

"You were at my grave today," his uncle said with a pleasant smile. "And you have a complaint against me."

"That's correct." R' Shalom went straight to the point. "My wife said that you stood in the way and prevented our pact from being fulfilled."

"Very true," his uncle confirmed. "Right now, you are living for me. You are very important to me in this world, and I can't give you up. That's why I pleaded with the Heavenly Court not to listen to Gittel."

"Why is it so important to you that I be alive?" R' Shalom asked in astonishment.

"You are the only member of the family who scrupulously observes the *yahrtzeits* of all your aunts and uncles. You visit our graves and say *Tehillim* and *Kaddish*. Our souls are very grateful to you, and it is important to us that you go on living."

Another person might have yielded at this point either because of all the praise or because of the legitimacy of the claim. But R' Shalom was not the kind of person to become overly excited by compliments. He countered at once: "And what about your only son, Yankel? Doesn't he observe your *yahrtzeit*?"

"No," his uncle stated flatly. "Go talk to him and you'll see."

"So how long will I remain in this world?" R' Shalom demanded.

"About another five years," his uncle replied — and vanished.

That morning, R' Shalom phoned his cousin Yankel and asked him if he had visited his father's grave on R' Moshe's last *yahrtzeit*. At first Yankel claimed that he had gone, and tried to counter-attack in response to the suspicion and insult he had incurred. In the face of R' Shalom's unyielding confidence, however, Yankel broke down and admitted limply that, in recent years, he had not visited his father's grave on the *yahrtzeit*. "I've been so busy," he said in self-justification. "I've gone to the grave a few days earlier or later instead."

It was now his turn to ask the questions. "Do you have *ruach hakodesh*? How did you know?"

"Your father told me in a dream," R' Shalom said.

His talk with his cousin verified for R' Shalom the dream's veracity, as well as his uncle's message. He understood that he still had five long years to live in this world. He would try to use the time for Torah and mitzvos and would refrain from troubling his wife's spirit any longer.

Five years later (in the year 5737/1977), at the ripe old age of nearly 90, R' Shalom passed away and was buried beside his wife. But before that — immediately after he had the dreams — he revealed their contents to a family member, who subsequently told us the whole story.

"A Kohen Suits Her"

THE FELDMAN FAMILY, THAT RESIDED IN JERUSALEM AT the edge of the Batei Ungarin neighborhood, was known as a warm, good family. The father was well respected in the city and his wife was descended from the famous *tzaddik*, R' Levi Yitzchak Leiber of Berditchev. It was because of this fact that the whole story took place, but let's not get ahead of ourselves.

The entire episode took place in about the year 5700 (1940), approximately 66 years ago. Miriam Feldman, a daughter of the family, was suggested as a match for an excellent *bachur* by the name of Tuvia Katz, from another illustrious Jerusalem family. It seemed to be a very fitting *shidduch*. The boy had been blessed with a wealth of fine qualities and had earned a good name for himself.

The *kallah's* father was about to give his consent to the match when a problem arose.

"Tell me," his wife said as they discussed how to finalize the *tenaim* between the *chasan's* family and themselves. "Are the Katzes by any chance *Kohanim*?"

"Of course they're *Kohanim* — and it's no coincidence," said R' Simchah Feldman. "The name 'Katz' is made up of the initials for '*Kohen tzedek.*' In fact, I've been privileged to receive the priestly blessing more than just once or twice, from both the *chasan*, Tuvia, and his father, R' Pinchas Katz."

"In that case," his wife said firmly, "the *shidduch* is off."

"Why?" her husband asked in shock.

"Because we are *Yisraelim* and the *chasan* is a *Kohen*. Have you forgotten that I'm the granddaughter of the great R' Leiber of Berditchev," she asked, "who cautioned his descendants not to marry *Kohanim* under any circumstances?"

R' Simchah had not known about R' Leiber's warning. The *shidduch* seemed very promising. How could they pass up such an exceptional boy, just because of a stricture that had probably expired by now?

"We have the holy *tzaddik*, R' Shloim'ke of Zhvil, right here in our city. Maybe we should consult with him?"

His wife agreed to this plan. That very day, they went to the Rebbe of Zhvil's small home in the Beis Yisrael neighborhood. The Rebbe, whose spiritual stature was of a kind that our own generation cannot fathom, was not surrounded by *gabbaim* and assistants. There were no receiving hours. Anyone with a pain in his heart or body, or a question on any topic, could drop into his house and ask his advice.

The couple entered the Rebbe's room and presented their question. The Rebbe listened to the details and the daughter's name, and said, "A *Kohen* suits her."

Surprised, the couple said nothing. The Rebbe continued, "You can go forward with the *shidduch*. There's no need to worry."

R' Simchah Feldman stood up eagerly. To his shock, he discovered that his wife was still staunch in her refusal. "Rebbe, I am a granddaughter of the great R' Leiber, who left behind a code of conduct for his descendants, in which he said not to marry *Kohanim*."

"It is impossible to decide that on your own. If it's hard for you to come to a decision about the *shidduch*, go consult with the *Mara D'Asra* of the neighborhood: the *gaon* R' Shimshon Aharon Polanski, the Rav of Teplik. He, too, is a grandson of the great R' Leiber of Berditchev."

(According to another version, it was the Rebbe of Zhvil himself who suggested the match, and when the girl's mother wished to decline on the above grounds, he sent her to the Rav of Teplik to ask his opinion.)

R' Simchah and his wife went to the home of the Rav of Teplik, who lived in the same neighborhood. They presented their query, telling of the proposed *shidduch* and its good points, and of the *kallah's* mother's strenuous objection. "We've come directly from the home of R' Shloim'ke of Zhvil, who sent us here to consult with your honor."

The Rav of Teplik did not hesitate for a second. "I, too, am a grandson of R' Leiber of Berditchev," he told the woman directly. "And I am telling you unequivocally that you may make this *shidduch* and have nothing to fear. Our great-grandfather's command was binding on previous generations, but there is no need to abide by it today."

Fine and good. What more was needed than the explicit approval of such an absolute spiritual authority as the Rebbe and the Rav? But Mrs. Feldman was still obstinate as a mule and refused to back down. "We will not make this *shidduch*, no matter what," she declared to her husband when they returned home. "Go to the honored *shadchan* and tell him that we're stepping back from this match. We have nothing against the *boy,* but because the *chasan* is a *Kohen*, we cannot go through with it."

A short while later, another *bachur* was suggested for Miriam Feldman. Yirmiyahu Dolman was his name. He was a *Yisrael* of good family, going back generations. Mrs. Feldman agreed to the match, and the *shidduch* was concluded between the two families.

Like the first boy, the *chasan* was an exceptionally learned *yeshivah bachur*, outstanding in Torah and *yiras Shamayim*. Everyone who knew him could not sing his praises enough. After a year-long engagement, as was the custom at that time, the *chasan* and *kallah* stood beneath the *chupah*.

Young Yirmiyahu learned in yeshivah and brought home a pittance. In those days, the concept of a *kollel* did not yet exist. Most young men went out to work after the wedding; those who thirsted for Torah and remained in yeshivah — be it Eitz Chaim or Toras Chaim in the Lithuanian style, or the chassidic Chayei Olam and "Toras Emes"— received a minuscule stipend, amounting, as said, to no more than pennies. A great deal of self-sacrifice was necessary to learn Torah all day.

Yirmiyahu Dolman had an uncle in America by the name of Jeffrey Nanson. Uncle Jeffrey was his mother's brother, and was a very wealthy man who owned a factory employing hundreds of workers. One day, Yirmiyahu received a thick letter covered with numerous American stamps and decorated with the postal seal of black, wavy lines. In the letter, his Uncle Jeffrey wrote, "All these years, I've been hearing about you from my sister — your mother. She's described you as a talented young man and successful in everything you do. Now I hear from her that you and your young wife are simply wasting away from hunger. I ask you, is this the purpose? Is this why you married, in order to starve your wife? Come work with me in my factory. I'm thinking good things about your future … Come to me, work and make good money, and let me take care of all your needs. I've prepared a spacious, beautiful apartment for the two of you to live in. You'll get a large weekly paycheck from me that will allow you to live very comfortably. And, of course, a pair of tickets for the ship to America is included in this envelope, as I am sure you noticed right away."

Indeed, the envelope contained two tickets for passage on a ship to the United States. They were made out in the names of Yirmiyahu and Miriam Dolman!

The young couple was thunderstruck. They had never expected such a letter. "It's as though the gates of *Gan Eden* opened in front of us," Yirmiyahu cried ecstatically.

Miriam was less enthusiastic. America was a distant and murky concept to her: a gigantic land at the ends of the earth. They debated for a long time about whether or not to make the trip, but the inducement was too dazzling to resist. Their destitute home had nothing. They were living a life of unmitigated poverty. For several days they walked around like drunkards, filled with doubts and questions until, in the end, they decided not to reject their American uncle's generosity. Yirmiyahu's mother continually encouraged them, telling them day and night about her brother's good heart and legendary wealth.

On the appointed day, they boarded the ship. Three weeks later, they set foot on American soil.

It was like a dream. Yirmiyahu and his wife could scarcely believe it was really happening. Compared to poverty-stricken Jerusalem, America seemed to glow and glisten. It was all beyond their wildest imaginings. Their home was large, beautiful, and tastefully furnished. The skyscrapers amazed them and they were entranced by the shop windows with their flashing neon lighting.

But all this was not the purpose for their coming. Uncle Jeffrey gave them a few days to feast their hungry eyes. Then, at the start of the following week, Yirmiyahu began working in the factory beside his uncle.

Jeffrey was all smiles. His investment had justified itself. Yirmiyahu proved to be an energetic and talented young man whose work was crowned with success.

That first Friday afternoon, Yirmiyahu was on edge. It was already past midday, but there was no sign of the workday coming to an end. The workers were glued to their machines and the assembly line kept rolling. Maybe here in America they worked a little later on Friday afternoons. But when another full hour had passed and nothing had changed, Yirmiyahu went to his uncle and asked in surprise, "Dear uncle, I don't understand. Is today Wednesday?"

"No, it's Friday."

"When does work end on Fridays?"

His uncle lifted his head and blinked. The trouble was starting …

"Listen, my dear boy, this is not Israel. This is America. Here we work seven days a week."

"Oh, no!" Yirmiyahu exclaimed.

Jeffrey stood up. Approaching his nephew, he placed a gentle hand on his shoulder. "I understand. I guessed that you wouldn't agree to work on Shabbos and I've thought it over. You'll be different from all my other employees. You're free from Friday afternoon till Sunday morning. Go home in peace now, and come back on Sunday."

Yirmiyahu put on his coat and walked, white faced, to the door. He was deeply shaken. Uncle Jeffrey motioned him over with a crook of his finger. "My dear Yirmiyahu, have you forgotten your weekly paycheck?" Smiling, he handed his nephew an envelope. "Inside you'll find a full week's salary. It'll be like this every week. You'll work five-and-a-half days and receive seven days' salary. Now, go home. *Ah gutten Shabbos* — and see you on Sunday, bright eyed and bushy tailed!"

Yirmiyahu walked around that Shabbos like a caged tiger. "Is this what we came to America for?" he roared from the depth of his broken heart. "To spend our time with people who are *mechalel Shabbos*? How is it that we didn't think of this before we came?"

"How can we enjoy our food and drink," his young wife said, gazing sadly toward the kitchen, from which wafted the good smells of Shabbos delicacies, "when the money for it comes from impure sources? From money earned through *chilul Shabbos*."

"And this beautiful apartment of ours." Yirmiyahu looked around at the spacious living room, the likes of which he had never seen before he came to this country. "It's all based on a crumbling foundation: a disregard of the sanctity of Shabbos."

On *Motza'ei Shabbos*, after 24 hours of painful struggle with his conscience, Yirmiyahu went to his Uncle Jeffrey's house and told him, with great emotion, that he had decided to leave the job. "I cannot earn my livelihood from a business that is open on Shabbos," he explained. "I don't want the apartment or the job. Your intentions were good, dear uncle, and I thank you for them from the bottom of my heart. But I cannot work with you as long as your employees work on Shabbos."

Jeffrey tried to argue with him. "You don't have to work on Shabbos; I told you that yesterday. Don't leave me. I can use your talent and ability, and I enjoy your company."

But Yirmiyahu stood his ground. "I simply can't, Uncle Jeffrey. It would contradict who I am: working for a company that desecrates the Shabbos, and earning my living from it."

"I was counting on you!" Jeffrey cried. "Your ideas can help my business. I can't give you up. Listen to me," he said quickly, trying to halt Yirmiyahu's slow retreat toward the door. "I'll make you a partner, with stock options. You'll get rich from me. It'll be well worth your while."

"I can't. I'm sorry. Hashem doesn't permit me to do it."

Yirmiyahu left his uncle reeling in shock. Jeffrey had never seen such a proud stance on behalf of a principle. All his prior thoughts and plans seemed to shatter on the rock of that principled attitude. It was a profound lesson in the laws of *shemiras Shabbos* and *yiras Shamayim*.

The following day, the young couple left the apartment, returned the keys, and rented a tiny, airless place in its stead. They did not have enough money for the trip back to Eretz Yisrael. Yirmiyahu looked for a job to help him earn the airfare. Being a man of ability and energy, he soon found new work as the *gabbai* of one of the *tzedakah* institutions in the city. Each week, he traveled to a different city in the United States to collect charitable funds.

Hidden are the ways of Hashem …

One day, as Yirmiyahu traveled between cities, his car was involved in a fatal accident. He was killed on the spot.

Within a short time, the young widow returned to her parents' home in Jerusalem. She had no husband and no children.

She was sunk in mourning for a lengthy period. After a while, her parents began to urge her to rebuild her life and marry again. This, they said, was the way of the world. The dead passed on and the living continued with their lives.

Industrious matchmakers began to offer various proposals. Out of all the rest, one suggestion seemed especially apt. He was a young man who was widowed and who, because he was a *Kohen*, was permitted to marry only a single girl or a widow, but not a divorced woman.

This time, Miriam's mother could not reject the match on the basis of her eternal claim that "We don't marry *Kohanim*." Her daughter was no longer in a position where she could throw away a fine suggestion with equanimity. Within a short time, a plate was broken amid cries of "Mazal tov!"

Only then did they recall the words of the holy Rebbe of Zhvil: "A *Kohen* suits her!"

[NOTE: *Hagaon* R' Avraham Dov Auerbach, *shlita*, Rav of Teveryah, relates that he once went to see his father, *Hagaon* R' Shlomo Zalman Auerbach, *ztk"l*, and found him at a loss. On his desk was a letter from a Jew in Antwerp, who said that a *shidduch* had been suggested for him with a woman from a family of *Kohanim*, but he was descended from the great R' Leiber who had forbidden his offspring from marrying *Kohanim*. The reason R' Leiber had issued this ban was because of a certain *Kohen*, a Torah leader of his generation, with whom R' Leiber did not wish to be aligned in marriage because that *Kohen* had refused to join three other *gedolei hador* who had accepted death as an atonement for *Klal Yisrael* in order to prevent the terrible massacres of "*Tach V'Tat*." (These were R' Shimshon of Ostropoli, R' Yechiel Michel of Nimerov, and the first R' Leiber the Great, of Berditchev. All three of these men died that same year.) It was because the fourth *gadol* had refused to join the others that the terrible suffering had befallen the people. It was for this reason that R' Leiber had forbidden his descendants from marrying *Kohanim* — to prevent their marrying the descendants of that *gadol*. The man from Antwerp wrote R' Shlomo Zalman Auerbach, saying that he had looked into the antecedents of the family of *Kohanim* with whom a match had been proposed, and had ascertained that they were not descended from that *gadol hador*. R' Shlomo Zalman told his son that he did not know what to answer. R' Avraham Dov then related to his father the above story involving R' Shloim'ke of Zhvil, and what the Rebbe and the Rav of Teplik had said. Hearing this, R' Shlomo Zalman said that he now had a source on whom to rely, and immediately wrote back to Antwerp, telling the man that he could go forward with the *shidduch* in a fortunate hour.]

He Who Courts Scorn

Jerusalem, 5708

THE NARROW STREETS OF THE MEAH SHEARIM AND BEIS Yisrael neighborhoods appeared deserted. A stranger, happening upon the place, would have made the mistake of thinking that no one lived there. Not a soul was to be seen anywhere. Even the street cats, inured to suffering the hurled rocks of Jerusalem's mischievous children, seemed to have fled for their lives.

The Jordanian Legionnaires' mortar shells, raining down on the city, had forced its residents to cower in bomb shelters. These were not the well-fortified and well-equipped rooms that we have today. Any rickety structure that was at least partially below ground level, and therefore not threatened directly by bullets and mortar attack, was deemed fit to protect the scores of Jerusalemites who cowered there until the danger had passed.

These were difficult times. With the whistle of bullets constantly overhead, anyone venturing out into the street was taking his life in his hands. And even staying indoors did not spell protection. From time to time, a person would stand at the window to check the situation outside. More than one of these became the target of an unerring bullet, which stole another life.

There were also calmer days, days when the shriek of mortar shells and the whine of rifle bullets were dampened. It was as if the enemy soldiers had grown weary and were giving up hope of defeating every Jewish man, woman, and child in the city, all in one day.

The Jews took advantage of the lull to go outside and obtain food and water. Then the terrifying noise would start up again, echoing through the streets and taking its merciless toll of human life. The Legionnaires were situated on the hills surrounding the city where, through their binoculars, they could see the residents of the city hastening to take advantage of the momentary calm. The snipers aimed directly into the crowd, killing and maiming indiscriminately: babies, small children, teenaged boys, and their righteous mothers. My father, *Hagaon* R' Shlomo Menachem Weinstock, *zt"l*, once told me that he was staying in the home of his oldest brother, *Hagaon Hatzaddik* and *mekubal* R' Moshe Yair Weinstock, *zt"l*, during a mortar attack. When a lull fell, he hurried outside to go to yeshivah. Within a moment, however, the street began to hum with threatening bullets. My father ran into some sort of inadequate shelter to wait out the attack. When silence fell once again, he emerged and went quickly to yeshivah.

The next day, he returned to his brother's house. Seeing him, the whole family sighed with relief. "We thought you were no longer among the living," they told him emotionally. "The shells started flying the minute you left the house, and there was no way to find out what had happened to you."

Such was the atmosphere and the situation at that time. Jewish Jerusalem was under heavy attack. Terror sharpened the air. No more than a heartbeat lay between the beleaguered city and the decimation of its entire population.

In one shelter, in the Beis Yisrael section of the city, dozens of neighborhood residents waited. The boom and crash of the mortar shells sowed a deathly fear in their hearts. No one knew where the next shell would land, or who would next fall victim to its devastating destructive power.

They sat in family groups within the "bomb shelter," which was actually nothing more than the basement level of one of the neighborhood shuls. Luckily, the place was airy and not too crowded. Every family chose its own corner and spread blankets on the floor on which to sleep at night. Kerosene lamps made an ineffectual attempt to shed light in the dim room.

The situation might have been a little easier to bear were it not for the presence of "Mad Tzipporah" (fictitious name). It had been the children who had given her that nickname, and there are no more astute judges of emotional health than children. They have been blessed with a keen intuition, so that when they notice a person deviating even a fraction from the norm, they stick to him like a magnet, never removing their eyes for an instant, waiting for his first slip.

Tzipporah made life in the shelter extremely unpleasant for those who were sharing it with her to the point where the shriek of the shells outside seemed preferable to her whining voice.

She was a bitter woman, a woman who had not found her way in life. The troubles she had suffered had addled her wits, but she was by no means dim witted. On the contrary, she was quite shrewd, and focused all her talent and keen eyesight on finding the flaws in others. During ordinary times, there was no need to endure the sting of her tongue. If she accosted you in a public place and began to enumerate your faults, all you had to do was walk away. Here in the shelter, the situation was quite different.

Tzipporah sat and looked around her, targeting her next victim. "Has anyone told you how fat you are?" she asked one of her neighbors, hunched fearfully amid his family. Tzipporah burst into a cackle of horrible laughter. "Tell me, how many loaves of bread do you eat in a day? Two? Three?"

The poor man was beside himself with mortification. Indeed, his midsection was spilling generously over his waistline. But did she have to embarrass him that way?

"Never mind," his wife whispered. "Yesterday she sucked Chaim Tobias' blood, and shamed him in front of everyone because he has a squint."

Those whose physical shortcomings Tzipporah earmarked could count themselves fortunate compared to the neighbors whom that sharp-eyed woman decided to publicly bring to task over secrets and other matters better left unspoken; all of it, of course, based on genuine fact.

In short, Tzipporah sowed pain wherever she went. Reuven was a hunchback and Shimon was bowlegged. Levi's nails were overgrown and Yehudah suffered from an infestation of lice ... The only thing they all had in common was the way they suffered in silence the terrible humiliation that Tzipporah heaped on their heads without pity, shaming them in front of their families. She seemed to derive pleasure from their discomfit.

After several days of torture, both from within and from without, the inhabitants of that shelter began to feel that they could not endure another moment. Though they were compassionate Jews, there was a limit to what they could bear. Spontaneously, they decided to evict Mad Tzipporah from the shelter. Let her find some other place to hide.

But before they took this step, they decided to ask the permission of the great *tzaddik* who was staying with them: the holy R' Gedaliah Moshe of Zhvil, seated in a corner with his family. At one point, when the madwoman had just finished another bloodletting in which a neighbor was thoroughly mortified in front of his wife and children — who didn't know where to look in their shame — the people's patience dissipated. Several spokesmen approached the Rebbe and whispered in his ear, "The Rebbe has no doubt seen and heard what's been happening here. We can't stand it any longer! We would like the Rebbe's permission to send her somewhere else. Maybe they'll be able to stop her wild tongue over there."

R' Gedaliah Moshe spent all his days poring over his *sefarim*, eyes fixed on the printed page. Despite this, he was neither blind nor deaf. He had seen and heard what was taking place around him. Perhaps, too, he knew the lashing of that unbalanced woman's tongue — which did not differentiate between a good man and a bad one — and of her anger and pain over her own miserable life which she poured over everyone else's head.

"What are you saying?" the Rebbe exclaimed softly. "Absolutely not! I do not agree to this. I will not allow you to send her out."

The others were stunned by his refusal. "We would not, Heaven forbid, expose her to danger. We would only transfer her to another shelter. Our own endurance is at an end."

R' Gedaliah Moshe remained firm. "Absolutely not!" he said forcefully. "And if you ask me why, I will tell you several things I heard from my holy father, R' Shlomo of Zhvil …

⟡

"It was back in the town of Zhvil, where my father, R' Shlomo, served in its heyday. He resided there in his splendid chassidic courtyard, which was like a royal palace.

"One day, my sister became ill. She was the Rebbe's youngest daughter, and her life was in danger. After all treatments failed, the doctors threw up their hands in despair and left the house. She was nearly at death's door.

"My father, R' Shlomo, put on his overcoat and prepared to go out into the street. 'Where are you going?' the family asked him.

"'To town,' he answered briefly.

"We knew that he was a man of mystery, one who spoke little and did much. I accompanied him, to see what would happen and to learn from his actions.

"Several of the houses in town were owned by the local Talmud Torah, who rented them out and used the income for the school. The rents were collected in a rather lackadaisical manner, and those who were short of funds often managed to avoid paying at all. It was to the home of a woman who had not paid her rent for a long period of time that R' Shlomo now proceeded.

"He knocked on the door. When it was opened, the Rebbe explained that he had come to collect the debt. He requested payment owed to the Talmud Torah for several years' back rent.

"The woman raised her voice in piercing shrieks. 'How dare the Rebbe come to a poor woman like me? The Rebbe receives *kvitlach* and donations every day. Money is plentiful for you while I don't have two pennies to rub together and am practically dying of starvation!'

"The woman's anger did not quickly subside. She heaped her fury on the Rebbe, who stood with bowed head, submitting to the tirade.

"Hearing her screams, many neighbors gathered around, and the humiliation increased sevenfold. Finally, the woman slammed her door furiously in the Rebbe's face, shouting that he had better not dare show his face at her door again!

"A contented expression settled over the Rebbe's face. He turned to me, his son, joyously. *"Baruch Hashem*, we can go home now. We have brought about a *refuah* for your little sister. We have endured more than enough mortification.'

"His words proved correct. I understood my father's intention only when we returned home, and witnessed a veritable miracle of *techiyas hameisim* (revival of the dead) when, contrary to all expectations, my sister recovered.

"But one does not always merit being mortified," R' Gedaliah Moshe concluded. He looked sad. "Some time later, her illness returned. My father told me that he was heading into town to seek humiliation. He went back to that same woman who had so shamed him the last time, knocked on her door, and requested payment of the outstanding rent. This time, though, she came out and stammered apologetically, 'I really have not behaved properly. Here, I've prepared a partial payment. And I also beg the Rebbe's forgiveness for the way I acted last time. Please forgive me, holy Rebbe!"

"Instead of scorn, my father reaped honor. He went around to other homes, but Heaven apparently did not wish him to be mortified. Everywhere he went, he was royally honored.

"My father's face darkened. Heaven did not wish to grant him the merit of humiliation, a sign that the decree had been signed and sealed. He returned home with slumped shoulders and sorrowful face, to find that his daughter's illness had worsened. Within a short time, she passed on to the world where all is good ...

"And if you say that all this happened only in Zhvil, but things are different here in Yerushalayim?" R' Gedaliah Moshe went on. In the dim bomb shelter, his face shone with a radiance that borrowed nothing from the feeble kerosene lamp. "Well, you all know my father's work with respect to *mikvaos*. Whenever he went to a *mikveh*, he would say, 'I'm going to settle my mind.' He would immerse himself frequently, reciting the names of the sick while in the water, and answering questions and offering counsel. People would stand outside and he would remain in the water for a long time, immersing himself and telling the questioner, 'Do this,' or 'Don't do that.' One day, they mentioned the name of a Jew who had become very ill and was dying. My father went to the *mikveh*, placed his clothing on a bench, and went down into the water.

"Unfortunately (or perhaps fortunately), he had placed his clothes beside those of a wealthy Jew from abroad who was immersing in the *mikveh* at that same time. The man, wrapped in a towel, came and saw that my father's simple clothes were touching his own crisp, pressed ones and that the man who had left them there was proceeding toward the *mikveh*. His face reddened with rage. 'You should be ashamed of yourself! How dare you place your rags near my clothes. Get them out of here at once!' Before anyone could react to his insolent words and explain whom he was addressing, he hurled my father's clothes angrily on the floor. My father walked calmly over to his clothes, picked them up, and placed them back on the bench, at a good distance from the tourist's sparkling ones. Then, without a word, he went to immerse himself.

"The moment he stepped out of the *mikveh*, my father told his companion, *Hagaon* R' Eliyahu Rata, *zt"l*, 'We've accomplished more with our humiliation today than with the *tevilah* itself.'

"On another occasion, a different Jew scolded him when, unfamiliar with my father's custom, he saw someone standing over him and asking question after question, which the Rebbe would answer after each immersion. 'What's the meaning of this? What kind of talk is this to take place in the *mikveh*?!'

"When my father did not look at him, the man became angry and began shouting, 'Reb Yid! We use the *mikveh* to dip and leave. This is no place for idle chatter!'

"This time, too, my father remarked to the man who had been asking him questions, 'We've accomplished much more than I thought at first — in the merit of the scorn.'

"And once, my father told me: 'Humiliation has the power to erase a death sentence!'"

⁓⊙∽

"Do you understand?" asked R' Gedaliah Moshe. "We are all in a difficult situation right now, and a very dangerous one. Seventy times a day, we hover between life and death, Heaven forbid. The mortar shells explode every hour, and no man's life is secure. *HaKadosh Baruch Hu* has sent us a cure before the dire decree: He has brought our salvation right here to this basement. This witless woman is heaping scorn and embarrassment on us without end. There is no need for us to go outside and risk our lives in order to seek the humiliation that will serve as a merit and save us. Hashem, in His infinite mercy, has brought the scorn right here to us. And you fools wish to take this miracle and throw it outside?"

⁓⊙∽

Actually, those who were close to the Rebbe understood that this was not his only reason for preventing the woman from being evicted; his fervor in the realm of "*bein adam l'chavero*" was like a devouring flame. All his life, R' Gedaliah Moshe was extremely scrupulous with regard to honoring his fellow man, and tried with all his might never to insult another Jew. When he lay on his deathbed, he said, "I am not afraid of my '*bein adam laMakom.*' *Baruch Hashem*, there I am completely clean. But '*bein adam l'chavero*' does worry me, lest I once wounded the honor of another Jew."

[Many thanks to the teller of this tale, my friend R' Shlomo Rosenbaum, *shlita*, son of the Zutchka Rebbe, *shlita*, and grandson of the hero of the story: the holy R' Gedaliah Moshe of Zhvil.]

Three Riddles — and Their Solutions

O NE OF THE FOREMOST CHABAD CHASSIDIM IN THE previous generation was R' Simchah Gorodetsky, *zt"l*, who — at the behest of his Rebbe, R' Yosef Yitzchak Schneerson — would travel on missions to disseminate Torah and *Yiddishkeit* throughout Russia.

R' Simchah was young when he began traveling the length and breadth of that enormous country at his Rebbe's command. Even before he was married, he had already traveled hundreds of kilometers, going from city to city and from town to town — to any place where there were Jews to be found.

This is how it came about.

When still a young *bachur*, R' Simchah studied in Yeshivas Tomchei Temimim, in Poltava. This was in the year 5683 (1923). The Russian economy was at an all-time low. The Bolsheviks had wrested the government from the Czarist monarchy, but the paradise they had promised after the revolution failed to materialize. In fact, things went from bad to worse. Complete chaos reigned in the land. Russia's citizens were hungry, the students of Yeshivas Tomchei Temimim no less than the rest.

It was during this period that the *bachur* Simchah Gorodetsky fell seriously ill. As his condition deteriorated, the *mashgiach,* R' Yechezkel Feigin, became alarmed. He took Simchah to a specialist in the city of Kharkov.

The doctor performed a thorough examination of the ailing youth, then called R' Feigin into the next room — out of Simchah's hearing — to render his conclusions.

"His heart is not functioning properly," he told the *mashgiach.* "His lungs have constricted and he is generally in very feeble health."

"What are his chances for recovery?" R' Feigin asked fearfully.

"To be perfectly frank, he has none. He has no chance of remaining alive!"

R' Feigin was stunned. He had known that the boy was very ill; that was why he had undertaken the trip to see the specialist. But the brutal truth was still very hard to accept. He breathed deeply, and when he had regained a measure of composure he returned to the next room, where his student waited.

"What did the doctor say?" Simchah asked the *mashgiach*.

R' Feigin tried to evade the question. "You need rest," he said. "Don't go back to yeshivah. Return to your parents' house and rest there until you get better."

He did not wish to worry the boy. On the other hand, it was clear to him that Simchah must not return to yeshivah in such a frail state of health.

Although Simchah had not heard the doctor speak of the gravity of his condition, he sensed it within himself. He made up his mind not to travel home but to go instead to his Rebbe, the holy R' Yosef Yitzchak Schneerson, then living in the city of Rostov. It was about a year since he had succeeded to his father's position as Rebbe.

The trip was not easily accomplished. Simchah was forced to argue at length with the *mashgiach*, R' Feigin. Both were adamant, but the boy's obstinacy overcame that of the *mashgiach*. They went to Rostov.

When they arrived at the Rebbe's house, R' Feigin entered first to speak privately with the Rebbe. He wished to tell the Rebbe the truth about Simchah's desperate situation, so that the Rebbe would urge the boy to hurry home to rest rather than return to yeshivah — a move that was liable to very rapidly make Simchah's health take a turn for the worse.

After the *mashgiach* finished his private interview, it was Simchah's turn to present himself to the Rebbe.

Before Simchah said a word, the Rebbe told him: "According to the *mashgiach*, R' Feigin, you must not continue learning in yeshivah."

The boy turned pale. The Rebbe's words landed on him like an exploding bomb.

The Rebbe continued. "And *I* am telling you" — his warm gaze caressed the boy — "that this is not so. You can remain a yeshivah student."

The color returned to Simchah's cheeks.

"But there is one difference between you and the other students," the Rebbe went on to explain. "The other *yeshivah bachurim* (the '*temimim*,' in the terminology of Chabad) learn a *seder* of eight hours of revealed Torah and four hours of Chassidus each day. You will have a different *seder*. Because the yeshivah is experiencing terrible financial difficulties, I wish to send you across the country, collecting money for the yeshivah's upkeep and improvement. And I promise you faithfully: If you heed what I say, you will be healthy and whole, *b'ezras Hashem*!"

And so, the sickly student, whose chances of survival had been rated by the great specialist as nil, set out to raise funds for the yeshivah from his fellow Jews. Not only did his extensive traveling not damage his health, they actually had the effect of curing him! Within a short time he had recovered his health completely, and the danger that had threatened his life vanished as though it had never been.

Ever since, R' Simchah had remained the Rebbe's faithful emissary. Every month or two he would return to report to the Rebbe on the state of the Jews he had met. He told the Rebbe everything he had seen and everything he knew: good things, and also painful ones. Whenever he had bad news to report, the Rebbe's eyes would fill with anguish and tears would fall from them, until R' Simchah's heart would be utterly broken. Unable to bear the Rebbe's pain a moment longer, he requested permission to transmit such news in writing.

Once, on his return to the Rebbe, he reported on his most recent trip. As they spoke, the *gabbai* entered and informed the Rebbe that the time had come for him to see the chassidim and others who were already lined up and waiting outside.

"Let them in," said the Rebbe.

R' Simchah began to retreat, wishing to leave the room when others entered to pour out their troubles to the Rebbe. But the Rebbe motioned for him to remain. "We're not done yet." R' Simchah felt extremely uncomfortable. How could he stay in the room and invade the privacy of those who had come to tell their personal troubles to their Rebbe? But he was a loyal chassid, and the Rebbe had ordered him to stay!

He found a compromise. He walked over to the very edge of the room, where he stood until the meetings were over. Many people came and went, and R' Simchah saw and heard them all. He placed a lock on his mouth and kept everything he knew sealed up within his heart.

Later in his life, however, R' Simchah related three unique episodes that he witnessed that day and their meaning, which he only came to understand after the passage of time.

～ ～

The first Jew entered the room. Approaching closer, he asked the Rebbe, "Rebbe, have I understood the sign correctly?"

The Rebbe nodded in agreement, saying, "Yes, yes, yes." The man heard the answer, left the room — and the first interview was over.

Right on his heels came a second Jew. His face was white as chalk and he was trembling violently. He emitted an emotional cry. "Rebbe, it's me!" With that, he sank to the floor in a dead faint. The *gabbai* was summoned. He came into the room, poured water on the man's face, and managed to rouse him from his faint. The man stood up, left the room — and the second meeting was concluded.

For the third meeting, a man came in whose appearance made it obvious that he did not belong to any chassidic group. He handed the Rebbe a *kvittel*, retaining a copy for himself, and together they went over all the questions written there. The Rebbe advised him what to do in each case, and how to act. But when he came to the last question, the Rebbe fell silent.

The man repeated the question.

"I'm not blind," the Rebbe responded. (In other words, "I've seen the question.")

The Rebbe did not wish to answer. But the questioner was stubborn, and begged him to respond. Finally, the Rebbe said, "I'm not deaf." (That is, "I heard you.")

Obstinately, the man importuned the Rebbe yet again not to leave him without an answer. At long last, the Rebbe said only, "Listen. There are many people waiting outside …"

At this point, the man understood that the Rebbe did not intend to answer his question. He left the room, shoulders bowed.

Three meetings — and three riddles.

Years passed. R' Simchah continued to travel across Russia. One day, as he walked down a street, whom did he see approaching but the man who had entered the Rebbe's room for the first private interview, the one who had asked the Rebbe if he had correctly understood "the sign"!

"I was in the Rebbe's room that day, and ever since then I've been wondering what it was all about. Perhaps you can explain to me what lay behind your mysterious words to the Rebbe," R' Simchah asked.

"I'll tell you the whole story," the man answered willingly enough.

"It happened many years ago, in the lifetime of the previous Rebbe (R' Shalom Ber Schneerson, father of R' Yosef Yitzchak). One day, the Rebbe summoned me and gave me a difficult mission. I was to go to Siberia and establish a Jewish presence in one of the cities there.

"Siberia! The ends of the earth! I had heard such terrible things about that place.

"Being a loyal chassid, I agreed at once. However, I did venture to ask one question. 'Rebbe, how long will I remain there? How will I know when my time is up?'

"The Rebbe answered with one short sentence: 'When the time comes, you will receive a sign!'

"I went out to a remote city in Siberia where I managed, with great difficulty, to establish a shul and the nucleus of a Jewish community. I drew many Jewish souls to a life of Torah and mitzvos, but my main satisfaction derived from a certain stubborn Jew who was very distant from *Yiddishkeit*, and who, with tremendous effort, I managed to turn into a genuine *baal teshuvah*. He abandoned his former life, which he had lived like a gentile, and became a true *oved Hashem*. We developed a rare and powerful friendship, a bond on the highest level. Neither one of us hid anything from the other.

"When the terrible news arrived of the Rebbe's death, I thought to myself that this might be the sign the Rebbe had mentioned, the sign that my mission here was over. I sent a letter to his son, who had taken the Rebbe's place, and asked if I could return to my own city and my own home. In response, the new Rebbe wrote something that stunned me: 'It seems to me my father said that, when the time comes, you will have a sign.' I trembled with wonder. The new Rebbe had not been present during my talk with his father, and I had never told him about it. How could he know what his father had told me in a private meeting?

"I continued my work in Siberia, and waited for a sign.

"One day, as I sat at home chatting with my good friend, the *baal teshuvah*, we heard a knock on the door. The mailman had brought me a letter from the Rebbe.

"I grew very excited. I washed my hands, wrapped my *gartel* around my waist, and, because there were no secrets between my friend and me, began to read the Rebbe's letter out loud.

"In the letter, the Rebbe had a request for me. He wanted me to help him in the matter of an *agunah* whose husband had deserted her. He described the absconding husband and asked me to do everything in my power to help locate the man.

"Why would the Rebbe turn to me, way out here in Siberia?" I wondered aloud.

"Up to that point, my eyes had been riveted to the letter and I had been unaware of what was happening around me. When I lifted them from the page, I was stunned.

"My friend's face was white as a sheet. He leaned back with sudden weakness, looking like a man in deep distress. Suddenly, I noticed that the Rebbe's description fit my friend perfectly!

"In short, my dear friend was none other than the deserting husband who had left his wife behind and made his way to Siberia. The Rebbe's eyes had seen all the way there! To send me a letter that would reach me at the precise moment when the man in question was seated beside me, so that I could compare the Rebbe's written description with the real face in front of me! On the spot, we both decided to travel together to see the Rebbe.

"The first man to walk into the Rebbe's room, as you stood by on the sidelines, was me. I asked the Rebbe, "Was this the sign?" and the Rebbe replied in the affirmative. The moment I left, my friend, the *baal teshuvah*, went in. Seeing the holiness shining from the Rebbe's countenance, he became very affected. All he could do was cry out, 'Rebbe, it's me!' before he fainted dead away."

But the secret of the third questioner was not yet revealed to R' Simchah.

⌒⌒⌒

Years passed.

One day, R' Simchah was walking down the street when he saw the "man with the *kvittel*" coming toward him. The moment he spotted R' Simchah, he recognized him as the man whom he had seen that day in the Rebbe's room.

He approached R' Simchah and asked eagerly, "Do you remember what took place during my meeting with the Rebbe that day?"

"Certainly," R' Simchah replied. He felt an enormous satisfaction because, at long last, he was about to learn the solution to that mystery.

The man cried out, "There's no one like him! There's no one like your Rebbe!" In his excitement, he repeated his own words. "No one in the world like your Rebbe!"

And then, he revealed his secret.

"As you will remember, I came with a note that was filled with questions. The Rebbe answered them all — except for the last one, which he refused to answer. Though I pleaded with him, he declined to have anything to do with the question, and I was at a loss to understand why. It was the most important question in the whole note! It was the main reason I had traveled all that way to see the Rebbe — to hear his opinion, despite the fact that I am not a chassid.

"Now I will tell you what the question said." The man smiled, enjoying the suspenseful interest in his listener's eyes. R' Simchah was clearly very curious. "This is what happened. At that time, I wished to remarry, and a woman was suggested who seemed to me a very likely prospect. I wanted to know if the Rebbe agreed. The question was obviously very close to my heart, as it touched my personal life.

"But, as you saw, the Rebbe evaded the question with all his might. He refused to answer. I couldn't understand it. But when I returned to my own city, I was shocked to learn how the Rebbe's eyes can send rays of light to distant places, and how all stands revealed before his gaze. The woman who had been suggested as a possible match for me had died suddenly, after I left town. At the time that I was standing in the Rebbe's room, she was no longer among the living. The Rebbe saw this with his *ruach hakodesh*, and did not wish to pain me by telling me. So he kept the news to himself and did not reveal the sad reality. But he also did not wish to answer the question, as it was no longer relevant."

R' Simchah Gorodetsky merited a long life. Eventually, he moved to Eretz Yisrael, where he established the Yeshivas HaBucharim in Kfar Chabad, which, after his death, was renamed Ohr Simchah in his honor. Four hundred students learn there to this very day!

[Many thanks to *Harav* Meyer Tabiv for this story, which he heard from *Harav* Michel Wissotsky of Kfar Chabad, who in turn heard it from R' Simchah himself.]

The Hidden Tzaddik From Tibet

THE INCIDENT TOOK PLACE AROUND PESACH, IN THE YEAR 5625 (1865). In those days, I, Akiva Yosef Schlesinger [this was the sainted *gaon*, author of the *Lev HaIvri*,] was living in the home of my father-in-law, the holy *gaon* R' Hillel Lichtenstein, *ztk"l*, of Kolomaya. We were in the midst of our final preparations for Pesach, and that night, after *bekidas chametz*, I went to bed very late.

Before dawn, I awoke with a *pasuk* on my lips: "*Ashrei tivchar u'tekarev yishkon chatzeirecha*" ("Praiseworthy is the one whom You choose and whom You draw near to dwell in Your courts"). I remembered the words of R' Yochanan, to the effect that if one awakens in the morning with a verse on his lips, this constitutes a small prophecy (*Berachos* 65b). All morning long, I waited expectantly for this prophecy to come true though I had no idea how it would come about.

A few hours later, after the *chametz* had already been burned, the riddle was answered. There was an unexpected knock on the door. We greeted the newcomer.

He was a tall, impressive-looking man with a black beard and blazing eyes. On his head he wore a turbanlike hat, of a sort not generally seen in our region, and he was wrapped in a light robe. From the first moment, I liked him. A sort of holy aura seemed to hover around him. He was welcomed into the house, where he set down his bundle and sat on the chair he was offered. His face was drawn and tired.

"My name is R' Eliezer ben R' Shimon Moshe," he began. "I have come from the land of Tibet, in Asia. My country lies between China and India, and I have come to you at the behest of my teachers and rabbis."

He turned to me. "I request a meeting with your father-in-law, Rabbeinu Hillel, *shlita*. My leaders have asked me to transmit a certain message to him."

I was very surprised. How did he know that I was R' Hillel's son-in-law and how, in far-off Tibet, had he even heard of my father-in-law, here in Hungary? And who were his "leaders"? The entire matter was veiled in mystery.

At once, I brought him to my father-in-law. Though the two had never met before and came from different countries and very different cultures, nevertheless they fell immediately into a flowing conversation, as though they had been friends for years.

"If I may, I would like to eat in your home over the Yom Tov," R' Eliezer requested of R' Hillel. "I must request permission to conduct my own Seder, alone, because my customs are different from yours."

My father-in-law willingly agreed. R' Eliezer, the mystery man, arranged to sleep in the home of a wealthy homeowner who lived nearby, and there he left his belongings. After a brief rest, he went to the shul and learned from a small *sefer* he had brought along, until the *davening* started.

When R' Hillel and his guest returned from shul, two separate Sedarim began. One was the usual Seder of my father-in-law, R' Hillel Lichtenstein; the other was the guest's.

What can I say? I had never seen a Seder like that in my life. Amazing! My father-in-law supplied him with matzos, wine, and all his other Seder needs, and the enigmatic guest conducted his own Seder. His face glowed as though lit by fire from within, and his entire Seder was like a flaming inferno. He read each portion of the Haggadah aloud, translating to himself in a language I could not identify. I listened to what he was saying, and heard him murmur, in Hebrew, words from the *Zohar* and *midrashim*, which he immediately translated into his own language. His quotes were accurate, word for word, letter for letter.

We tried to offer him delicacies for his pleasure, but the man would not accept the smallest thing from anyone. He was incredibly ascetic. He ate very little; it was no wonder he was so terribly thin. All skin and bones was he, but strong as a lion to carry out the will of his Father in Heaven.

I decided to uncover his secret. On one of the days of Chol HaMoed, as he sat in my father-in-law's home, I struck up a conversation with him, speaking both directly and indirectly.

R' Eliezer was a very smart man. He was very careful in what he said, and did not reveal anything that he did not wish to reveal. No question of mine succeeded in luring him over the line he had drawn for himself. But the picture he painted with his words was at the same time fascinating and cloaked in mystery.

R' Eliezer had been sent to Hungary by order of the "leaders" to whom he had referred earlier, on a mission which only my father-in-law knew. I knew nothing. The "leaders" was his name for the men who headed the communities of Jews scattered through the countries of the Far East. From R' Eliezer I learned that there were a great many Jews there. Merely in his own community, he said, there were 96,000 Jews, leading their lives the way the Jewish nation led theirs in the

Sinai desert. There were leaders appointed over every 10 men, every 50 men, every 100, and every 1,000. Over every 10 men was a minor leader known as the *Sar Asarah*. The others gave him one-tenth of their salaries and some income from the fruits of their fields and orchards. Thus absolved from earning a living, the *Sar Asarah* was able to wholly engage in Torah and service of Hashem. All of his time was devoted to spiritual matters. On Shabbos and Yom Tov, he would learn individually with the 10 men in his care, each according to his ability; this was apart from the *shiurim* that he delivered to them as a group. Every 10 Jews were united with their *sar*, and above him with their *Sar HaChamishim, Sar HaMeios,* and *Sar HaElef*.

The numerous communities that were run this way were all subject to the supreme authority of the leader of leaders — a great *mekubal* and possessor of *ruach hakodesh* who governed all the Jews in the Far East. This man decided all important matters, and nothing was done without consulting with him first. R' Eliezer did not reveal to me the name of this leader, but I understood from him that the leader had, with his *ruach hakodesh*, known my father-in-law without ever having seen him or heard of him in his life! Therefore, he had sent R' Eliezer to transmit several secret messages to R' Hillel.

The leader had a *sefer* called the *Aviv* — the acronym of *Acheinu Bnei Yisrael Bagolah* (Our Jewish Brethren in the Diaspora). The book contained instructions regarding conduct and behavior for all Diasporan Jews. I understood from R' Eliezer that this was actually a sort of yearly calendar that included practical rules for every holiday and festival. Apparently, my father-in-law had received a copy of this marvelous book but when I asked if I could see it, he became evasive. And so, I am unable to write down what the *sefer* included.

Over the course of the holiday, I had several conversations with R' Eliezer. He evinced a lively interest in the poetry of R' Eliezer HaKalir, and when I taught him those poems, he showed me how it is possible to interpret every one of them according to the secret Torah and the writings of the *Arizal*. He explained it all according to the *sefarim Eitz*

Chaim, Pri Eitz Chaim, Shemoneh Shearim, and similar works. With a radiant face, he sat and explained each of the poems in the light of such deep kabbalistic concepts that my mind could not encompass them all. He spoke of everything: of the roots of *gilgulim* (reincarnated souls) and the rotation of *gilgulim* in Heaven, and the methods of creation in the upper worlds, and the movements of the angels. Depths upon depth …

By expounding upon the meaning of soul roots, as brought down in the *sefer Shaar HaGilgulim* on the *Arizal's* generation, he revealed to me the secret of the reincarnation of souls in our own times. I reached the point where I felt that I could no longer follow him, and asked him to stop at a certain stage. But the little that I did manage to hear from him, I will reveal here. The *tzaddik* from Tibet knew all the *gilgulei neshamos* of the *gedolei hador* of our generation, and told me that some of the leaders of that portion of the Jewish world that was breaking away were reincarnations of the Shabtai Tzvi cult and its followers, for whom outside wisdom had proved a stumbling block and on whom, therefore, it had been decreed that they return again as outsiders. He revealed to me some secrets written in the *sefer* entitled *Aviv*:

R' Nosson Adler and his foremost *talmid*, R' Moshe Sofer, author of the *Chasam Sofer*, were secret *mekubalim*. R' Nosson Adler wished to expose the corruption of the *shochtim* in his city of Frankfurt-am-Main, and to deflect the *Sitra Achra* that had overpowered these corrupt *shochtim*. Had R' Nosson Adler actualized his wish, the *Mashiach* would have come, but the enemy set some of Frankfurt's butchers upon him, forcing him to flee the city. His *talmid*, R' Moshe Sofer, ran after him on foot for a considerable distance, as is known.

About the author of the *Noda B'Yehudah*, the *sefer* said, "And his eye was like an electric eye," and about R' Meshulam Igra of Tismanitz it said that he had the soul of a *saraf*. The *sefer* warned that Bohemia — the area known today as Czechoslovakia, Austria, and portions of Germany — is stamped with the seal of the Satan, and one must protect himself by not passing through there. Nevertheless, though their sins were grievous, nothing stands in the way of *teshuvah*. About the city of Prague, it said that as long as the Noda B'Yehudah lived there, the Satan was not able to enter except as a guest; now, however, he reigned there in full strength, and the destruction began when they introduced a cantor with a choir and organ into Prague shuls. The *sefer* said that prayer in the new Reform "temples," that had introduced the organ into shul, falls into the category of a prayer of abomination.

$$\sim\!\!\sigma\,\odot\!\!\sim$$

Ruach hakodesh emerged from the throat of R' Eliezer of Tibet. Glancing at a book — any book — from the outside, he knew at once whether or not it was a holy work. With my own eyes I witnessed the way he once looked at two books, lying side by side. They appeared identical in every way. They were of the same thickness and both had a black binding. R' Eliezer kissed one *sefer*, while he hurled the second onto the floor in disgust. I opened both books. The *sefer* that he had kissed was a *Midrash Rabbah*, while the one he had thrown on the floor was a work of the Haskalah! It had been printed in Hebrew letters and looked just like a holy book. But our guest knew the secret of "sniffing out" *yiras Hashem*.

I've been very careful not to write anything too extraordinary about the visit of that mysterious guest from Tibet. But there is one fact that I cannot leave out.

For a long period of time, we had been "honored" by visits from a large, black dog that entered the house like an uninvited guest. All of our efforts to evict it were useless. It did not harm anyone or anything in the house. It only followed my father-in-law around, everywhere he went. When my father-in-law returned home, so did the black dog. It would park itself under the table and wait for my father-in-law to finish his meal. It ran after him to the *beis medrash* and waited outside until he had finished *davening*, then raced after him again all the way home. The black dog was rejected and beaten by various members of the household, but no stick or strap made the slightest impression on it. It seemed to crave closeness with my father-in-law, who didn't know what to do with the creature.

Such was the situation until the arrival of our visitor, R' Eliezer of Tibet.

On the very first day of Pesach, R' Eliezer noticed the dog walking after my father-in-law. He followed the animal with his eyes and turned to me in surprise. "Why doesn't your father-in-law do something? That dog carries the soul of a person who had sinned and is waiting for your father to rectify its soul. So long as he doesn't help, it won't rest easy!"

"I don't know who it is," I replied in astonishment.

R' Eliezer was even more amazed. "Don't you remember *Harav* So-and-so, son of So-and-so?"

I slapped my forehead and cried excitedly, "Of course I remember. He was a 'Rav' of the *maskilim*. Very distant from *yiras Shamayim*, and he always spoke secularly."

"Your father-in-law cursed him," R' Eliezer said gently, as though he had been there to witness the event.

"True!" I confirmed. "My father-in-law saw that he was destroying *Yiddishkeit*, and cursed him vigorously."

"And, as a result, he died a short time later," our guest told me. "And it was decreed that he return as a barking dog, because he spoke foreign tongues. People who speak *lashon hara* also return as barking dogs. (It also says in the *sefer Yalkut Reuveni* that one who speaks *lashon hara* or informs on other Jews is reincarnated as a barking dog.) You have an obligation to tell this to your father-in-law."

But I did not dare tell such a terrible thing to my father-in-law. Instead, I waited to see how the matter would play itself out.

Just two days later, on one of the days of Chol HaMoed, my father-in-law took a trip on a mitzvah-related matter. He set out and, as usual, the dog followed. Several hours later, my father-in-law returned from his mission. Looking out the window, I saw a carriage pulling up in front of the house. I went out at once to welcome him. Before my very eyes, something amazing occurred.

The moment my father-in-law stepped out of the carriage, the black dog bounded forward to greet him. It bent its knees as though bowing, whimpered, seized the hem of my father-in-law's coat — and kissed it! Had I not seen it for myself, I would not have believed it.

My father-in-law, too, was stunned. He did not know how to react to the dog's strange behavior. At this point, I felt bound to share with him what the mysterious man from Tibet had told me.

My father-in-law became very excited. He looked at the dog kneeling before him and told me humbly, "I don't know what *tikkun* (rectification) to give this reincarnated dog."

I agreed to serve as the middleman between my father-in-law and the visitor from Tibet, who told me at once what needed to be done in order to bring the unfortunate soul to a state of rectification.

My father-in-law did as R' Eliezer had instructed, and from that moment the black dog disappeared and was not seen again.

After the holiday, our visitor parted from us to continue on to the city of Kashoi, and from there to Poland and Russia, on the secret mission of his "leaders" in Tibet. Together with seventy of my yeshivah students, I accompanied him as he left. We gazed at his retreating form as it dwindled into the distance, until he had vanished from sight.

I have written here only a small part of the secrets and amazing things that I witnessed during that Pesach of the year 5625 together with my holy father-in-law, when we merited a glimpse into an unknown part of the Jewish world in the Far East.

[Adapted from the memoirs of *Hagaon Hakadosh* R' Akiva Yosef Schlesinger, author of the *Lev HaIvri*, as they appeared in a small anthology entitled *Shimru Mishpat: Concepts, Poems, Essays*, printed in Jerusalem about 90 years ago. My thanks to R' Shmuel Tzvi Pearl, who gave us access to this rare volume.

"The mystery man" is the way R' Akiva Yosef referred to the visitor from Tibet in his writings. The year was 5625. Sikus was the city in which R' Hillel Lichtenstein lived before Kolomaya. He refers to the episode in his *sefer Toras Yechiel al HaTorah*, in *Parashas Noach*, p. 90, and *Parashas Balak*, p. 320. From his writings, it appears that the matter made a powerful impression on him — and that he wrote down far less than he chose not to write. And what he did write was just the tip of the iceberg. Many more secrets remained hidden and cloaked.]

The Rebbe's Accounting

Physical suffering was the lot of the holy Rebbe, R' Yitzchak Isaac Rosenbaum of Zutchka, *zt"l* (who passed from this world on 14 Tammuz 5760). Looking at him, all were able to see the fulfillment of our Sages' words: "He whom *HaKadosh Baruch Hu* desires, He oppresses with suffering" (*Berachos* 5). After surviving the Holocaust, he developed a leg ailment that frequently caused him great pain. He kept his suffering to himself, so that even his family and closest friends had no idea how much he was suffering. He always wore an expression of tranquility, even when — according to professional medical testimony — he ought to have been screaming in agony. Not only did he not sigh or give any sign of his suffering, he would chat calmly with the doctors as though he knew nothing of pain. This tremendous courage was a constant thread throughout all of his long and Torah-filled life.

After years of suffering, the condition of his legs deteriorated. Before, he had suffered from painful sores. Now they developed abscesses. After trying various treatments, the doctors conceded defeat. Just one hope remained: to amputate both legs in order to save the Rebbe's life.

"It's a difficult thing, and we understand your anguish," the doctors explained to the shaken family. "But there's no choice. If we do not amputate, the infection will spread to his entire body. Which do you choose? A father whose intact body is lying in a grave or a father without legs, but alive?"

The words were harsh, and the choice was harsher. But, as the doctors had said, there really was no choice. The Rebbe's family understood the gravity of the situation only too well. With heavy hearts, they agreed to the operation that would remove both of the

Rebbe's legs, and decided to share that decision with the Rebbe himself.

The Rebbe received the news without blinking an eye, as though they were not speaking about him at all. Outwardly, he did not react, though we may assume that he was feeling vastly different on the inside. Who can hear such a thing and remain unshaken? Yet his self-control was total, like that of a young lion at the height of his power.

The Rebbe lay in his bed in Ichilov Hospital, while around him preparations were being made for the difficult operation scheduled for the next day.

Night fell. The Rebbe had already *davened Minchah* and *Maariv.* Now he began to conduct a *cheshbon hanefesh,* an accounting with himself.

The *cheshbon hanefesh* of a *gadol!*

Out in the hospital corridors, the usual bustle of activity was taking place. Medicine-laden carts were being wheeled from room to room, where doctors were examining their patients and nurses were distributing medicines. This one received one pill and that one, two. This patient received an injection while another had his dressing changed.

And all the while, the Rebbe lay in his sickbed and conducted his personal accounting.

Suddenly, he rose up in a turmoil. Yes! He knew why this terrible thing had befallen him. He put on his clothes and slipped out of the room. Several minutes later he was standing in the noisy street, outside the hospital gates, an arm outflung to hail a taxi.

"Where to?" asked the driver.

"Rechov Hapalmach 40, in the Yad Eliyahu neighborhood," answered the Rebbe.

Back in his room, several white-clad medical staff had just come in to give him the appropriate medicines and instructions for his upcoming grueling surgery. To their shock, they found his bed empty. A search was conducted, but the Rebbe had vanished.

The hospital was in an uproar. Had such a thing ever been heard of? A patient fleeing the hospital on the night before an operation that was slated to save his life?!

The doctors were angry. Some of them, who had come to recognize the patient's spiritual greatness, were astonished but silent. They realized that there must be some reason behind the Rebbe's sudden disappearance. Soon enough, they surmised, they would be privy to the mystery that lay behind this strange event.

But none of them knew the extent of his courage or the extent of his self-sacrifice.

The Rebbe had already demonstrated both these traits decades earlier — under far more difficult circumstances. Under the auspices of the Nazi brutality …

∽ଡ଼୵

At that time, the Rebbe had been living in the city of Chernowitz, in Bukovina (the Ukraine). The accursed Nazis had already spread their tentacles into the area; now they marched into Chernowitz as well. The Rebbe and his family fled the city, traveling a great distance on foot until they reached the Ukrainian border. Slipping secretly across the border, they found refuge in a house in the city of Balta.

But here, too, they were not permitted to remain safe for long. They were like a man who flees the bear, only to encounter the leopard. The Germans had reached the Ukraine.

SS soldiers went house to house, seizing men and drafting them into forced labor. One day they arrived at the Rebbe's house. Being told that a great rabbi lived there, they politely told him that, by military orders, the family of "*rabbiners*" were not to be touched.

In a flash, the news spread throughout the district. Within days, the Rebbe's home was transformed into a shelter housing forty-five Jews. There was no safer place to be than the "*rabbiner's*" house. No one would check here or recruit men for forced labor that would end with a bullet to the heart.

When dealing with beasts of prey like the Nazi Gestapo, however, even a refuge like the Rebbe's house was not safe for long. The Nazi thirst for Jewish blood was insatiable. When all the other houses had been emptied of their residents, they would return to the one place that had been granted an exemption.

One day, as the Rebbe sat and pored over his *Gemara*, armed German soldiers burst into the house. Apart from their rifles, they held thick ropes, whose tragic purpose would soon become all too evident. No one knew why they had been so abruptly summoned. Perhaps a rumor had leaked that the Rebbe's house had become refuge to scores of Jews. With deafening shouts, the soldiers passed from room to room to flush out their prey.

At first, the soldiers paid no attention to the Rebbe sitting and learning at his table. They merely passed through his room on their way to the rest of the house. But when they had been everywhere else, they returned to the Rebbe's room.

The rebbetzin and the children sensed danger, and raced to the Rebbe's room to find him surrounded by soldiers. At the sight, they burst into heartrending cries.

"*Shtill* (silence)!" screamed the captain. "You're disturbing us."

The rebbetzin and children were chased out of the house with brandished weapons. The Rebbe remained alone with the armed soldiers.

The spectacle of the Rebbe, whose unflappable calm did not abandon him for a moment, enraged the Nazi captain. He snatched the *Gemara* and slammed it shut. "Let's see what you do now, *rabbiner*," he snarled mockingly.

The Rebbe said nothing. A small *sefer Tehillim* sprouted in his hand. His eyes scanned the precious words and his lips began to move.

"And what are you doing now?" the captain shouted in a fury. He could not bear to see how unafraid the Rebbe was. Usually, people cowered in fear of him and his men. He enjoyed seeing their wide, stricken eyes, the white tongue vainly licking lips gone terribly dry; and their rapid breathing was music to his ears. But the Rebbe showed no sign of fear. He demonstrated a level of self-control that even the captain's trained soldiers had not achieved.

The Rebbe stopped his whispering. Quietly, he answered, "I am praying to G-d."

"You have a G-d?" The captain grew angrier still.

The Rebbe looked him firmly in the eye. "Certainly."

The Nazi smiled satanically. "Let's just see about that!" he crowed triumphantly. Snatching up the little *Tehillim*, he threw it out the window. "Now we'll see if your G-d can save you."

His fingers caressed the thick rope. Quick as a wink, a noose appeared at one end. He approached the Rebbe and stood poised to drape the noose over his neck.

Even now, with the Nazi about to hang him and end his life, the Rebbe evinced no sign of fear. Nevertheless, he did not passively submit to the wicked man's will. He tried to resist the murderous officer, but the German was far stronger than he and easily managed to subdue the Jewish *rabbiner*. Around the Rebbe's neck went the suffocating "necktie," firmly knotted.

The situation seemed hopeless. The Rebbe was alone with five or six young soldiers and their leader, who surrounded him on all sides. His life was lost — apparently.

The officer adjusted the knot around the Rebbe's neck, stood the Rebbe up on a chair, and screamed, "I permit you to pray to your G-d before I push away this chair from under you. Let's see your G-d save you now!"

"Needless to say, I was not afraid at all," the Rebbe was to say fifty years later to his honored visitor, the Vizhnitzer Rebbe, *shlita*, who had come to celebrate the miracle of his rescue on that day, the 5th of Nissan, 5754.

"And how was the Zutchka Rebbe saved?" asked the Vizhnitzer Rebbe, deeply moved.

"Here is how it happened ..." The Zutchka Rebbe continued his reminiscences half a century later.

As the Rebbe began to whisper the words of the *viduy*, the Nazi commander gazed upward, like the wicked Titus in the *Kodesh HaKodashim* in his time. He seemed to be looking to see where the heavenly messenger would appear from, to rescue the Jew whose fate he held in his hands.

The Rebbe silently whispered the *viduy* until he came to the words "*rachum v'chanun*," while the Nazi continued to lift his eyes up, heavenward. Suddenly, he said, "Enough. That's enough," still gazing upward.

No one will ever know what took place in that cruel man's heart that day. But the miracle happened. A moment later, he stated, as though to himself, "All right. We'll leave him alive!"

The noose was removed from around the Rebbe's neck, and he was permitted to step from the chair. His life had been handed back to him.

But it wouldn't do to let him off scot-free. One of the soldiers thrust a pair of scissors into the captain's hand. At least let the rabbi's *peyos* be cut off, as was their practice.

To the soldiers' surprise, the captain seemed to have had a change of heart. He pushed away the scissors and yelled angrily at the soldier, "I said no, so it's no!"

Alarmed, the soldier beat a hasty retreat.

On their way out, another soldier approached the commander and asked, "Why is today different from any other day? Why did you leave the Jew alive?"

The captain was not ashamed to admit the truth: "I was afraid that G-d would punish me!"

So someone *had* been afraid in that room, only it wasn't the feeble, unarmed Jew. It had been the powerful Nazi who had been afraid. The Jewish spirit had triumphed over evil.

Nearly thirty years later, a different sort of danger threatened the Rebbe. The danger did not emanate from a Nazi soldier this time, but from the hands of the hospital surgeons who wished to save his life.

The taxi arrived at the Rebbe's *beis medrash* on Rechov Hapalmach 40, in the Yad Eliyahu neighborhood. The Rebbe paid the driver and bid him farewell. With an energetic step he entered the *beis medrash* and went directly to one side, where the bookbinder's tools stood. He pulled out a spool of thick thread and a needle, then went over to the *aron kodesh*. Opening the doors, he removed one of the *Sifrei Torah* standing in the second tier — the inner row.

He placed the *Sefer Torah* on the table and, with unnatural strength, unrolled it to its beginning. When he came to the edge of the first panel, he checked the stitches. They were extremely frayed and consequently the parchment was almost detached from the wooden pole.

The Rebbe threaded the needle with the thick thread and began to sew the panel, until it was firmly attached to the wood. He rewound the Torah to the end of *Sefer Devarim*, then repeated his sewing on the other side.

Now the *Sefer Torah* was fixed at both ends. The ragged panels were firmly attached to the "*atzei chayim.*"

He replaced the *Sefer Torah* in its place and returned to the hospital the same way he had left it. Quietly, he slipped into his bed, and waited.

Late that night, word spread throughout the hospital that the patient who had run away had "returned of his own free will, and placed himself in his doctors' hands." When asked why he had left and why he had returned, the Rebbe said nothing.

The next morning, when the surgeon came to his room shortly before the scheduled surgery, the Rebbe surprised him by saying, "I'd like you to check my legs again."

To the doctor, this was a useless request — an attempt to deny reality. He tried to explain this to the patient, but the Rebbe told him firmly, "If you do not re-examine my legs, I will not agree to have this operation under any circumstances!"

"What's this?" the doctor said angrily. "Are you giving me orders?"

The situation was saved by one of the hospital administrators, a pious Jew by the name of R' Nosson Brecher, who had been a chassid of the Rebbe's father, R' Isamar, the old Nadvorner Rebbe. R' Nosson was summoned to the Rebbe's room where, after hearing the argument, he threw his weight into backing up the Rebbe's request for a re-examination.

The doctors' surprise was boundless.

A slight improvement was clearly evident in the condition of his legs. The infection was receding. Amputation was no longer urgent and immediate, as it had been before. The doctors recommended a simple, conservative treatment using ointments and bandages.

Several days later, the Rebbe was released from the hospital — walking on his own two feet!

"Why are you surprised?" the Rebbe asked his stunned family and friends. "That night, before the scheduled operation, I did a *cheshbon hanefesh*. Our teachers have taught us that a Jew is obligated to think about why he has arrived at the situation in which he finds himself. I conducted my own personal accounting and suddenly remembered a *Sefer Torah* in the second row in the *aron kodesh* of our *beis medrash*. For some time now, I've known that the parchment panels were practically detached from the wooden poles. I wanted to deal with this at once, but because of my crowded schedule I did not manage to get around to it.

"I thought to myself: *HaKadosh Baruch Hu* deals with us *middah k'neged middah*. I neglected to attach the *sefer* to its 'feet' — so I, the one responsible, was struck with an appropriate consequence. It was as though *Middas HaDin* was crying out, 'Just as you did not attach the *atzei chayim*, so, too, will your legs be detached from your body!' Heaven forbid. So I hurried over to quickly make the repairs. And, indeed, when the *atzei chayim* were attached to the Torah, my legs were no longer in danger of being cut off!"

The River Rises

T HE SUN WAS SETTING OVER CRACOW, CASTING GENEROUS orange rays over the waters of the Vistula River as they wound their way through the city. Winter was over. That year, endless snows had fallen, to the point where the populace had despaired of ever seeing the last of the pristine white flakes slated to end as mire beneath the feet of man and beast. In the final analysis, however, it was a good thing that the snow had been so plentiful, for as winter drew to an end the sun's warmth began to thaw the heaps and banks of snow so that they streamed toward the river from every direction. The melted snow raised the Vistula's water level until it ran strong and powerful.

Berel the *shochet* and Feivel the tailor came out of the *beis medrash* at the same time, to catch a breath of fresh air and to stretch their limbs. Berel glanced at the water and started. "Look at that river," he said fearfully. "Look how red its water is."

Feivel laughed. "Berel, Berel, see how far your profession has colored your thoughts? You see blood everywhere."

Berel stared at the racing river, then repeated forcefully, "If only I were joking, Feivel. We live among gentiles and are worth less than a garlic peel in their eyes. I've learned from experience that anything bad that happens can only be to our detriment. No rainfall? It's the Jews' fault. Too much rain or snow? The Jews suffer for it. It's like a law of nature. I see the rushing water and remember the eternal words of Dovid HaMelech, *a"h*: '*Lulei Hashem shehayah lanu b'kum aleinu adam ... azei hamayim shetafunu ... azei avar al nafsheinu hamayim hazeidonim*' ('Had not Hashem been with us when men rose up against us ... then the waters would have inundated us ... then they would have surged across our soul — the treacherous waters'). Feivel, I'm getting away from this river, lest the treacherous waters rise up against us!"

Again, Feivel the tailor laughed out loud. "Berel, I'm afraid that maybe one of the oxen you slaughtered yesterday attacked you and banged your head a little ... Or maybe one of the cows you slaughtered with your sharp knife, so that it might be kosher and placed in a Jewish *cholent* pot, came to you in a dream and demanded your blood. Eh, Berel?"

"Feivel, I'm speaking from a pained heart, and you're making fun of me?" The *shochet* sighed. "I am a man of sensibility, and my heart foretells something bad."

"Berel," the tailor persisted, "go to the end of the *Tehillim* you quoted. See what it says next: '*Baruch Hashem shelo nesananu teref l'shineihem … hapach nishbar va'anachnu nimlatnu*' ('Blessed is Hashem, Who did not present us as prey for their teeth … the snare broke, and we escaped'). Don't worry. No evil will befall us."

Berel gazed glumly at the reddish waters, splashing in the air and foaming into frothy waves.

"If only that were true," he sighed.

Only two days after this conversation between *shochet* and tailor on the riverbank, Berel was proved right.

It was noon, on a day in early Nissan. Through the heavy iron gates of the large Catholic cathedral came a group of theological students. It was a gentile holiday, and the day had been chosen for the distribution of the students' certificates. Dressed in black cassocks, they had the appearance of a flock of crows. They passed through the large market square, talking to one another in loud voices amid bursts of raucous laughter. Several of them were in possession of small bottles of whiskey hidden in the sleeves of their cassocks.

Zalman Zeidel, the *melamed*, concluded his lesson in the narrow room in his house. He brought his hand down on a wooden board as a sign that his students were free to go.

Nine boys happily left the *melamed's* house and started for their homes. Their curly black *peyos*, pointed yarmulkes, flapping *tzitzis,* and bright, intelligent eyes seemed to send a challenge to the flock of Christian seminary students they passed.

"Look at those Jews," one of them called. "How small they are, and how insolent."

"What's the problem?" his friend asked, a bubble of drink appearing at the corner of his mouth and dribbling down his chin. "Have they done something to you?"

"They sure did!" rejoined the first. "They hung our savior on the cross! Look at their brazen air. Walking among us as though Cracow belonged to them. We've got to teach them a lesson!"

As the innocent children carefully sidestepped a horse that was pawing the road nervously beneath the hot sun — staying well clear of the kicking hooves — the two black-robed students sneaked up behind them, a malicious gleam in their eyes.

Shmerel, son of Eliezer the bath attendant, was the first to fall victim to the students' wickedness. He was trotting after his friends on his shorter legs when he was suddenly seized with hands of iron. The gentiles covered his mouth and lifted him up into the air. Before Shmerel could cry out more than the single word, "*Shema*," he was tossed into the river.

His friends did not notice his absence, or see his hands waving frantically above the current. And so, none of them were able to explain to Slava, Eliezer's wife, why her son did not return home that day.

The night that fell on the home of Eliezer and Slava brought tears and wailing. Many of the Jews in Cracow's Jewish quarter hastened to help search for the lost boy, but they searched in vain. Shmerel was nowhere to be found.

While Cracow's Jews had no idea of the tragedy that had taken place in their midst, the Christian students, well pleased with the success of their ploy, began planning a second drowning. Why not? It was so easy to snatch a helpless Jewish child and throw him into the turbulent river and to watch, with satanic smiles, how the young boy, unable to swim, thrashed despairingly in the water until he succumbed.

The next afternoon, the Catholics lay in wait for Zalman Zeidel's students as they returned home for lunch. Yankele, son of Chaim Chaikel the water carrier, and Lipman Meir, son of Riva the widow, were chosen as the next sacrificial victims: pure, innocent children, untouched by sin. Because they had no idea what had happened to their friend the day before, they did not know who or what to fear.

Once again the Jewish boys passed close by the flock of crows. All too soon, the two children were screaming with all their might in the river, as they battled feebly against the treacherous waters.

This time, their friends heard the cries. Their stricken eyes were forced to watch their friends' desperation and see them sink to their deaths.

That day, the Jewish ghetto of Cracow was like a pressure cooker. The cat was out of the bag now. The disappearance of little Shmerel the day before was now explained. To everyone's horror, they later learned that, at that same moment, other Catholic students had stood all along the river, tossing another ten Jewish children into its depths. Cracow was in an uproar.

The city's Jews gathered together, as Jews will do in times of trouble, for a day of fasting and reciting *Selichos* in shul. "*Rabbosai!* Evil hands have taken hold of us," cried R' Reuven, the community leader. "The holiday of Pesach, which is fast approaching, reminds our enemy of what Pharaoh did in his time — tossing every male child into the river ..."

Every eye was raised to the eastern wall where, wrapped in his *tallis* and weeping bitterly, sat the *mekubal* R' Eliyahu, author of *Hatzoref*. He was a holy man, one of Cracow's great rabbinical figures of three centuries ago. Members of the community told amazing stories about him. Those in the know claimed that he was conversant with the secrets of practical kabbalah and could modify nature at will. The community hoped that he would reveal his powers and save them in a miraculous fashion.

But R' Eliyahu did not choose to exercise his supernatural ability then. He set his sights on the down-to-earth ways of nature. "We must follow our forefathers' example," he told Cracow's fearful residents. "They made efforts and spoke in a language of appeasement. So must we."

The heads of the community heeded his advice and walked with quaking knees to the large cathedral, closing their eyes at the sight of crosses and statuary on every side. They reached the lecture hall, where they spoke to the student leaders and even with their teachers, pleading, persuading.

The students mocked them. They denied any involvement in the drowning of Jewish children in the river, and chased the Jews from their seminary with curses and epithets.

The community heads then had recourse to the law, as instructed by R' Eliyahu the *mekubal*. But, like the students, the law-enforcement officials were not prepared to hear their complaints and treated them with total dismissal. Next, the Jews turned to government ministers, but the Catholic students were so powerful that the government itself feared them, for the students were backed by the mighty Catholic Church that intimidated all of Poland.

Meanwhile, the students continued to attack Jewish children. Cracow's Jewish population lived in terror. Any Jewish child walking through the city's streets without adult protection was liable to find himself in the depths of the river.

Their anguish reached the heavens.

R' Eliyahu saw how dire the situation had become, and that there would soon not be a Jewish home in the city without its dead. He said: "They are coming at us with sword and spear. We will come in the Name of Hashem, G-d of Israel."

He closeted himself in his room, putting his exalted secrets into practice and doing what must be done to save Jewish children who had never tasted sin. Then he went down to the river along with two of the city's rabbis. Standing on the riverbank, he cried:

"River! River! I hereby decree that any child tossed into your depths be spat out at once, still alive, and that you raise your waters at once against the man who threw him in. Wash over him with your angry waves and swallow him alive."

He finished speaking and returned home with his companions.

The next day, several of the Catholic students left the cathedral and stepped into the city streets. They hid behind a pile of rubbish for a while, until they saw a small Jewish child approaching them, alone.

They pounced, seized the boy in their strong arms, and hurled him cruelly into the river.

The students stood on the riverbank to derive bloodthirsty enjoyment from the child's agony and drowning. To their shock, the water rose from its usual confines, climbing onto the bank and roaring toward them. A wave swept over the student who had thrown the Jewish child in, engulfing him and sweeping him away as though he had been no heavier than a walnut shell. The student bellowed with fear until, a moment later, he vanished from sight and sank to the depths.

The Jewish lad, meanwhile, floated on the water's surface until he reached the riverbank. From there he climbed back onto the street, safe and whole. Shaking himself to get rid of some of the water that soaked his clothes, he raced home as fast as his short legs could carry him.

From that day, things were different in Cracow. Whenever any Jewish child was tossed into the water, the river would rise in a mighty storm to seize the wicked student and drag him back into the depths, while the child escaped unscathed.

The theological students were afraid. But they were also wicked, filled with hatred toward the Jews and insatiable in their murderous hunger. They began to weave plots for killing Jewish children without incurring the river's wrath. They understood that the Jews' wise men must have sworn the river to exact vengeance for the killings by drowning the student who threw the children in. But they had not sworn the river to do the same to someone who drowned a Jewish child by other means or messengers.

The ambushes continued. The Catholic students grabbed a few Jewish children and threw them into the river from a distance, using a form of slingshot that hurled the child straight into the water without the student's touching him. But the ploy proved useless. The same water that spat the child out onto dry land swept furiously over the student and his friends who had sent him into the river, sending them to their doom.

Seeing that the G-d of the Jews was fighting their battle, the students were filled with terror. There came a grateful lull in the lives of Cracow's Jews.

For two years, no evil befell a Jewish child. Then came *bedikas chametz* night. Immediately after sunset, several young Jewish men walked out of shul with their children, heading to the spring of water just outside the city walls. They drew *mayim chayim* with clean earthenware vessels, and walked quietly and confidently back to the city.

The night was peaceful. Darkness fell and the mid-month moon shone with brilliant purity. From the distance came the whisper of the Vistula River as it flowed slowly beneath the white moonlight.

Suddenly, a bloodcurdling scream split the air.

"What happened?" the young men asked each other, turning toward the river.

"That was a child's voice," said Shmelke, son of Michael the bookbinder. "Tatty, I think that was Gedaliah's voice — my school friend!"

His father removed the heavy jug from his shoulder and peered at the river, as though trying to understand the meaning of the terrible scream.

In the silence and the darkness, they all stood and waited. They were afraid to utter a word. Only Shmelke whimpered in terror, and whispered to his father, "Tatty, those evil men have drowned Gedaliah in the river!"

"Don't open your mouth to the Satan," his father warned, shushing him. But his son's fears had affected him. Confused and frightened, they returned home and put the jugs of water in a corner till the morning, when they would be used to bake *matzos mitzvah* on *erev Pesach*.

Word of the tragedy reached them that same night. Young Shemlke had been right. Bloodthirsty Catholic students had ambushed Cracow's children in the dark. Gedaliah had wandered away from his father in the open field and strayed right into the students' wide-open arms. In a flash, he was hurled into the Vistula, and the river — apparently having no recollection of its orders from the *mekubal*, R' Eliyahu — had drowned the child in its waves without exacting revenge on the evil one who had thrown him in.

The next day, after the *chametz* was burned, R' Eliyahu went out to the river, followed by all the Jews of Cracow. Their gentile neighbors, seeing the enormous procession making its way to the river, hastened to join the throng.

R' Eliyahu stood on the riverbank, closed his eyes, and said:

"River! River! You have forgotten the oath to which I swore you. You drowned a Jewish child and did not exact vengeance on his enemy. I hereby decree on you, in the name of Hashem, that you will uproot from your usual route, which you have followed since the six days of Creation, and will flow in a different place, following a different route, far from the city. Someplace where those who hate us will not be able to torture us and drown our children."

Before the eyes of thousands of witnesses, both Jews and non-Jews, the river moved from its accustomed place with a mighty roar, and its waters began to seek a new path. They flowed away until they found a new channel, far from the city — leaving behind in Cracow a damp, swampy riverbed that quickly dried.

For years afterward, Cracow's residents would point out the Vistula River's old channel until, in time, large, beautiful houses were erected on the spot, and the story was forgotten.

[This story was told by *Harav Hakadosh* R' Yitzchak of Skvere, and is cited in his name in the s*efer, Ma'asiyos U'maamarim Yekarim,* Zitomir, 5663. For more on the holy R' Eliyahu, author of *Hatzoref,* see *Shem Hagedolim Hechadash.*]

In the Merit of Shabbos

D AVID EISBERG WOULD NEVER FORGET THE MOMENT HE heard about the collapse of the Twin Towers. He had risen early that morning, as he did on all the days when *Selichos* were recited, and after *davening*, he still had a full hour left in which to learn the *daf yomi*. Glancing at his watch when the *shiur* was over, he planned the start of his workday. David was a veteran employee of the General Maintenance Corporation, one of the largest firms in the state of Georgia and a leading business in Atlanta. (Note: This story is completely true, though all details and names have been changed, including company names.)

In Georgia, as in many states, when someone has a leaky faucet, or a broken windowpane, or some sort of electrical problem at home, he does not summon an electrician now and a plumber another time. There is a single phone number to dial: that of a maintenance firm responsible for the building or for the general area. The firm would dispatch the appropriate worker to deal with the problem. David had worked for General Maintenance for years, and was well versed in every kind of home repair and maintenance job.

David sat behind the steering wheel of his car and consulted his electronic daily calendar. The first job that awaited him was in a large apartment building, where a water main had burst and had been fixed the day before. An hour ago, however, a woman residing in the house had called, furious, to complain that water was once again leaking into her apartment.

He arrived at the building and waited by the elevator. Outside, he heard someone yell hysterically about a "plane crashing into the building."

David raced outside to the street. "What happened?" It wasn't possible that a plane had crashed into *this* building. There had been no unusual noise in the last few seconds.

A group of people had collected on the sidewalk, all talking animatedly. He approached at a rapid clip. The woman could wait a little longer for her repair job. He had to find out what had happened.

That's how David Eisberg learned that a large passenger plane had taken a self-destructive flight right into one of New York's Twin Towers. Shortly thereafter, as he was trying to figure out the nature of the water-main problem and why the pipe continued dripping, David heard that a second plane had crashed into the second tower. Along with the rest of the United States, and the world, he listened in shock and horror to the unbelievable news that both towers — once viewed as the symbol of America's pride and strength — had crumbled to the ground.

David never imagined that the terrible news would impact on his own life. But that was exactly what happened. As is known, the United States suffered severe economic setbacks on the heels of the fatal terrorist attack on the World Trade Center. The damage affected only a limited circle of people and corporations at first, but with the passage of time the effect of Bin Laden's action began to be felt on a much broader scale than anyone might have expected. A domino effect was set in motion, with ever-widening circles affecting more and more people.

The entire United States entered a slowdown period after the towers fell. There was a wave of firings. The General Maintenance Corporation discharged hundreds of workers. Among them was David Eisberg, who had been considered an exceptionally fine employee. But his good reputation did not spare him the loss of his job. The firm wanted to tighten up and downsize, leaving only the most indispensable workers and the heads of various special projects. All the rest were sent home, armed with letters of recommendation.

David, too, came home with glowing letters of recommendation and certificates testifying to his excellence on the job. The problem was that all these fine papers did not enable him to bring as much as a carton of milk home from the supermarket. David found himself on the verge of a crisis. He had never believed the day would come when he would lose his job. He had been a dedicated and energetic worker who had never been idle and had always supported his family nicely. How had he reached this state? It was awful. To wake up one morning and realize that he had no reason to hurry … and, what was worse, that all too soon he would have no money to take to the supermarket.

David began to search for a solution.

∽໑∾

Along with David, as said, hundreds of other employees were laid off. David, however, was in worse straits than those others. Many of them managed to find new jobs in various manpower positions. Although David likewise proffered his resume, no firm wanted to hire him.

David Eisberg was a Shabbos-observant Jew. He wore a yarmulke on his head that testified to his commitment to his faith. Everywhere he went for an interview, he would state that he could work only six days a week. And that the sixth day would have to be shortened.

The Eisbergs were a religious family. David had a brother learning in a *kollel* in Israel and a sister who had strayed from her heritage and now classified herself as "non-observant." She, too, lived in Atlanta.

David's sister was upset when she heard that the reason her brother was finding it impossible to obtain work was because he would tell potential employers that he was Shabbos observant.

"David, you're making a big mistake," she scolded him over the phone, when she called yet again to find out whether he had found a job. "Why do you have to tell everyone that you're *shomer Shabbos*?"

David didn't understand. "What else should I say? It's the truth."

"O.K.," his sister agreed. "No one's saying that it's not. But why do you have to talk about it?"

"I don't have to say a word," David smiled. "The yarmulke on my head says it all."

His sister was impatient. "Then take it off. There are lots of good Jews out there who don't wear a yarmulke all day."

"How are you talking?" David responded, becoming angry. "Do you imagine that the United States will ever throw its flag into the trash? You're asking me to do the same thing. Take my yarmulke off my head? It's — it's my badge!"

"Your badge is causing you big problems," his sister remarked. "If you weren't observant, you'd have found work long ago. Do you think this is smart? What are you going to do about your wife and children? Are you waiting to go on welfare? You — who had an excellent senior position and supported your family respectably — go on the dole? Put your wife on the phone, David. I want to talk to her and hear how *she* feels about the situation."

"My wife is with me all the way," David said heatedly. "She's ready to sacrifice a great deal for the Torah and our faith."

But his sister would not back down. Distress over his financial situation and his family disturbed her deeply. Sincerely concerned, she could not understand what would be so bad about David's working on Shabbos. The important thing was for him to have a good job and a decent income, so that his children would not be forced to live like paupers.

She chose a moment when David was not at home. It was the hour of his *daf yomi* class. She called to speak to David's wife. In the course of their long conversation, she was surprised to find her sister-in-law even more obstinate than her brother.

"Work on Shabbos?" David's wife nearly shot to her feet. "What are you talking about? Why don't you just suggest that we convert, Heaven forbid?"

"It's not the same thing."

"It is, for us. Shabbos is equal to the entire Torah, and anyone who does not observe it is like a non-Jew. I know that my words will insult you, so I beg your pardon at the start, but my first obligation is to honor the One Who created me, and only after that to honor His creatures. And, with all due respect to you, I have not yet heard from Hashem that He permits David to work on Shabbos."

"Well, that's the point, isn't it?" David's sister laughed. "I'm an atheist. I don't believe in anything. But I think that you two have old-fashioned beliefs that don't fit the modern world."

The debate continued for a long time, turning into a philosophical discussion between the sisters-in-law. On one side stood a woman imbued with deep faith, who was prepared to pay a steep price for that faith. On the other was a secular woman who had lost faith in her youth — who claimed that *HaKadosh Baruch Hu* had never revealed Himself to her, so she didn't believe in Him.

"You know what?" the sister concluded, when the conversation had reached a dead end. "I'm prepared to make you a bet that David will never find a job with any manpower firm as long as he lets them know ahead of time that he's Shabbos observant."

"And I promise you that he will find a job," Mrs. Eisberg declared. "And a lot sooner than you think!"

"I wish that were true," David's sister sighed. "This slowdown is hitting us hard. Unemployment is on the rise, and I know what's happening in the market. You're living in a dreamworld, my dear sister-in-law. So let David switch professions to something Jewish — like becoming a school principal, or a *shochet*, or a *cheder rebbe*. Knowing my brother, though, he would not be suited to any of those jobs. He's developed an expertise in a specialized field over the years, and that's building maintenance. If he doesn't find work with that kind of company soon, you're all simply going to starve!"

"And I say that David *will* find work," David's wife maintained. "Hashem has given us an ordeal at the moment, but He doesn't want to punish us for clinging to His Torah."

"Again you're talking about G-d as if you saw Him just yesterday!"

"I see Him every day," her sister-in-law said with a smile. "Of course, no one can actually see Him, because He has no form. But *HaKadosh Baruch Hu* reveals Himself to us constantly, in all sorts of ways. A believing Jew sees the hand of Providence everywhere. The heretic, on the other hand, puts a black bag over his head and screams, 'I don't see anything. It's all dark!' But Hashem doesn't give up on anyone. He brings every person to a point where he has no choice but to say, 'Now I see that Hashem is the One Who brought this about.'"

"If that ever happens," David's sister rejoined. "I'll be prepared to reassess my life."

"Remember what you just said," her sister-in-law said. "Because the day is fast approaching ..."

The picture grew very bleak. David and his family were forced to struggle with a reality they had never faced before. The manager of the Eisbergs' bank called them in for an angry meeting after several of their checks bounced because of insufficient funds. David's wife didn't have the money for basic necessities. Day by day, the situation grew more difficult.

David would not step over the firm line he had drawn for himself. At every job interview, he would bring along a lengthy list of recommendations — and a declaration: "I work only six days a week!"

And all the firms, without exception, informed him that they were sorry, but "We cannot hire you for a job in our company."

The reason was simple. What maintenance firms could be counted on to provide was not only professionalism but also speed. A housewife, phoning the company because of a problem in her house, expected an experienced worker on the premises within a short while to effect the necessary repairs. The manager of a maintenance operation had an up-to-date list of workers in every area, with whom he was in constant touch so that he knew who was doing what at any given moment. If some housewife in David's area phoned urgently from her home to announce that the house was plunged into darkness, what would he answer? "Sorry, but our worker will not be able to come for another day, because it's Shabbos and he's an Orthodox Jew"?

This was the reason the maintenance firms turned David away empty-handed. Once, luck had seemed to smile on him. It had been years before, when he had begun working for General Maintenance and asked for permission to be free on Shabbos. The company manager, familiar with David's outstanding talent, had agreed, substituting a non-Jewish worker on Shabbos and thus solving the problem. But this pleasing arrangement ended on the day David was fired, and now he was groping in a fog. Every few days he would receive another negative response. Undaunted, he went on with his search, setting up new interviews just to receive new rejections.

Each rejection was like a slap in the face. Mrs. Eisberg secretly chewed her lips with anxiety. She knew that her sister-in-law was observing it all, waiting to see if the *Ribono Shel Olam* would indeed reveal Himself. In the depths of her heart, she whispered a prayer to her Creator, begging Him to find her husband a good source of livelihood; not least, so that His great Name might be publicly sanctified!

√≈≈

One day, David presented himself as a job applicant at a maintenance firm he had not yet tried. An interview was arranged with the local manager of the Atlanta branch.

Before the interview, David collected all his references and recommendations, then got into his car and set off with a hopeful heart. If only, this time, he would not return empty-handed!

On the way, his cell phone rang. "Mr. Eisberg?"

"Yes?"

"This is the secretary of our local manager. I wanted to let you know that there's been a change in his calendar and he will not be able to see you at the time we spoke about. In fact, he won't be able to see you at all."

A cold sweat covered David's forehead. Was this a simple evasive maneuver: the ringing slap, administered earlier than usual?

"Are you saying that I shouldn't bother coming in?" he asked sadly.

"The interview has been moved to a different branch of our firm," the secretary said dryly. "The Atlanta manager will not be able to see you. In his place, you will be interviewed by ..." She named a different branch manager, and gave David the address. "Please come at the appointed time."

The situation was not as bad as he had thought. He had to make a sharp turn and travel to a different part of Atlanta, much farther away. But it would all be worth the effort, if only they would hire him.

If only ...

He drove quickly, and was greeted by the female manager of the branch to which he had been directed. She busied herself with his paperwork. When she finally lifted her head, there was a question in her eyes.

"I don't understand. The impression I get from all these glowing recommendations and your work log, which I received from the

General Maintenance Corporation, is that you are an excellent worker — even one of the best in the field. How is it possible that three months have passed since you were laid off, and no other firm has hired you yet?"

David spread his hands and answered candidly, "I am a religious Jew. Everywhere I go, I state up front that I do not work on the Sabbath. Saturday is simply out of bounds for me. Because of this, I've been turned down by every firm."

"I see," the woman said, shaking her head in distress. "I also must tell you that, if you're not prepared to work on Shabbos (she used the Jewish term), there's nothing for you here."

With bowed head, David stood up. His face was white as chalk. This time, it felt as though his cup of bitterness had overflowed. The manager looked past David's shoulder to the door, which had just opened. Suddenly, David heard a new voice, asking, "What, you won't work on Shabbos?"

David turned around.

In the doorway stood a tall Jew, dressed in an expensive, three-piece suit, and with long, curly *peyos*, and a full beard!

"Who are you?" David asked in astonishment.

"I am the new owner of this company," the man introduced himself. "Nice to meet you. My name is Efraim Flatman, and I live in Monsey."

An astounding story unfolded. The new owner of the firm in which he was seeking a job — the "big boss" himself — was a chassidic Jew who was presently traveling from city to city and state to state, inspecting all the branches of the giant corporation he had recently acquired. "I wasn't supposed to be here today. I was meant to be in a different branch, in another city," he explained to David. "I don't know why, but I felt drawn to come here to Atlanta today."

He glanced briefly at David's references, then turned decisively to the branch manager. "Listen, this man has got a job in this firm. Starting now!"

The manager was stunned. "Mr. Flatman, we still haven't conducted the blood test (all workers were requested to submit to a blood test to check for drug or alcohol abuse). On what grounds are you prepared to hire him without a test?"

The chassid from Monsey searched David's face with a good-natured smile. "It's all right," he said, chuckling. "He's just passed all of *my* tests and those are the ones that count!"

With that, he shook David's hand warmly and told him, in Yiddish, "Listen, these *goyim* don't understand anything about Shabbos and Yamim Tovim. Here's my personal card. If you have any problems, you can call me at any time. I'm at your service."

David's sister had a problem. As she put it, "I don't know what to do. I'll have to change my entire lifestyle. Hashem has shown Himself here in such an open way. It's almost as if He did it just to show an atheist like me, 'Here I am. Will you accept the yoke of serving Heaven?' Such a strange concatenation of circumstances … changing the location of the interview with no explanation, bringing the firm's new owner in without explanation, right where he needed to be … having the two believing Jews meet in such a way, so that my brother David would get a job. And all because of *shemiras Shabbos* … and so that his sister would have no more excuses!"

[Special thanks to my friend (name withheld for privacy), who heard this story from his brother — the hero of this story.]

If You Give ...

MEIR KAUFMAN AND HIS WIFE, CHAVA, HAD ALL sorts of plans for that day. They also had all sorts of plans and endless dreams for their future, both short term and long range. They were young and energetic, and they were filled with rosy optimism.

But on that black day, their dreams for the future went up in smoke. In a fatal car accident that flattened their car, the couple lost their lives and left their three young children orphaned and helpless.

R' Chaim Shalom Kaufman, R' Meir's older brother, was the one to whom everyone turned at this difficult time. The *mashgiach* of a well-known yeshivah, he was also a noted community activist and a man of stature and good sense, which was why everyone hoped he would come up with answers for the shattered family. He had eight children of his own but surely someone who offered help to so many could offer assistance to his own flesh and blood!

R' Chaim Shalom Kaufman never had another thought in his head. Even before his brother's funeral, when all those around him were unable to lift a finger in their shock and grief over the sudden tragedy, he arranged for a babysitter to care for Ditza and Penina, his brother's daughters, aged 2 and 4½, and made a host of phone calls to arrange whatever else was necessary. He and his wife, Malka, did not need to discuss the fact that, from that day on, they would become the orphaned girls' adoptive parents. It was understood between them.

R' Kaufman sounded calm and restrained during that painful time, but when he rose to eulogize his brother and sister-in-law, thousands of people wailed in unison with him.

R' Kaufman's primary concern was for his brother's oldest child, 9-year-old Elimelech. He was a perceptive boy, and a sensitive one. How would he cope with the loss? Something that Elimelech had said before the funeral troubled the uncle. He had spoken with the boy briefly, preparing him to say *Kaddish* for his parents. Elimelech had said: "Isn't it true that uncles are not the same as parents?"

R' Chaim Shalom, unprepared for such a simple and penetrating comment, had replied, "That depends on who the uncle is. Malka and I will try to be like real parents, I promise."

Elimelech's round, dark eyes held a gaze that was mature before his time. It was a look that would accompany him from that day on. "My father and mother didn't have to try," he said. "They were just my father and mother."

These words were to haunt the Kaufmans. R' Chaim Shalom and Malka did their utmost to serve as the best possible substitute for the parents whose lives had been so tragically cut short. The little girls were amenable and cooperative, and treated their uncle and aunt just as if they were their parents. But Elimelech was a problem. He was not especially gifted academically, and instead of taking trouble over his schoolwork he turned his pain and grief inward and acted up both at home and in *cheder*. The saying, "*HaKadosh Baruch Hu* prepares the cure before the ailment," proved itself many times over the course of the years: Each time Elimelech had a problem, his activist uncle pulled all the strings at his disposal in order to repair the damage and cover up for the boy's antics, which had their source in his anguish and frustration, and were usually both provocative and infuriating.

Elimelech's bar mitzvah was celebrated with a lavish affair in a big hall. Had his parents been alive, they would not have acquiesced to such an elaborate event. R' Chaim Shalom Kaufman's own sons did not merit a celebration on that scale. But Elimelech was something else. There was a powerful desire to compensate for what had been taken from him — not only in his uncle's heart but also, apparently, in the hearts of the hundreds of invited guests who made the effort to attend. Well-known *rabbanim, roshei yeshivah, mashgichim* — the cream of the yeshivah world — came to celebrate with Elimelech as he assumed the yoke of mitzvos.

Half a year later, Elimelech entered *yeshivah ketanah* — Yeshivas Yodei Binah, the large institution where his uncle served as *mashgiach*. There are those who supervise the whole world but fail to notice what is taking place inside their own household. R' Kaufman was definitely not of this ilk. If he did not keep a close eye on Elimelech, who knew what the boy might get up to? Much better to keep him close, to quench the flames while they were still small. That there would be many fires, R' Kaufman was certain. Elimelech's nature practically guaranteed it.

He wasn't wrong. Elimelech stirred things up everywhere he went. If not for his uncle, he would have been invited to leave yeshivah just a short time after he began there. Thanks to R' Chaim Shalom, however, the faculty members of the *yeshivah ketanah* were forced to swallow their ire time after time.

"What do you want from us?" the *rebbeim* would complain bitterly to R' Kaufman. "We understand that you have to suffer his behavior. But why should we — or the *bachurim* — have to?"

R' Chaim Shalom, of course, did not enjoy hearing such criticism leveled at him — but he was optimistic about the future. "You'll see … '*Hazor'im b'dimah, b'rinah yiktzoru*! Those who sow in tears shall reap in joy.' In the end, Elimelech will be a good boy."

Over the next three years, the curve on Elimelech's graph generally plunged, and only occasionally registered a slight rise. By fighting like a tiger, R' Chaim Shalom succeeded valiantly in keeping him within the yeshivah's framework, despite the fact that Elimelech had a rebellious and anti-authority nature that made the yeshivah seem like a prison. "He should go out and get a job," his *rebbeim* claimed again and again. "He and the *Gemara* will never be a match!"

R' Kaufman was a believer. The day would yet come when Elimelech would change. He was waiting for the day when his nephew would enter *yeshivah gedolah*. Then, he was sure, things would start looking up.

And, in the end, the day finally came. On *Rosh Chodesh Elul*, Elimelech walked through the portals of Yeshivas Yodei Binah's upper school — the *yeshivah gedolah*. His uncle awaited him at the door, a broad smile across his face, just as though he hadn't fixed him a cup of coffee at home that morning, or packed Elimelech's bag with his own two hands! This was the day when Elimelech would start to become a *mensch*!

After a week in which Elimelech genuinely tried, without success, to learn for two consecutive hours at a stretch, the boy broke down. With tear-filled eyes, he stood before his uncle and pleaded, "Yeshivah doesn't suit me. Please let me go out to work. I promise that I will remain a *frum* Jew. I'm not, *chas v'shalom*, going off the *derech*. I just can't sit and learn!"

Here was R' Kaufman's other persona's shining hour. As a member of the neighborhood committee dealing with the disbursement of charity to families in need, he was a big believer in *tzedakah* — in the power of *tzedakah* and its ability to change nature.

"Have you tried *davening* about this?" he asked Elimelech. "You know, we were all created in order to learn Torah. That is our purpose — not reading newspapers, however religious. In the end, all of us will die and return to the place we came from — the upper world. We must prepare now for a journey lasting billions upon billions of years. Your friends are preparing *Gemara, Rashi, Tosafos, Rishonim,* and *Acharonim.* What are you preparing to bring? A stack of newspapers? A sack of excuses? 'I had a headache; I had a *yetzer hara*, I couldn't learn, I'm not built for *Gemara.*' All fine and good, but in *Olam Haba* you will remain a pauper, a pitiable figure. You'll go there naked and barefoot, and you'll wail bitterly, 'Where was my good sense while I was still among the living? Why didn't I want to learn?' Everyone will pity you, but no one will be able to help you, for if you are not for yourself, who will be for you? Only you can do something now: Pick up a *Gemara* and learn!"

For the first time in his life, Elimelech got the message. The gleam of self-pity and self-indulgence that had settled in his round, dark eyes gave way to shock, as he studied his life and found a deep, empty hole, plunging down into a dark abyss.

"Uncle Chaim Shalom," he whispered, ashen. "I really want to change. Tell me how to overcome my *yetzer hara.*"

"*Tzedakah,*" his uncle whispered back. "Every morning, give a few *shekels* to *tzedakah* and ask Hashem, from the depths of your heart, 'Please, Hashem, You created me in order to learn Your holy Torah, but

You also created a *yetzer hara* in me. Give me the strength to overcome it.' I promise you that it will help."

"How many *shekels* every morning? And where will I get the money?" his nephew asked.

"If you give, you will have," his uncle said tranquilly. "*Tzedakah* always comes back to you."

And so, near Elimelech's bed at home, next to his Discman and the pile of religious weekend newspapers, stood a round *tzedakah* box. Each morning Elimelech would put in several *shekels* and *daven* that he have the desire to learn Torah that day, and not waste his time in idle talk.

His prayers were accepted. Elimelech suddenly discovered the sweetness in Torah study, the beauty of every *Rashi* and *Tosafos*.

The change did not happen overnight. There were many hard days and anguished hours when he felt as though he were grinding gravel between his teeth. Sometimes his *Gemara* was like a beloved friend, and at other times all he saw were long, alien rows of meaningless black squares. He had his ups and he had his downs — the latter far outnumbering the former.

After several months of struggle, the results were plain to see. Elimelech was now capable of learning *Gemara* for several hours at a stretch, as well as understanding and even enjoying the simple meanings of the commentaries. Unable to suppress his restless nature, he still found it necessary to get up and walk around now and again, lest he go out of his mind.

In a convoluted chain of reasoning, Elimelech interpreted his uncle's praise of *tzedakah* in a unique way. From being a giver, he became a taker — to speak plainly, a *schnorrer*!

"Tell me, have you lost your mind? I can't believe it. You're going around the *shteiblach* asking for *tzedakah*? What are you lacking at home? Had I not heard the same story from several reliable people, I'd have thought it slander. Is it true that you go around the shuls and ask everyone, 'Maybe you have a *shekel* for me?' Is it true or not?"

"It's true."

"Do you want to bury me alive? Why are you causing me this embarrassment?"

"But Uncle Chaim Shalom, you taught me how important *tzedakah* is," Elimelech whispered, shamefaced.

"How important it is to *give!*" his uncle expostulated. "Not take!"

"I read that what the poor person does for the *baal habayis* is greater than what the *baal habayis* does for the poor person," Elimelech said. "You put me in the first grade of *tzedakah* and I've moved up to the second grade. What's wrong with that?"

"But you're not poor," R' Kaufman nearly exploded. "You have everything you need. You lack for nothing!"

"You can give me anything I want," his nephew agreed, "except for one thing: the joy of action. I feel that joy when I go around collecting donations. I feel a great feeling of satisfaction because I'm giving people the merit of giving *tzedakah*. Besides, you've given me so much over the years. I want to repay some of it. All the money that I collect goes into my pocket, and I'm going to donate it all to our neighborhood *tzedakah* that you, dear uncle, help run. Your committee has four or five fund-raising drives each year, don't you? Well, I'm collecting funds all year round!"

For the first time in the history of their debates, Elimelech had the last word. R' Kaufman was forced to swallow his mortification and adjust painfully to the fact that his brother's son had become a *schnorrer*. Later, he came to understand that the orphan was seeking in this way to fill an emotional void. Still later, he began to see Elimelech's actions in a positive light. Their store of charity funds were often depleted, and the large sums that Elimelech managed to amass saved more than one destitute family when times were hard.

Elimelech reached the age of marriage. R' Kaufman did not expect too many offers for his nephew, and in this he was proved correct. Though Elimelech was a pleasant-spoken young man with good *middos*, gentle and good hearted, and even to a certain extent a *talmid chacham,* his practice of canvassing every shul had earned him the label of *schnorrer* — a label that impacted on *shidduchim* the way an effective repellant acts upon mosquitoes.

At last, however, his day came. He became engaged to a girl in his own situation: an orphan who had lost her father and didn't have a penny to her name. Like the *chasan*, the *kallah* was filled to the brim with good *middos* and the emotional delicacy of those whose walk through life has not been a bed of roses.

Elimelech's uncle, R' Chaim Shalom Kaufman, sat at the engagement celebration with a cheerful face and a worried heart. Where was he to find the money with which to marry off the young couple?

He was a member of an important neighborhood committee and a well-known *gemach*, you will say. He must have millions rolling around in his pockets ...

R' Kaufman could only laugh in pain. Who, better than he, knew the meaning of the saying, "All shoemakers go barefoot"? His neighborhood committee would certainly donate something to his nephew. After all, Elimelech was no less deserving than any other unfortunate living in their midst. The question was: How to marry off a couple on $5,000?

The *chasan* himself can take care of covering the wedding expenses, you will say. After all, that's what he does best! Let him make the rounds of the shuls and collect the necessary funds.

The problem was, the *chasan* was adamant on one point: He would not collect money on his own behalf. Ever since he had begun collecting donations for *tzedakah*, he had given every last penny to his uncle's charity committee. Take the money for himself? Heaven forbid!

Two months before the wedding date, the coffers were still empty. R' Kaufman's heart was filled with anguish. How could this golden-hearted young man who cared for the whole world find himself in such a situation? The injustice of it screamed up to Heaven!

He had no way of knowing that neighborhood activists — his fellow committee members — had met without him in an emergency conclave. The topic under discussion: Elimelech Kaufman.

"How can we be satisfied with the usual allotment for that boy?" asked R' Rachamim Ben Shushan, an energetic activist who lived in the area. "Is the very person who cares for the poor all the time to suffer now?"

"Certainly not," said R' Segolevski of the salt-and-pepper beard. "We must give him more than we give anyone else. The question is: How much? Even double the usual amount will not be enough. The *chasan* and *kallah* are indeed a match made in Heaven! Neither one of them has a thing."

How much to give? The committee members scratched their heads over the question.

The neighborhood Rav, R' Kalman Kleingarten, said after some thought, "It seems to me that we ought to reciprocate, *middah k'neged middah*. For every *shekel* that Elimelech has brought us to this day, we give him a *shekel* in return!"

This brilliant notion was accepted unanimously.

The list of Elimelech's donations was brought into the room and a pocket calculator put to work to figure sums. It turned out that, over the years, Elimelech had brought the committee a sum large enough to marry off a young couple in style.

No one asked, "Where will we obtain the funds?" No one asked anything else, or raised any sort of objection at the extraordinary allocation. All the committee members threw themselves into the great mitzvah, feverishly but quietly collecting the enormous sum.

Two weeks before Elimelech's wedding, as he and his uncle paced the house with hunched shoulders and creased brows, two committee representatives arrived with a large suitcase. Without a word, they counted out onto the table all the money that had been collected outside the normal framework of the committee's activities.

Elimelech Kaufman stepped under his *chupah* with an erect bearing and a happy heart. Beside him stood his uncle and adoptive father, R' Chaim Shalom Kaufman, eyes brimming over like a spring.

"If you give, you will have," he had told his young nephew years before. And, indeed, for the great mitzvah he had undertaken then, Elimelech had been unstintingly, and joyously, repaid in full.

From the Depths to the Heights

SIMCHAH, THE INNKEEPER, NEVER HAD AN EASY TIME paying his rent. The inn that he managed was owned by a *poritz* who was only interested in extracting the maximum rent, but not at all interested in ever spending a penny maintaining the property.

Simchah's inn served partly as a rest stop for weary passersby and partly as a tavern where the local peasants imbibed alcoholic beverages freely. The road to the inn was not paved, however, and this made the inn very difficult to access. Travelers who wished to stop at the inn would often become mired in pits or ditches, their wagons suffering broken wheels and broken axles. Because the road to the inn was so treacherous, people avoided it. And without guests, there was no income for Simchah.

Many times, Simchah begged the *poritz* to pave the road to the inn, but the *poritz* always refused. Instead, he would just charge an even greater rent every year.

Each month, Simchah struggled to pay the exorbitant rent that the *poritz* demanded. One month, when the *poritz* came to collect his money, Simchah told him that he just could not come up with the rent. The *poritz* warned Simchah that if he did not come up with the 28 golden coins that he owed by the next day, he and his family would be forcibly evicted from the inn.

The only possession of value that Simchah owned was a cow that provided his family with fresh milk to drink and some extra milk to sell. With a heavy heart, Simchah went and sold the cow for 28 gold coins. The cow was worth more than that, he knew, but he was too desperate for the money to be in a good bargaining position.

From now on, his children would not have milk to drink, and Simchah would not have that bit of side income that came from selling the extra milk. But at least they would have a roof over their heads.

Understandably, Simchah felt down and depressed. He wished that he could pour his heart out to the holy Baal Shem Tov. *I need to go to Mezhibozh*, he told himself. *The Baal Shem Tov could give me advice how to get out of this terrible situation.*

Toward evening, Simchah heard the welcome sounds of wagon wheels and the clip-clop of a horse approaching his inn. He went out to the courtyard to greet the visitor. To his surprise, he discovered that the visitor was none other than the Baal Shem Tov himself, accompanied by his student Rabbi Wolf Kitzes and Alexei, the wagon-driver, who was in a deep slumber. Alexei had fallen asleep at the reins, and the horse had found its way to Simchah's inn on its own.

Rabbi Yisrael Baal Shem Tov emerged from the wagon and entered Simchah's inn. Reeling from the shock of the unexpected visit, Simchah began groping for the words with which to explain his situation to the Baal Shem Tov.

Before Simchah could open his mouth, however, the Baal Shem Tov addressed him.

"Simchah, do you have money in the house?"

"Rebbe, what just happened to me should not happen to any Jew," he replied, grateful for the opportunity to recount his tale of woe. "I have become so destitute that today I had to sell my only cow just so that I can pay the *poritz* the 28 gold coins I have to give him for rent. Otherwise, he threatened to throw me and my family out onto the street."

"So you have 28 gold coins," the Baal Shem Tov said happily. "I need the money for *pidyon shevuyim*, redeeming captives. Saving Jews from captivity is a great mitzvah."

Simchah froze. He stared at the Baal Shem Tov, uncomprehending, for a moment. But only for a moment. His rock-solid *emunas chachamim* did not allow him to object to the Baal Shem Tov's request. He recovered his composure quickly, and immediately went inside to retrieve the pouch of money he had received from the sale of the cow.

Simchah's wife, Rivka, almost fainted when she saw her husband giving the Rebbe the money that he had prepared to give to the *poritz*. But she, too, was a pious woman, and she did not say a word until the Baal Shem Tov took the money from Simchah and continued on his way to free the captives.

As the Baal Shem Tov's wagon disappeared down the dirt road, Rivka began to weep. "You could have at least asked the Rebbe to stay overnight," she said reproachfully. "Maybe he could have said something to the *poritz*. Simchah, I'm afraid."

✦

Even Rabbi Wolf Kitzes, the Baal Shem Tov's loyal disciple, was surprised when he saw the Baal Shem Tov take the money designated for the innkeeper's rent. He wanted to ask the Rebbe how he could allow Simchah and his family to be thrown out onto the street the next day; but he knew better than to question the Rebbe's actions.

That night, Simchah did not sleep a wink. He tossed and turned on his straw mattress restlessly, terrified of the treatment he would receive at the hands of the *poritz* the next day.

His fears were not unfounded. In the morning, the servants of the *poritz* arrived. When they heard that Simchah did not have the rent money, they grabbed him by the arms and pushed him out of the inn. They had no pity on Simchah's young children, either. They chased the entire family out of the inn, and then threw Simchah's furniture and belongings out the window.

The brokenhearted Simchah shepherded his wife and children to an empty barn owned by a kindhearted neighbor. "I have to go to Mezhibozh to get a *berachah* from the Baal Shem Tov," he told his wife. "What else can we do?"

Simchah set out on foot to Mezhibozh. He removed his shoes — why ruin the soles? — tied them onto a branch and threw them over his shoulder. In some places, the ground was muddy; in other places, rocky. Simchah walked slowly, absorbed in his anguish, while pebbles pierced the soles of his feet.

After walking for several hours, he heard the sound of an approaching wagon. He didn't bother turning his head in the direction of the wagon. Even if the wagon-driver would have room to take him in, he did not have a penny to pay for the trip.

The wagon pulled up alongside Simchah. "Reb Yid, why are you walking alone?" the wagon-driver asked jovially. "Come, join me on the wagon. Where are you heading?"

"To the place where all Jews go, to Mezhibozh. But I have no money to pay you."

Leizer, the wagon-driver, chortled. "Who asked for money? Jump in. Two are better than one. I'm also heading for Mezhibozh, and I could use some company."

By the time the wagon arrived in Mezhibozh, it was filled with Jews that Leizer had picked up along the way. These Jews were all traveling to Mezhibozh to seek the Baal Shem Tov's guidance and blessing.

They reached the Baal Shem Tov's court, where Reb Hirsch, the *gabbai*, was sitting and writing *kvitlach*, as was customary. "Baruch ben Sarah Shoshana for a *refuah sheleimah*," he wrote, and handed the *kvittel* to the Jew standing before him.

When Leizer's group entered, Reb Hirsch gestured to Simchah to come forward. But Simchah wished to show his appreciation to Leizer, so he motioned to Reb Hirsch to allow Leizer to go ahead of him.

Leizer said to Reb Hirsch, "My name is Eliezer ben Rachel, but I haven't come to ask anything for myself. I am here on behalf of my *kehillah*, and I wish to ask for a *berachah* for a *refuah sheleimah* for someone."

"What's the name?" Reb Hirsch inquired.

"His name is Kazimizh, but I don't know his mother's name. He's not Jewish. He's the *poritz* of our town."

"A *poritz*?" Reb Hirsch asked, puzzled. Why did the Baal Shem Tov have to be bothered with the problems of a rich *poritz*, when there were so many poor Jews who were waiting for a *berachah*? He was about to motion to Simchah to enter instead of Leizer, but the Baal Shem Tov stood up, walked over to the doorway and beckoned to Leizer to enter.

"He's here to ask for a *goy*," Reb Hirsch told him.

"Hashem's mercy is on all of His creations," the Baal Shem Tov answered calmly. "Let us hear what you have to say," he said, turning to Leizer.

"The Rebbe should forgive me," Leizer said. "I am here to ask on behalf of our sick *poritz* who needs a great *yeshuah*."

"Tell me about your *poritz*," the Baal Shem Tov urged.

"The *poritz* is one of the world's righteous gentiles," Leizer began. "He's a goodhearted, generous person who gives the Jews in his jurisdiction everything they need. He provides us with ample *parnassah*, protects us, and gives us free land on which to build our houses. He even gave our *kehillah* land for a shul and a *mikveh*.

"But his sons are not like him. They are wild, young men, and they give their father a great deal of trouble. Our *poritz* became so upset about his sons' behavior that he began drinking too much. Eventually, he became ill. Now, he is coughing up blood and suffering from internal bleeding. If he dies, his evil sons will inherit his property and we are all afraid of what will happen to our *kehillah*."

After hearing Leizer's story, the Baal Shem Tov turned to Simchah and asked him to say what was bothering him, as though he did not recognize him. Simchah told the story of how the *poritz* had evicted him, and how he no longer had a home or a *parnassah*. "I need advice," he told the Rebbe.

"Advice? Leizer already gave you advice!" the Baal Shem Tov replied.

"Leizer?" Simchah asked in confusion. "He only talked about his sick *poritz*."

"He told of an honest, goodhearted *poritz* who provides *parnassah* generously to an entire town of Jews," the Baal Shem Tov said. "There's room for another Jew to earn a livelihood there."

The Baal Shem Tov turned to Leizer. "Take Simchah and his family in your wagon to your town," he instructed.

"The wagon is too small," Simchah objected. "Maybe it has room for my wife and children, but for the furniture and other belongings there won't be enough room."

"So sell the furniture," the Baal Shem Tov responded. "And when you get to Leizer's town, go to the animal market and buy a cow with the money from the sale of the furniture."

With that, the Baal Shem Tov turned to Leizer again. "Tell the *poritz* that he should stop drinking alcohol and drink only milk instead, and the Healer of all Flesh will send him a *refuah* soon."

∽◦∾

On the way back to his village, Simchah realized that selling his furniture was not such a simple proposition. The furniture was old and dilapidated, and he was sure that no one would be willing to buy it after the treatment it had received at the hands of the *poritz*'s servants.

To his surprise, however, when he arrived at his inn he saw that the furniture was intact.

"It's a miracle," he told his wife Rivka. He collected the furniture, took it to the market, and managed to sell it for 8½ gold coins.

Rivka wrung her hands together. "We can't even buy a goat with 8½ gold coins," she protested.

"If old furniture doesn't break after being flung out the window, 8½ gold coins can bring us the *yeshuah* we need," Simchah comforted her.

∽◦∾

When Simchah and his family arrived in Leizer's town, Leizer found them an abandoned shack on the outskirts of the village. Simchah settled his family in the shack as best as he could, and then headed for the animal market. He could not afford any of the cows that were for sale, however. Finally, he saw a short farmer leading a small, thin cow.

"How much do you want for this calf?" Simchah asked the farmer.

"Calf?" the farmer replied indignantly. "Are you joking? This cow already has grandchildren giving milk."

"Does she give milk?" Simchah asked skeptically.

The farmer pulled himself up to his full height, which was not very tall. "I'm also short and small, but I manage to do in one day of work what three, big and tall farmers would not be able to do. My cow is like her owner — small, but productive. She gives lots of milk."

"So how much do you want for her?" Simchah asked.

"How much money do you have?"

"Eight-and-a-half gold coins."

The farmer extended his hand. "It's a deal," he said. "The cow is yours."

Simchah led the small cow after him. On his way back to his shack, he began having second thoughts. How did he know that the cow really gave milk? Why had he bought it so hastily? What would Rivka say?

When Rivka saw the little cow, she began laughing bitterly. "Well, I guess 8½ gold coins wasn't going to get you anything better. But even a goat would have been preferable to this bag of bones."

"The Baal Shem Tov told me to buy a cow," Simchah answered with more confidence than he felt.

Rivka pointed to the pathetic-looking animal her husband had bought. "You call this a cow?"

"Let's try milking it," Simchah suggested. He reached for a small pot and began milking the cow. A minute later, he called out excitedly, "Bring me the big bucket, the pot is almost full."

Rivka ran to get the bucket, and saw that the cow was giving a generous amount of milk. When Simchah finished milking the cow, he carried the bucket into the little shack. The children drank their fill, and there was plenty left over to sell.

Leizer came to the house of the sick *poritz*, who was on the verge of death. At first, the servants refused to allow him entry. "The *poritz* is very ill, go away," they told him.

Leizer was persistent. He shouted, "Enlightened, kind *poritz*, I went to our holy rabbi, and he told me what you need to do to get better."

The *poritz*'s son heard Leizer shouting. He took his club and was about to go outside and chase Leizer away, but his father stopped him. "Tell the Jew to come inside," he commanded. Grudgingly, the *poritz*'s son told Leizer to enter.

The Baal Shem Tov had earned a reputation as a miracle worker even among the *goyim*. "What did the rabbi say?" the *poritz* wanted to know.

"He said that if you stop drinking alcohol and drink only milk, you will get better," Leizer told him.

The *poritz* took the Baal Shem Tov's advice very seriously. From that moment on, he swore off all wine, beer, and vodka. Instead, he began drinking only milk. His internal bleeding stopped and he began to feel much better. Soon, he was able to walk again.

One morning, when his servant brought him the jug of milk, the *poritz* swallowed a bit and then immediately spit it out. "This milk is spoiled," he declared.

The servant ran to bring the *poritz* milk from a different cow, but the *poritz* declared that milk to be spoiled, too. The servant ran to the barn, milked a cow himself and brought the *poritz* the fresh milk, but still, the *poritz* insisted that the milk was spoiled.

The *poritz*'s servant brought him milk from every cow in the entire village, but no milk met with his approval. "It's all spoiled," he said.

In his search for a cow whose milk would satisfy the *poritz*, the servant knocked on the door of Simchah's shack and asked if he had a cow that could give milk for the *poritz*. Simchah nodded and pointed to the cow standing outside his shack.

When the servant saw the gaunt creature, he refused to take the milk Simchah was offering him. But Simchah begged him to bring a cup of milk from his cow to the *poritz*. "What do you have to lose?" he argued. The servant reluctantly agreed.

Hesitantly, the servant brought the milk to the *poritz*. "Where did you get this milk from?" the *poritz* asked joyfully. "Finally, milk that I can drink, instead of horrible, spoiled milk."

From that day on, the servants brought the milk from the little cow straight to the *poritz* each morning.

The *poritz* was concerned that the cow should continue to give good milk, and so he told his servants to provide Simchah with vast expanses of grass where the little cow could graze as she desired.

Slowly, the *poritz* got to know Simchah, and he was impressed by his honesty and humility. After a while, the *poritz* put Simchah in charge of some of his estates. Later, he appointed Simchah to manage large portions of the village, and eventually he made him a *poritz* in his own right.

Simchah, the Jewish *poritz*, began renting plots of land to others, and he eventually became a wealthy man. Several years later, he married off his daughter.

Rabbi Wolf Kitzes was in attendance at the wedding. *How*, he wondered, *could a Jew become so wealthy?*

Simchah was happy to tell him the whole story. When Simchah began describing how he had been evicted from his inn, Reb Wolf remembered how he himself had silently questioned the Baal Shem Tov's taking the last pennies from the poor Jew for *pidyon shevuyim*.

"The Baal Shem Tov lowered you to the depths, so that you should rise to the heights," he told Simchah.

A Matter of Milk and Meat

R EB BARUCH NEUSTADTER SAT IN HIS WAGON, HUMMING cheerily under his breath. He was on his way to visit his Rebbe, Reb Elimelech of Lizhensk, the legendary "Noam Elimelech." It was a sunny, cool day, the type of day when the whole world seemed to be smiling. Reb Baruch could not help but smile back.

Here he was, on his way to his beloved Rebbe — not, like so many others, to beg the Rebbe for a *berachah* for health, or children, or *parnassah*, but simply to bask in the Rebbe's holy light and drink from his fountain of Torah and *avodas Hashem*. *Indeed,* Reb Baruch told himself, *I have much to be grateful for.*

In his youth, Reb Baruch had been considered a promising young scholar. He had known complete *masechtos* of *Gemara* by heart, and he was familiar with *Rashi* and *Tosafos* on half of *Shas*. He had studied all four parts of the *Shulchan Aruch* and he could quote entire sections with ease.

When he married, Reb Baruch had no choice but to go out to work; the alternative, in those days, was starvation. Poland at the time boasted a working class that included many learned Jews — carpenters who occasionally sawed their tables crooked because their heads were buried in a *Ketzos*, storeowners who stole a few seconds between customers to learn Mishnayos, and shoemakers who recited *Tehillim* as they pounded leather into shoes.

Reb Baruch was a member of this group. No matter how busy he was with his textile business, his mind was always on some *sugya* in *Gemara* or some halachah in *Shulchan Aruch*. Like a fish out of water, he longed to return to the *beis medrash* and open his *Gemara* once again. His work drained his energies and demanded much of his time, but he nevertheless always managed to make it to the *beis medrash* at the end of the day. There, he would thirstily pore over the ancient tomes. His tired eyes would strain to read the words, but once he began, he would invariably get a second wind, and with renewed vigor, he would start to plumb the depths of the *sugya* he was learning.

Reb Baruch never spoke about himself to the Rebbe, but Reb Elimelech knew very well what this chassid was all about. When Reb Baruch would arrive, the Rebbe would look at him lovingly and caress his hand warmly. Often, the Rebbe would ask him questions about *Gemara*, or delve into *chiddushei Torah* with him. Reb Baruch was privileged to enjoy something that many of his counterparts did not: to learn Torah with the great Noam Elimelech.

Every few weeks, Reb Baruch would make his way from his village to Lizhensk, bask in the holy atmosphere of the Rebbe's court, and then return to his home with the spiritual energy to tide him over until the next visit.

During this trip, as always, Reb Baruch planned to stay in Lizhensk for a few days. The highlight, of course, would be Shabbos with the Rebbe, after which he would make his way back to his village.

When Reb Baruch was about to leave Lizhensk, he entered the Rebbe's room to receive his blessing.

The Rebbe greeted him warmly, and wished him a heartfelt "*Tzeischem l'shalom.*" As Reb Baruch was making his way to the door, however, the Rebbe motioned for him to come back.

"I have noticed, my dear Reb Baruch, that during your many visits to me you have never asked for anything. You always come and leave without telling me anything about yourself. If you are afraid to burden me with your needs, you should know that it is not a burden at all. This is my job, to make sure that every Jew has only the best in both spiritual and material realms. Is there anything that you need?"

Surprised by the question, Reb Baruch smiled abashedly. "The reason I have not asked for anything is not because I am afraid to trouble the Rebbe, but simply because I do not lack anything. Hashem has blessed me with everything I need — my family and I are all healthy, *baruch Hashem*, and I have ample *parnassah*. I'm not a rich man, but why would I want to be rich? A rich person is someone who is happy with his lot, and if Hashem gave me adequate *parnassah* and also gave me time to sit in the *beis medrash* and learn two or three *blatt* of *Gemara* every day, I am satisfied. What more do I need?"

"You sound just like Eisav the *rasha*," the Rebbe rebuked Reb Baruch. "Eisav told Yaakov, 'I have a lot, my brother, I don't need anything more.' If that is the case, why do you bother coming here? You're perfect in *gashmiyus* and in *ruchniyus* and you are not missing *anything*?"

For a moment, Reb Baruch was stunned. He recovered quickly, however. "Heaven forbid," he rushed to assure the Rebbe. "I did not mean that I don't need anything. The reason I come here is because I feel an intense yearning to learn Torah and *avodas Hashem* from the Rebbe. I know that everything I have has its source here, and the Torah that I absorb here is like life-giving dew on parched earth. If I wouldn't come here, I would really be missing something."

The Rebbe rested his holy gaze on Reb Baruch. "Is that so? You come here to hear *divrei Torah*? In that case, I will tell you a *dvar Torah*.

"You should know that the mitzvos in the Torah were given to the Jewish people to live by — as it says, '*V'chai bahem.*' Take the mitzvah of not eating milk and meat together, for instance. A good Jew is careful not to violate this prohibition in the slightest — but he doesn't realize that in doing so, he is not only performing the will of his Creator, he is guarding his health in the process as well. A Jew who is scrupulous about not eating milk and meat is physically unable to swallow such a mixture. In fact, were a mixture of milk and meat to come into his mouth, Heaven forbid, he would not be able to swallow it, but would cough it out and expel it."

With that, the Rebbe wished Reb Baruch a safe trip, stretched out his hand to him, and escorted him to the door.

Reb Baruch left the Rebbe, his head spinning. What did the Rebbe want from him? Why did he call him back a second time, and what on earth did he mean with his cryptic words about milk and meat? Of course Reb Baruch knew that the Torah was given to live by, and that observance of mitzvos not only nourished the soul but sustained the body as well. Did the Rebbe suspect him of not being scrupulous enough in this matter?

Reb Baruch did not deem it proper to ask the Rebbe what he meant, nor did he see any scholarly chassidim in the vicinity who could help him figure out what the Rebbe was trying to convey to him. He decided to turn his mind to other things, for the meantime. *When I return home, I will have the presence of mind to try to decipher the Rebbe's words,* he reasoned.

But when Reb Baruch returned home, he immediately became involved with some urgent business matters, and the Rebbe's mysterious words were all but forgotten.

Several months passed. Usually, Reb Baruch visited the Rebbe every few weeks, but this time of year was very busy, and his business occupied so much of his time that he simply could not get away.

One evening, just as Reb Baruch was settling himself in the *beis medrash* to learn his daily portion of *Gemara*, the door to the *beis medrash* was flung open, and Sholom'ke, Reb Baruch's 10-year-old son, ran in. When Sholom'ke saw his father, he burst into tears. "Father, Father, come home quickly. Mother —"

Sholom'ke was too distraught to get the words out.

"What happened?" Reb Baruch asked in concern.

"She's lying on the ground," Sholom'ke managed to say between sobs.

"But what happened to her?"

Sholom'ke took a deep breath and tried to calm down. "We were eating supper. Mother was feeding the little ones, and she also ate a little. Suddenly she started choking. Her face turned blue and she fell onto the ground. She can't talk and she's making these funny sounds. Father, you have to come save her, or else ..."

Sholom'ke did not want to say what he was thinking.

Reb Baruch bolted from the *beis medrash* and ran as fast as he could to his house, where a few neighbors had already gathered.

He sprinted across the yard in front of his house, bumping into Ella, the goat, who was placidly chewing on some fresh hay. The surprised Ella turned her velvety eyes toward her owner. For years, Ella had supplied the family with warm, sweet milk every day, and she had always known Reb Baruch to be kind and gentle. But now, Reb Baruch almost pushed her away in his haste to get into the house and attempt to revive his wife.

His heart racing, Reb Baruch entered his house. When he saw his wife, Hinda, lying on the ground, her face was a deathly shade of blue. His first thought was that he had arrived too late. But then Reb Baruch heard some wheezing noises coming from Hinda's throat. She was still alive. Apparently, her airway was not completely obstructed, and she was fighting for breath. Some air was still managing to make it into her lungs. It was obvious, however, that if the piece of meat blocking her throat would not be removed soon, she would suffocate.

The neighbors were trying all sorts of misguided first aid on Hinda. One stuck a finger into her throat, in a futile attempt to dislodge the meat. Another began breathing into her mouth. A third had run to call the local doctor, Yankel, whose medical training consisted of reading a few books on the subject of stomach ailments.

Yankel arrived at about the same time as Reb Baruch, and pulled out a long pair of tweezers from his impressive-looking black bag. Carefully, he put the tweezers into Hinda's mouth, but he was unable to reach the piece of meat that was stuck.

Reb Baruch was at a loss. If his wife would not cough up the meat, he knew she would suffocate within a few minutes. *If only I could run and ask the Rebbe*, he thought. *He would surely be able to daven and save Hinda.*

For a moment, Reb Baruch pictured himself standing in front of the Rebbe, beseeching him to *daven* for his wife. In his mind's eye, he could see the Rebbe. The Rebbe seemed to be telling him something.

"If a mixture of milk and meat would come into the mouth of a Jew who was careful with the laws of forbidden mixtures, he would not be able to swallow it, but would cough it out and expel it."

All of a sudden, Reb Baruch understood what the Rebbe had been trying to tell him. He grabbed a cup and bolted from the house, heading straight for Ella, the goat.

With trembling hands, he milked the goat until the cup was about halfway full. Then he ran back into the house and poured the liquid straight into Hinda's mouth.

Suddenly, Hinda began coughing. First, she coughed up droplets of milk and then, finally, she gave a loud cough. The piece of meat dislodged itself from her throat and flew across the room. Her airway unblocked, she began breathing again, and slowly her face took on a healthy pink tinge.

Several days later, Reb Baruch traveled to Lizhensk to tell the Rebbe about the miracle that had taken place. But when he stepped into the Rebbe's room, the Rebbe's face wore a knowing smile.

"Didn't I tell you that the throat of a Jew who is careful with the prohibition of eating milk and meat cannot tolerate such a mixture?" he asked.

The Power of Kevias Itim

I N ISTANBUL OF 400 YEARS AGO, WHEN SOMEONE WANTED TO describe the highest level of true friendship, they would say, "like the friendship of Menachem Elkarif and Avraham Benveniste."

Menachem and Avraham were the David and Yonasan of Istanbul.

These two friends were opposites in many ways. Menachem was quiet and reserved, a deep thinker, but not very imaginative or creative. He had a very logical, analytical mind, but his mental faculties were not exceptional in any way. Avraham, on the other hand, was outgoing, even fiery, a genius with a razor-sharp mind and lightning-quick comprehension.

In temperament and abilities, the two were as different as could be. So it was a bit surprising when the two developed a friendship, and even more surprising when they became inseparable buddies.

The friendship began when the two young boys began to learn Torah from their Rebbe, Chacham Yosef Chajaj, zt"l, who taught a class of young children in the Bnei Shimon Beit Midrash.

The two boys would walk home together and review Chacham Yosef's *shiur* on the way. When they arrived home, they could not bear to part from one another, and so they would alternate — one day, they would spend together in Menachem's house, and the next day they would spend in Avraham's house.

The two were always together. Wherever you saw Menachem, you saw Avraham; wherever you saw Avraham, you saw Menachem.

Both sets of parents were convinced that the intense friendship was a passing phase. While they did not actively encourage the friendship, they did not discourage it either. Admittedly, the friendship was exclusive of all others, but on the other hand, the two were good boys and good *chavrusas*. So why separate them? With time, the parents were sure, the friendship would lose its intensity and possibly dissolve completely. After all, there really was little that the two had in common.

As the boys grew older, however, it became apparent that the introverted Menachem and the extroverted Avraham complemented each other very well, and that the friendship was not going to dissolve. Everyone thought, however, that the friendship could last only as long as the two were unmarried and it was possible for them to spend the entire day learning together in yeshivah.

When the two reached marriageable age, a *shidduch* was made between Menachem Elkarif and Rosa Bensanior. Naftali Bensanior, Rosa's father, was a simple Jew who earned a modest livelihood from his store, where he sold choice, silk-embroidered fabrics. He was not a scholar, but he managed to imbue his entire family with a love of Torah.

Menachem preferred to remain in the *beis medrash* rather than enter the business world, and Naftali was happy to support him. In those days, the concept of *kollelim* did not exist, but many newly married men continued their Torah studies while being provided for by their in-laws.

The Bensanior family committed to maintaining Menachem for ten years. The plan was that Rosa would join her father in the store, so that she could learn the business and be able to assist in supporting her husband in learning.

But these well-intentioned plans did not come to fruition. A mere two months after Menachem and Rosa's wedding, Naftali Bensanior's store fell on hard times. Several competitors opened in the area, and the store, which had not been exceptionally profitable to begin with, began to show loss after loss.

At first, Naftali tried to make believe that everything was fine. He did not say a word to his son-in-law, who sat and learned in the Zohar HaRakia Beit Medrash day and night.

But the situation rapidly worsened. One evening, during a family dinner, Naftali mused aloud, "Maybe Menachem would want to join the business."

The idea was not appealing to Menachem, nor to his wife Rosa. But as rumors about the store's imminent closing began to circulate, pressure mounted on Naftali, and Menachem and Rosa were forced to reevaluate. Was it right for them to continue being helped by her parents, who were collapsing under the financial burden of the failing store?

Finally, Menachem reluctantly agreed to join his father-in-law's business and attempt to salvage the store from ruin. It quickly became apparent that Menachem's logical, analytical mind was perfectly suited to the business world, and it did not take long before the store began showing modest profits again.

Menachem tried very hard not to become too involved in the running of the business. He still wished to spend the majority of his day learning, and he made great efforts to keep his involvement in the store to a minimum. But the nature of business does not allow for just minimal involvement. Menachem had to throw himself into the business completely, to ensure that it would remain profitable.

At first, Menachem took over his father-in-law's store because he had no choice. But eventually, the intoxicating taste of business success made him start to enjoy it. Little by little, he found himself neglecting his Torah studies.

⁓ৡৡ⁓

Avraham Benveniste, the genius Torah scholar, also found a suitable match. His *kallah* was the daughter of Rabbi Natan Pardo, a rich man, and one of the greatest scholars in Istanbul as well.

Rabbi Natan had three daughters, all of whom he married off to *talmidei chachamim*. His eldest son-in-law, Rabbi Rachamim Cohen, was a *dayan* in Istanbul; his second son-in-law, Rabbi Chaim Aderet, was also a noted scholar.

Now Avraham Benveniste joined this prestigious family. Despite his reputation as an outstanding scholar, he felt pressure to live up to the family standard, and he threw himself into his learning with redoubled efforts.

The Pardo family owned a beautiful shul, where many of the community's leaders *davened*. Rabbi Natan served as the Rav of the shul. After observing his son-in-law's exceptional abilities, he decided to open a yeshivah in his shul and appoint Avraham *rosh yeshivah*. Avraham rose to the challenge and began giving a *shiur* to a group of gifted *bachurim* and married men.

With Menachem busy with his father-in-law's store and Avraham absorbed in his duties as *rosh yeshivah*, it seemed unlikely that their friendship could continue.

⚬⚬

Menachem found himself drawn into a world in which he never thought he would be a part. His learning hours dwindled steadily, to the point where he was barely learning an hour in the morning and an hour at night. But a nagging voice kept on admonishing him that if he would continue on this path, he would lose any connection he had to the world of Torah and eternity.

Menachem was determined to maintain the connection. Late one night, after a tiring day at the store that had not left him a minute to open a *sefer*, he decided to do something to reverse the course his life was taking. He made his way to his friend Avraham's house and explained his situation to his friend.

"Please, do me a favor. Make a *seder* with me," he pleaded. Avraham could not turn his friend down. They agreed to begin learning together for four hours every day.

Menachem would leave the store in the afternoon and sit down to learn with Avraham. No one was happier than the two friends during the time when they were learning together, and nothing could disturb that sacred time.

The friendship between the two became even stronger as a result of the joint learning *seder*, which continued for sixty years unabated.

When Menachem and Avraham entered their 80's, both with many descendants and a rich life of Torah behind them, they began thinking about their impending journeys to the next world.

One day, as the two were learning, Menachem turned to Avraham and said, "Tomorrow will be my 82nd birthday. I sense that my days in this world are numbered."

Tears glistened in Avraham's eyes. "Our friendship has lasted almost eighty years," he reflected. "Who knows how much time we have left together? But how can we allow death to separate us?"

Even the normally stoic Menachem displayed signs of emotion. "I wish we could go together to the next world, rather than one of us leaving the other behind," he mused.

Avraham shook his head. "It's not up to us," he said sadly. Then he had a bold idea. "Let's shake hands and promise each other that whichever one of us dies first will come down to the other and tell him everything that happened after he came before the Heavenly Court. This way we can keep the ties of friendship alive."

Menachem was taken aback by the idea, and he tried to dissuade Avraham from making such a promise. This type of promise was unusual, dangerous, and possibly even prohibited by halachah, he argued.

But Avraham was not to be swayed. Finally, Menachem agreed, and the two made a solemn pact.

Ten years passed.

One night, Menachem Elkarif passed away suddenly, in his sleep. The afternoon before that he had learned with Avraham, as usual.

Avraham Benveniste cried bitterly. A part of him had been severed, and he felt an enormous void. But he comforted himself with the thought that Menachem would surely appear to him soon. *A handshake is not something trivial,* he told himself. *I am certain that Menachem will honor it.*

About a month later, Avraham was sitting and learning *Gemara* when he suddenly sensed the presence of his friend Menachem.

"What happened with your judgment?" Avraham asked him, trembling. "And what goes on in the World of Truth?"

"You should know," Menachem responded, "that once a *neshamah* goes up to Heaven, it no longer has any connection to this world, and it does not have the right to come down to this world again. But because of our pledge, I had to come back down. I do not have authorization to tell you what goes on in the World of Truth, however, only what happened to me personally.

"After I died, all of my relatives whose deaths preceded me gathered to meet me — my parents, my brothers and sisters, my brothers-in-law and sisters-in-law. They announced, 'Whoever can testify about this person from the days of his youth should come forward and testify.'

"Immediately, good angels and bad angels gathered to testify to my good deeds and bad deeds. Then they announced that whoever knows about my deeds in my later years should come testify. Angels of destruction created from every sin that I ever committed shouted at me and embarrassed me in front of my ancestors and family members. I wanted to hide because of the shame, but I had nowhere to go. The black angels listed all of my sins one by one and approached me menacingly, threatening to envelop and destroy me. I was terrified by the sight.

"Suddenly, a high wall appeared, separating me from the destroying angels. Then a voice announced that I had been acquitted in my judgment.

"I was astonished. After such a long, detailed list of sins, how had I been acquitted?

"I was told that the wall that had saved me from the destroying angels had been created in the merit of *kevias itim laTorah* — setting set times for learning Torah. We never canceled our time of *limud Torah* — winter or summer, hot or cold, snow or rain, even on days of family *simchahs* and other busy times.

"Had the wall been punctured by *bitul Torah* and interruptions, the angels of destruction would have been able to penetrate the holes and take hold of me. But because the wall was solid and whole, they could not reach me.

"They allowed me to come down from the World of Truth to tell you this so that you should know the power of *kevias itim laTorah* and so that you should publicize it."

(This story was recounted by Rabbi Tzvi Michel Shapiro, *zt"l*, of Yerushalayim, the author of *Tzvi LaTzaddik*. It was printed in the pamphlet *Hilchos Kevias Itim*, published by Mifal HaTorah of Toldos Aharon in the year 5764.)

More Precious Than Gold (Threads)

ZEFAS, 1903. THE ARCHED ALLEYWAYS OF THE MYSTICAL city were shrouded in a peaceful afternoon stillness. Reb Mordechai Zeide Ludmir, the son of the *tzaddik,* Rabbi Shimon Ludmir, closed the door to his house softly and began making his way to his store. On the way, he ran his hands over the blue paint covering the ancient walls, his lips whispering a silent thanks to the *Ribono Shel Olam* for allowing him to spend the majority of his day learning Torah.

Reb Mordechai Zeide opened his store for only a few hours in the later part of the afternoon. His occupation as a merchant was almost coincidental, nothing more than a concession to the need to earn a living.

He would awaken before dawn and begin learning Torah to the sound of the birds chirping. As the sun rose, dispelling the morning mist, Reb Mordechai Zeide would *daven Shacharis*. Then he would hurry to the *beis medrash*, where he would deliver his daily *shiur* to a group of attentive students.

The *shiur* would typically last three to four hours, beginning with *Gemara, Rashi,* and *Tosafos,* and then continuing with the *Rashba,* the *Maharsha,* the *Pnei Yehoshua* and other commentaries. These hours of undiluted learning were Reb Mordechai Zeide's *raison d'etre*.

Reb Mordechai Zeide's wife and children knew better than to disturb him during this time. Nothing, nothing was important enough to draw Reb Mordechai Zeide out of the *beis medrash*. His neighbors used to quip that when Reb Mordechai Zeide sits and learns, the whole world could be destroyed and he would not even notice.

One day, a merchant arrived in Tzefas with a caravan of donkeys loaded with gold thread. The merchant entered Reb Mordechai Zeide's store and offered to sell him the gold thread at what he deemed a bargain price. "Gold thread has many uses, and it never loses its value," the merchant said enthusiastically. "It's a guaranteed investment, since you can always melt it back into solid gold."

Reb Mordechai Zeide mulled over the merchant's words. He was not in the gold business, but he was an astute businessman, and he could appreciate the eternal value of gold. The risks seemed to be minimal, so he decided to accept the merchant's offer.

The merchant quickly unloaded all of his gold thread at Reb Mordechai Zeide's small store. Reb Mordechai Zeide hurried to collect as much cash as he could to pay for his purchase.

"You should be able to sell the thread within a few days," the merchant assured Reb Mordechai Zeide. With that, he rode off and disappeared.

The expected demand for gold thread did not materialize, however. Reb Mordechai Zeide began to advertise his merchandise, but the advertisements did not seem to generate any interest. Reb Mordechai Zeide was a patient man, and he was willing to wait for customers. But as time passed, it became obvious that no customers were going to be found. Finally, Reb Mordechai Zeide decided to sell the gold thread at a loss, just to get rid of it. Still, no one was interested.

In the meantime, Reb Mordechai Zeide had no remaining cash with which to buy other merchandise. Unable to get rid of his inventory of gold thread, and unable to purchase new inventory, his business began tottering on the verge of collapse.

For the first time, food was scarce in the Ludmir household.

The caravan of camels making its way from Beirut toward Tzefas did not seem, at first glance, to be the harbinger of salvation. In those days, the border between Eretz Yisrael and Lebanon was open, filled with an endless retinue of merchants selling their wares. Caravans traveled freely between the two cities, and commerce flourished.

On one of the camels in this particular caravan sat a Lebanese gold merchant. He led his caravan into the city of Tzefas early one morning, and began inquiring where he could buy gold thread.

It was not long before Reb Mordechai Zeide's name was mentioned to the merchant. He asked for directions to Reb Mordechai Zeide's store, and was told that the store was open only in the afternoon. Undeterred, he headed for the Ludmir residence.

"I am a gold merchant from Beirut," the Arab introduced himself. "Where is Chavajah Ludmir?"

"He is in the synagogue," Reb Mordechai Zeide's wife answered.

"He is praying? Well then, I'll wait until he returns," the Arab replied.

"No, no," Reb Mordechai Zeide's wife hurried to explain. "He finished praying long ago. Now he is studying."

"Can you call him from the synagogue, then?" the Arab asked.

"I'm sorry. My husband cannot be interrupted during his studies," Reb Mordechai Zeide's wife answered.

The Arab seemed impatient. "Listen, I have a business deal to offer your husband. I need gold thread — a lot of it — and he seems to be the only one around who has it. I'm willing to pay nicely for the merchandise. But I'm in a rush. I need to leave here very soon, and I can't wait around all day."

Reb Mordechai Zeide's wife hesitated. She had never dared to disturb her husband while he was in the *beis medrash*. But then again, she had never heard such a tantalizing offer. Why, this one business deal could put an immediate end to the financial woes they had been experiencing for months.

"Run to Abba," she whispered to her son, "and tell him to come home right away. There's a merchant here who wants to buy all the gold thread."

The child ran over to the *beis medrash* and conveyed the message to his father.

Reb Mordechai Zeide was displeased. "I do not wish to be disturbed in middle of the *shiur*," he said sternly.

"But Ima said that it's urgent," the child answered.

"Whatever it is, it can wait until this afternoon," Reb Mordechai Zeide said calmly.

The child returned home and told his mother what Reb Mordechai Zeide had said. "He said he'll be home in three hours, and he'll be happy to speak with the merchant then," the child concluded.

The merchant crossed his arms across his broad chest. "I can't wait three hours," he said. "It's now or never."

Reb Mordechai Zeide's wife was beside herself. Before her stood a buyer for the gold thread her husband had been stuck with for months. She pictured herself being able to go out and buy food and clothing for her family once again.

"Just wait a few more minutes," she told the Arab. "I'll go speak to my husband."

Hurriedly, she made her way over to the *beis medrash*. She stood outside until she saw a man entering. "Could you please call my husband, Reb Mordechai Zeide?" she asked.

Reb Mordechai Zeide came out of the *beis medrash*, surprised to find his wife standing there.

"There's an Arab merchant who wants to buy the gold thread," she said excitedly, "but he has to leave back to Beirut right away."

Reb Mordechai Zeide shook his head firmly. "Not while I'm learning," he said.

"Wait," his wife pleaded. "Can't you interrupt your *shiur* for a short time, just this once? If you're worried about *bitul Torah*, don't you think it will be worse *bitul Torah* if we don't have food to eat and you can't concentrate on your learning? Don't you want to finally get rid of that gold thread that's been sitting in the store for so long?"

But Reb Mordechai Zeide was not interested in the business deal. "Absolutely not," he replied. "Tell the Arab merchant that if he's willing to wait until the afternoon, I'll be happy to talk to him. Until then, I'm not available."

Tears filled Mrs. Ludmir's eyes as she envisioned this one-time opportunity slipping away from under her fingers. Reb Mordechai Zeide noticed her distress. "Do you think a Lebanese merchant is the one providing us with our *parnassah*?" he asked gently. "Do not worry. Hashem will send our *yeshuah* from somewhere else, not at the expense of my learning."

Reb Mordechai Zeide's wife turned back toward her house, dragging her feet.

Reb Mordechai Zeide's students were no less puzzled. "Why can't the Rebbe interrupt the *shiur*, just this once?" they asked. "Isn't it worth a small amount of *bitul Torah* to save a lot of *bitul Torah* later?"

Reb Mordechai Zeide smiled. "You might understand the *Gemara*, my dear *talmidim*, but you do not understand the *yetzer hara* at all. Who do you think sent the merchant here? It was none other than the *yetzer hara*!

"Do you think the *yetzer hara* is pleased with what goes on here in the *beis medrash*?" Reb Mordechai Zeide continued. "He gnashes his teeth when he sees us learning without any disturbances. So what does he do? He sends a merchant all the way from Beirut with an irresistible offer: 'Just a small amount of *bitul Torah*, and then you'll be able to learn in peace. You'll be saved from poverty, and then you will have all the money in the world so you can learn as much as you want.' He coats the *bitul Torah* with a thick layer of honeyed enticements. 'Just one time,' he urges.

"Do you know what would have happened if I would have listened to my wife and gone home? Tomorrow, the *yetzer hara* would have sent me other merchants, with even more enticing offers. Then, I would not have been able to say no. The *yetzer hara* would tell me, 'You interrupted your learning yesterday — why is today any different?'

"No, I can't interrupt the *shiur* even once. Hashem is the One Who sustains the whole world — He will send my salvation from elsewhere," Reb Mordechai Zeide concluded confidently.

The Lebanese merchant left the Ludmir house, disappointed and irritated. He packed up his camels and began leading his caravan out of the city.

As the camels slowly meandered through the narrow paths that led through the mountains surrounding Tzefas, the cool breeze that had been blowing all morning suddenly whipped itself into a hot, fierce wind that carried sand and dust into the camels' eyes.

Within minutes, the sand became a swirling haze of yellow and brown that made it impossible to see more than a few inches ahead. The camels snorted in fear and refused to continue moving ahead.

"It's a sandstorm," shouted the Arab to the other members of the caravan. "We can't go on. We have no choice but to go back to Tzefas until the dust settles."

The caravan turned around and headed back into the city of Tzefas. *Well,* the Arab thought, *if I can't return to Beirut this morning anyway, I might as well buy the gold thread.*

Early in the afternoon, the Arab returned to the Ludmir home. Reb Mordechai Zeide and his family were just sitting down to lunch when they heard the knock at the door.

"Chavajah Ludmir, Al-lah loves you," the Arab said as he greeted Reb Mordechai Zeide. "Look what he did just to bring me back here." He pointed outside, where swirls of dust and sand were blowing wildly.

Reb Mordechai Zeide began negotiating with the Arab over the gold thread. Soon, Reb Mordechai Zeide's store was empty of the thread that had been waiting for months for a buyer, and his pockets were laden with the small fortune that the Arab had paid. From that day on, the Ludmir family became known for its wealth, which remained with the family for many generations.

Rothschild Encounters the Gvir

THE CARRIAGE OF THE FAMED ANSCHEL ROTHSCHILD WAS not particularly elaborate. It was well-equipped and strong, the horses leading it were swift, and the driver was skilled. But there was nothing about the wagon that would lead anyone to believe that it belonged to Rothschild.

The truly rich, they say, hide their wealth, for they have nothing to prove to anyone, and therefore no reason to flaunt their riches.

Strong as the carriage was, it was not unbreakable. One Friday afternoon, Rothschild was riding in his carriage when a loud noise was heard from beneath. One of the wheels had broken off its axle, and the carriage began keeling over on its side.

Rothschild, his secretary, and his driver emerged from the carriage unhurt. The driver examined the damage, and determined that the necessary repair could not be completed before Shabbos.

There was a village not far away with a sizable Jewish population, and Rothschild sent his secretary to secure a place to stay at an inn in the village. There was no need to caution the secretary not to reveal the identity of his employer; the secretary had internalized the Rothschild penchant for modesty, and he knew better than to draw undue attention to his employer.

When the arrangements for Shabbos were made, Anschel Rothschild settled himself in his lodgings and then made his way to the local shul. It was still early, and the women of the village had not yet lit Shabbos candles.

Rothschild looked around for a place to sit. Although he could have purchased the entire shul without batting an eyelash, he did not look for a seat at the *mizrach* wall, but instead found a seat toward the back, on a bench that did not have anyone's name written on it.

He found a *siddur* and began reciting *Shir HaShirim* slowly and deliberately, in a singsong voice. When he finished, he took a *Chumash* to learn the *parashah* of the week with *Rashi*.

As sunset approached, the shul filled up. Rothschild closed his *Chumash* and waited for *Minchah* to begin. But the *amud* remained empty. Rothschild glanced at the nearby window, and noticed that the sun was just about to set. He could not understand why the *davening* did not begin. The shul was full, the Rav was in his place, the *gabbai* seemed to be there — so why the delay?

Concerned that it would soon be too late for *Minchah*, Rothschild approached the person who looked like the *gabbai* and asked him why he wasn't sending someone to the *amud* to be the *chazan*.

The *gabbai* looked at him strangely. "It seems that you're new to this village," he said. "*Shalom aleichem*. We are waiting for the *gvir*."

"The *gvir*?" Rothschild asked, bewildered.

The *gabbai* chortled. "It seems that you don't know much about *gvirim*," he said condescendingly. "Our village has a *gvir* — or, more precisely, our *gvir* has a village. The *gvir* owns the entire village. Everything you see — from this shul to the chicken coop at the outskirts of the village — belongs to the *gvir*, Reb Chaim Zelig, may he live long."

The legendary Rothschild, who had never in his life lorded over anyone, shrugged his shoulders silently. At that moment, one of the congregants entered and announced. "Shh, the *gvir* is here."

The chattering of the congregants stopped instantly.

Rothschild watched as a short, portly man dressed in the finest silk clothing and a deluxe *streimel* made his way self-importantly into the shul. He strolled over to the *mizrach* wall and took his place next to the *Aron Kodesh*, huffing and puffing from the exertion of his regal entrance. The Rav's place, Rothschild noticed, was second in importance to the *gvir's*.

Now the *davening* would begin, Rothschild thought. But instead of going up to the *amud*, the *chazan* approached the *gvir* humbly. "What does my master, the *gvir* think?" he asked submissively. "Can we start *davening*?"

The *gvir* made a show of peering out the window. He nodded his head. "*Chazan*, go forward," the *gvir* announced.

The *chazan* walked away from the *gvir* backwards, respectfully, facing the *gvir* the entire time until he reached the *amud*. He donned a *tallis* and began to *daven*.

When the *davening* was over, all of the congregants assembled to wish the *gvir* "Gut Shabbos." To a very few who had some ranking in the community, the *gvir* extended his hand, while the rest he merely acknowledged with a nod of his head.

Rothschild was flabbergasted. This is no *gvir*, he thought. It's a Jewish *poritz*. No, not a *poritz*, but a king!

"How did the *gvir* come to have so much power?" he inquired of the innkeeper later at the Shabbos *seudah*.

The innkeeper looked surprised. "You mean you don't know about Reb Chaim Zelig? He's one of the richest, most influential Jews in the world!"

"What does he do, this Chaim Zelig?" Rothschild pressed.

The innkeeper laid his spoon down next to his bowl of soup. "Reb Chaim Zelig runs the entire village," he said proudly. "He makes all of the decisions here. We depend on him for everything. He supports the shul, the *beis medrash*, and all of the local charity funds. He has to approve every step that is made in this village — no one can even be buried here without his express approval."

Rothschild did not seem impressed. This bothered the innkeeper, who continued to regale Rothschild with descriptions of Reb Chaim Zelig's wealth and power. "From the time Chaim Zelig was a young man, it was obvious that he was blessed with unusual abilities, and that he would become a community leader and a great *baal chesed*.

"For years, he has been collecting money from the rich to distribute to the poor," the innkeeper said with obvious pride in his voice. He then went on to describe the prestigious *shidduchim* that the *gvir* had made, with the sons and daughters of the greatest *rabbanim* and wealthiest Jews in Europe. "The bottom line is, there is no one like Reb Chaim Zelig. Such a generous man, such a visionary," he concluded.

"Tell me more about his generosity," Rothschild urged.

"Well, there's the local *tzedakah* fund that the *gvir* runs, for instance," the innkeeper replied. "He makes sure that every person of means contributes handsomely to the fund. Anyone who does not, runs the risk of getting a resounding slap when he meets up with the *gvir*.

"Then there was the time that the *gvir* married off his daughter. There was enough meat at that wedding to feed all of the people in this village — and that is what the *gvir*, in his kindness, was planning to do. But then the *mechutan* informed him that he does not eat meat unless he himself saw it being slaughtered. So the *gvir* sent all of the meat to the *goyim* — to the police officers, to the priest, to the mayor, to the judges. Then he made a *milchig* wedding feast the likes of which the world has never seen."

The next morning, Rothschild awoke early and went to shul. This time, the *davening* began at the designated time. But when the *chazan* reached *Baruch She'amar*, he stopped suddenly and took his seat.

What is going on, wondered Rothschild. A look at the front of the shul where the *gvir* sat confirmed his suspicions. The *gvir* had not yet arrived.

A few minutes later, the *gvir* made his grand entrance. Once again, the *chazan* made his way over to the *gvir* and asked his permission to continue *davening*.

When it was time for *krias haTorah*, the *gabbai* went over to the *gvir* and asked him who should be called to the Torah for *Kohen*, *Levi* and the remaining *aliyos*. "There's a guest in shul," the *gabbai* added.

Reb Chaim Zelig turned to inspect the guest. He looked Rothschild up and down for a few seconds, and then told the *gabbai* to give him *Shevi'i*, the sixth *aliyah*. The *gvir* himself was called to the Torah for the third *aliyah*, the prestigious *Shelishi*.

When it was time for Rothschild's *aliyah*, the *gabbai* recited a *Mi Shebeirach*, then paused to allow the guest to make a pledge to the shul.

But Rothschild was quiet. "Nu," the *gabbai* said impatiently.

"*Chai* times *chai* against the *gvir's* estate," Rothschild said calmly.

The *gabbai* did a double take. "What did you say?"

"18 times 18 against the *gvir's* estate," Rothschild repeated. "Whatever the *gvir* Chaim Zelig owns, I will give 324 times that amount to the shul and to the Jews in this village. For instance, if Chaim Zelig has a million *rubles* in his treasure houses, I will donate 324 million *rubles* to the shul and to the Jews of the village."

The congregants began asking one another what the guest had said. In moments, the shul was in an uproar. This fellow must be insane, the congregants concluded. Why, even Rothschild himself did not own 324 times the wealth of the *gvir*!

Nevertheless, the remote possibility that the guest actually meant what he said was a tantalizing one. Was it possible that this inconspicuous guest was really a wealthy man?

After *davening*, the congregants surrounded the innkeeper and began peppering him with questions about his guest. The innkeeper admitted that he was as baffled as the rest of them. He had not noticed anything unusual about the guest, who seemed to be an average Jew. He had not requested special accommodations or special food, and there was no reason to believe that he was unusually wealthy.

When Shabbos was over, the townspeople gathered at the inn, curious to see how the guest planned to fulfill his pledge.

Rothschild was sitting in his room and calmly reciting the verses of *V'yitein lecha*. When the innkeeper knocked on his door and informed him that all of the townspeople were waiting outside for him, he closed his *siddur* and left his room.

"What would you like?" he asked in amusement when he saw the crowd that had gathered.

One of the community leaders spoke up. "We are here to collect the money you promised during your *aliyah* today," he said.

Rothschild nodded. "I will pay my pledge," he said. "But I am a businessman, and when a businessman makes a deal, he investigates the merchandise first. I will return home, and then I will dispatch a representative to determine the precise value of *chai* times *chai* against the *gvir's* estate. If you have any hesitations, take my business card."

The business card was passed around and an audible gasp rose from the crowd. "Why, it's Rothschild himself!" the townspeople whispered excitedly.

Word of the guest's identity spread quickly, and the entire village began rejoicing at its good fortune. The townspeople made all sorts of grand plans about what to do with the money that would stream into their pockets. Why, they could pave the streets with gold after Rothschild paid up his pledge, they told one another.

Within a few days, a new guest came to town. It was Rothschild's representative.

The representative found lodgings in the same inn where his master had stayed previously. He immediately began performing an audit of Chaim Zelig's property in order to assess his net worth.

After staying in the village for several weeks scrutinizing Chaim Zelig's financial records, the representative left the village with a ledger full of notes.

His findings: Chaim Zelig did not have a single penny to his name. Everything he owned — his house, his businesses, his fields — had been bought with public funds. All of the money in his treasure houses came from taxes that his servants and relatives had collected and pocketed. Never in his entire life had he earned anything of his own.

In the end, *chai* times *chai* against the *gvir's* estate amounted to — nothing.

"I am not surprised at all," Rothschild mused. "It is just as I thought. A true *gvir* could never act like that."

A Letter for the Future

A CARAVAN OF WAGONS MADE ITS WAY ALONG A NARROW dirt road, kicking up dust as it slowly creaked along. Within the wagons were scores of chassidim eagerly anticipating their upcoming visit to the Rebbe of Lublin, the holy Chozeh.

Among the men traveling to Lublin was a young man named Tuvia. Tuvia did not consider himself a chassid, and he had never made the trip to Lublin before. He had heard so much about the Rebbe of Lublin, however, that he had finally decided to spend a Shabbos with the holy Rebbe and see for himself why so many people thronged to his court.

Tuvia was not disappointed. The Shabbos he spent in the Rebbe's presence was truly a taste of *Gan Eden*. All Shabbos, Tuvia felt as though he were immersed in a sea of pure spirituality. For the first time in his life, he found himself *davening* that the Shabbos would not end.

On *Motza'ei Shabbos*, as the Chozeh was preparing to return to his chambers, his penetrating eyes passed over the faces of the many chassidim who had gathered around him. He smiled and wished each chassid, in turn, "A gutte voch."

When the Rebbe's eyes rested on Tuvia, he paused. "Please come here," he requested.

Tuvia began to tremble. Why was he being singled out? The Rebbe had never set eyes on him before this Shabbos, and he did not even know Tuvia's name.

The other chassidim were equally puzzled.

Tuvia nervously approached the Rebbe, who extended his hand and shook Tuvia's. "What is your name and where are you from?" the Rebbe inquired.

Tuvia responded in a soft voice.

"Come into my chamber," the Rebbe told Tuvia. Inside the chamber, the Rebbe said, "I have a request to make of you. There is an important letter I received from someone, and it needs to be safeguarded carefully. Are you able to take this letter home and watch it well?"

Tuvia was completely bewildered, but he nodded.

The Rebbe opened a drawer and removed a sealed envelope. "This is the letter. Are you able to keep it in your house?"

"Of course," Tuvia replied. "I will guard it like a precious jewel and return it as soon as the Rebbe asks for it."

The Rebbe gave Tuvia the letter and bade him farewell.

When Tuvia left the Rebbe's room, he was immediately surrounded by hordes of curious chassidim who wished to know what the Rebbe had wanted of him. But Tuvia only fueled their curiosity further when he told them about the mysterious letter that the Rebbe had given him. No one dared ask the Rebbe what the letter said, who it was from or for whom it was intended.

Later that evening, Tuvia and the group of chassidim with whom he had come left Lublin and returned to their village. As soon as Tuvia arrived home, he placed the Rebbe's letter in a locked drawer together with his wife's *kesubah*, his will, and other important documents.

Two months later, Tuvia traveled again to Lublin, and a few months later he visited Lublin a third time. By then, he considered himself an avid follower of the Rebbe of Lublin.

Each time Tuvia visited the Rebbe, he waited for the Rebbe to tell him what to do with the letter. But the Rebbe never brought up the subject.

Ten years passed. Tuvia rose to prominence among the chassidim in Lublin and in his own village as well. His business became very successful, and he began distributing large amounts of *tzedakah*, earning a reputation as a generous *baal chesed*.

Occasionally, he thought about the contents of the letter and wondered why the Rebbe had given it to him. *Had the Rebbe forgotten about it*, he asked himself.

Tishah b'Av 5575 (1815) was a bitter day indeed for Tuvia and for his fellow chassidim. The holy Rebbe of Lublin passed away, leaving behind a flock of followers mourning his passing and the destruction of the two *Batei Mikdash* simultaneously.

"We are orphans," the chassidim cried.

Compounding Tuvia's grief was the knowledge that the Rebbe would never be able to explain what the letter was and why he had given it to Tuvia. For years, Tuvia had waited for the day when the Rebbe would let him in on the secret — but now, the Rebbe had left the world without giving him any instructions about what to do with the letter.

Time passed, and eventually, the subject of the letter faded from Tuvia's consciousness.

Tuvia's stature in the community rose steadily, until eventually he was appointed the *Rosh HaKahal*, the leader of his community. He filled his position admirably, earning the respect and trust of his entire *kehillah*.

Tuvia lived in a small village owned by an elderly *poritz*, Anton Bezhinski. A righteous gentile, Bezhinski willingly rented out his properties to the Jews in his village, and he allowed them to expand their homes and communal facilities freely. Whenever the local priest would incite the villagers against the Jews in his hate-filled sermons, the *poritz* would send his security forces to disperse the mob before any hint of a pogrom could start.

The Jews of the village prayed that the *poritz* should live many long years, which indeed he did. But eventually, his time came.

The *poritz* did not have any children, so upon his death, his entire estate reverted to his nephew, Vadim Bezhinski. The new, young *poritz* was the antithesis of his uncle: he abhorred Jews.

The Jews in the village prayed for the best, hoping that Vadim would not live up to his reputation as a rabid Jew-hater. But it did not take long for Vadim to corroborate the Jews' worst fears. He barely had a chance to ride through the village one fine morning before he summoned the *Rosh HaKahal* to his palace.

Tuvia trembled as he entered the presence of the new *poritz*. "Listen, Jew," Vadim said spitefully. "I took a little tour through the village today, and I saw far too many Jews here. I don't want to have to look at you people, and so I'm expelling you from my village. I should really send you out this minute, but because I'm a kind person, I'll give you six months to sell your property and arrange your affairs. But after six months, not a single Jew will be allowed to live in this village. Do you understand?"

Vadim grabbed Tuvia by the collar and shoved him out the door, as if to stress his point.

As the news of the uncalled-for expulsion spread, a pall descended on the *kehillah*.

"Perhaps we can convince the *poritz* to reconsider," the Jews told one another. "If we arrange an impressive gift and send a delegation to discuss matters with him peacefully, perhaps he will reconsider."

A respectable delegation was promptly organized. The Rav, the *dayanim*, and the wealthy members of the community joined Tuvia on a trip to the *poritz's* palace, holding a magnificent crystal decanter filled with the finest wine. The decanter stood atop a base made of solid gold, upon which was engraved the *poritz's* name.

The *poritz* kicked the gift when it was presented to him. "You think you can bribe me?" he sneered. "I don't need anything from you miserable Jews. All I need from you is to get out of my village. Leave my palace, and never return." The *poritz* then motioned to his servants to remove the Jewish delegation from his palace.

The Jews prayed fervently for the decree to be reversed. But even the most optimistic members of the *kehillah* sorrowfully agreed that there was no chance of changing the *poritz's* mind. This was a bona fide Haman they were dealing with, and it would take a miracle almost as great as the miracle of Purim to save them.

Tuvia, the *Rosh HaKahal*, was more perturbed than anyone else. He was the leader of the *kehillah*, after all, and he felt a responsibility to ensure that every individual was taken care of. If only the Rebbe of Lublin were alive, he thought sadly. He would surely be able to bring about a *yeshuah* for our *kehillah*.

It was then that Tuvia remembered the letter sitting in his drawer. The Rebbe had asked him to safeguard it, and he had done so faithfully for fifteen years. If there was ever a time that he was in need of a communication from the Rebbe, it was now. Would the Rebbe have wanted him to open the letter at this time?

There was no way to know. The Rebbe could not ask for it back, that was for sure. But without the Rebbe's explicit instruction, how could he open the letter?

Tuvia debated for a long time whether to open the letter. Finally, he decided to read the letter, despite his reservations.

The letter was written in Polish, a language that Tuvia knew well. It read:

"To whom it may concern:

I, the undersigned, do hereby declare that when this letter is brought before me, I will fulfill the wish of its bearer in full. I hereby append my signature as proof of my solemn pledge."

The signature was clear: Vadim Bezhinski.

Tuvia broke out in a cold sweat as he began making frenzied calculations. The letter was lying in his house for fifteen years. The young *poritz* could not be older than 31 or 32. If so, he must have written the letter when he was no more than a teenager. What had possessed him to write these words, and how had the holy Rebbe of Lublin gotten hold of it?

That night, Tuvia did not sleep a wink. Instead, he lay awake planning his next steps. Did he dare approach the *poritz* with the letter? Twice he had been chased from the *poritz's* palace, and he was loath to risk the *poritz's* wrath again. On the other hand, he was holding a document that could potentially save his entire *kehillah*. No, there really was no question what he should do.

After *Shacharis* the next morning, Tuvia gave money to *tzedakah* and set out for the *poritz's* palace once more, the letter safely ensconced in his pocket. He bribed the guard with a few *rubles*, and swiftly made his way into Vadim's room. Before Vadim could open his mouth, Tuvia thrust the letter into his hands.

Vadim glanced at the paper, and his face turned pale. "How did you get this?" he demanded.

"The Rebbe of Lublin gave it to me fifteen years ago," Tuvia said calmly. "It has been waiting in my house all this time."

"You got it fifteen years ago?" Vadim cried out in anguish. "That was when I wrote it, fifteen years ago.

Vadim slapped his face agitatedly as he began reminiscing to himself. "I was about 16 years old, I remember clearly, and I was very sick. No doctors could help me. But a Jew who knew my father told him that in Lublin there is a rabbi who performs miracles. They said that the rabbi was almost like a prophet.

"The Jew took my father and me to the rabbi. I was brought into the rabbi's room on a stretcher, and my father begged him to heal me. When I saw the rabbi, I thought I was looking at an angel.

"The rabbi took a cup of water and told me to drink it. I began to feel better. My father was so grateful, he wanted to give the rabbi a purse full of gold coins, but the rabbi refused. 'I don't take money for healing people,' he said humbly. 'All I ask is that the boy should sign a paper for me. I might one day need a favor from him, and I might not be able to come in person to ask for it.'

"At that time I would have done anything the rabbi asked," Vadim recalled. "I didn't think twice about signing a promise to fulfill the wish of whoever would bring me this paper. Afterwards, I forgot about it completely. But I guess the rabbi didn't. How did he know to give it to you? He must have been a true prophet."

Vadim sighed. "And now you want me to withdraw the expulsion order. I would not do it, but I am afraid to start up with that holy rabbi. He knew fifteen years ago that this was going to happen."

And then Tuvia heard Vadim mutter, "Fine, all of you can stay."

A sense of calm descended on Tuvia, and a smile appeared on his face.

This volume is part of
THE ARTSCROLL SERIES®
an ongoing project of
translations, commentaries and expositions
on Scripture, Mishnah, Talmud, Halachah,
liturgy, history, the classic Rabbinic writings,
biographies and thought.

For a brochure of current publications
visit your local Hebrew bookseller
or contact the publisher:

Mesorah Publications, ltd

4401 Second Avenue
Brooklyn, New York 11232
(718) 921-9000
www.artscroll.com